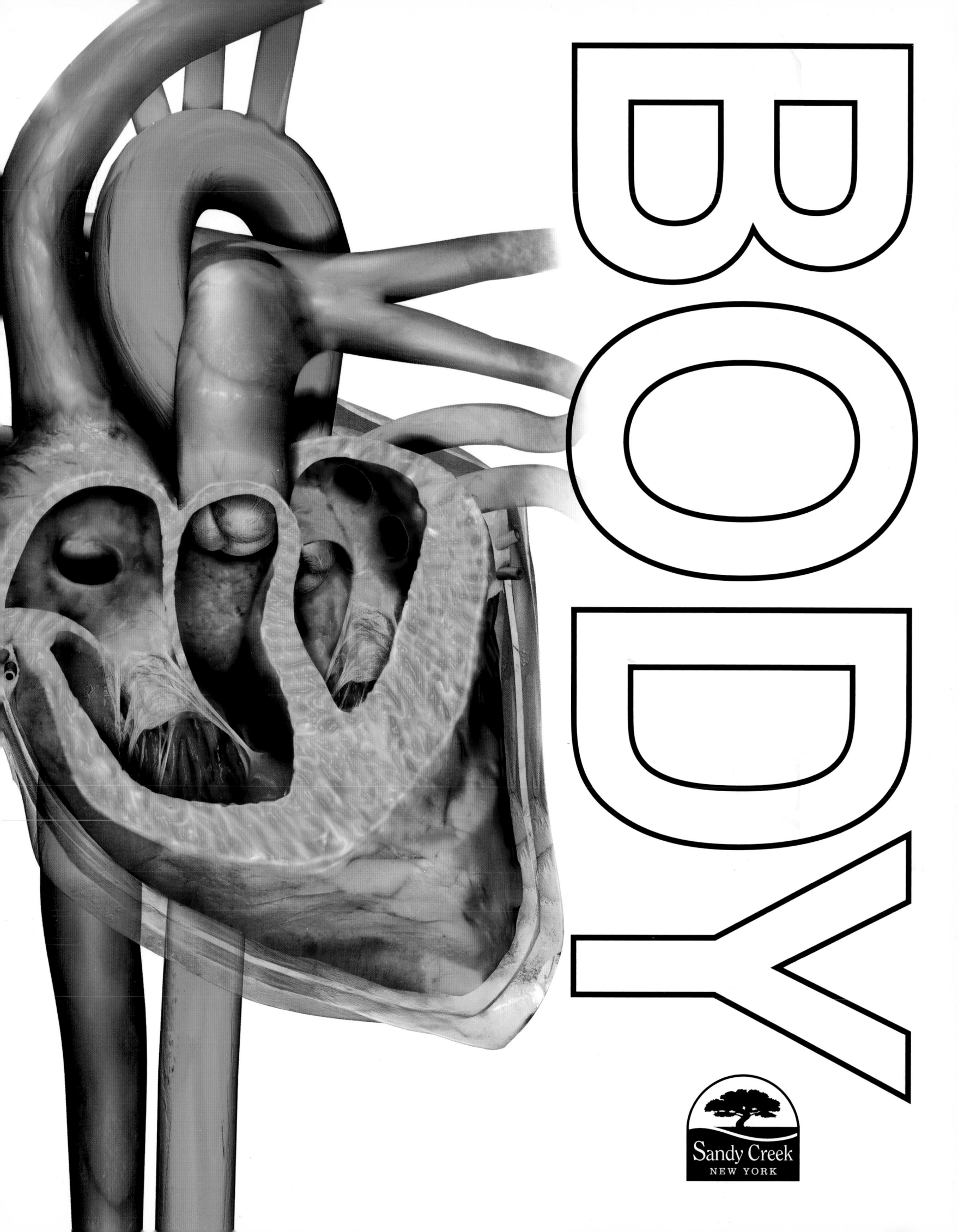

BODY

Sandy Creek
NEW YORK

Sandy Creek
NEW YORK

An Imprint of Sterling Publishing
387 Park Avenue South
New York, NY 10016

Senior editor Shaila Brown

Senior art editor Stefan Podhorodecki

Editors Fran Jones, Hazel Beynon
Art editor Nicola Harrison

Managing editor Linda Esposito
Managing art editor Diane Thistlethwaite

Picture research Julia Harris-Voss
DK picture library Rose Horridge
DTP designer Siu Yin Chan
Jacket designer Natalie Godwin
Production Shivani Pandey

For Primal Pictures
Consultant anatomists Pippa Chadfield and
Lorna Stevenson
Images rendered by Simon Barrick

ISBN 978-1-4351-5684-5

Manufactured in Hong Kong, China
Lot #:
2 4 6 8 10 9 7 5 3 1
08/14

Contents

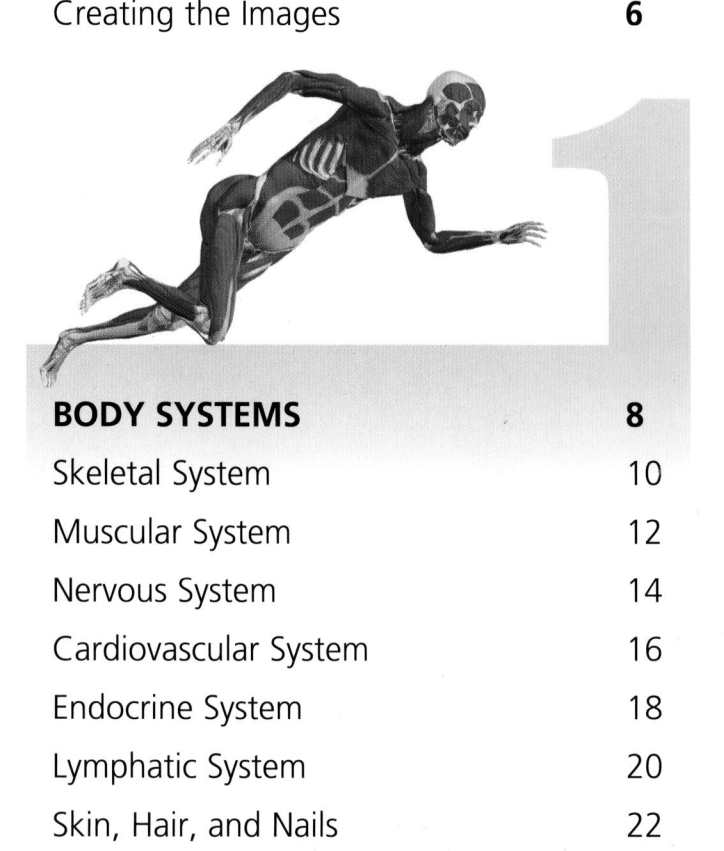

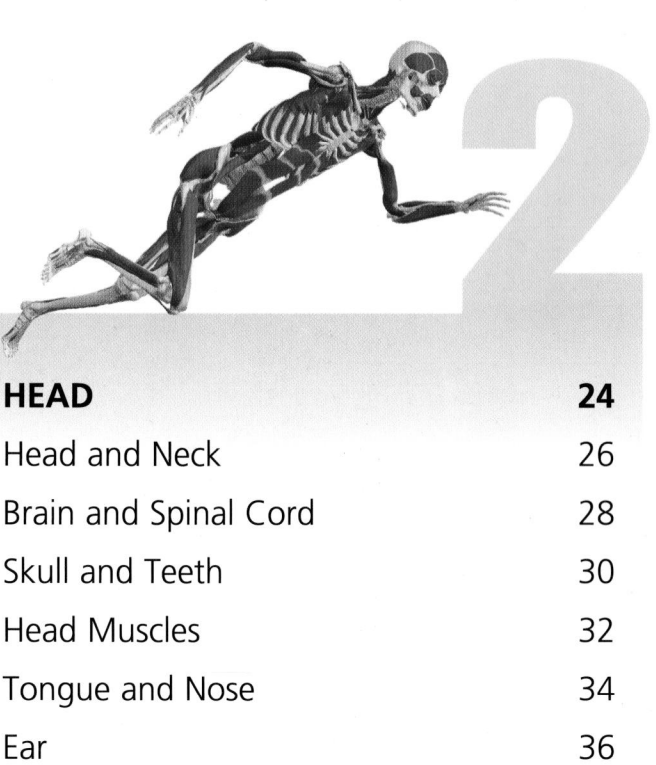

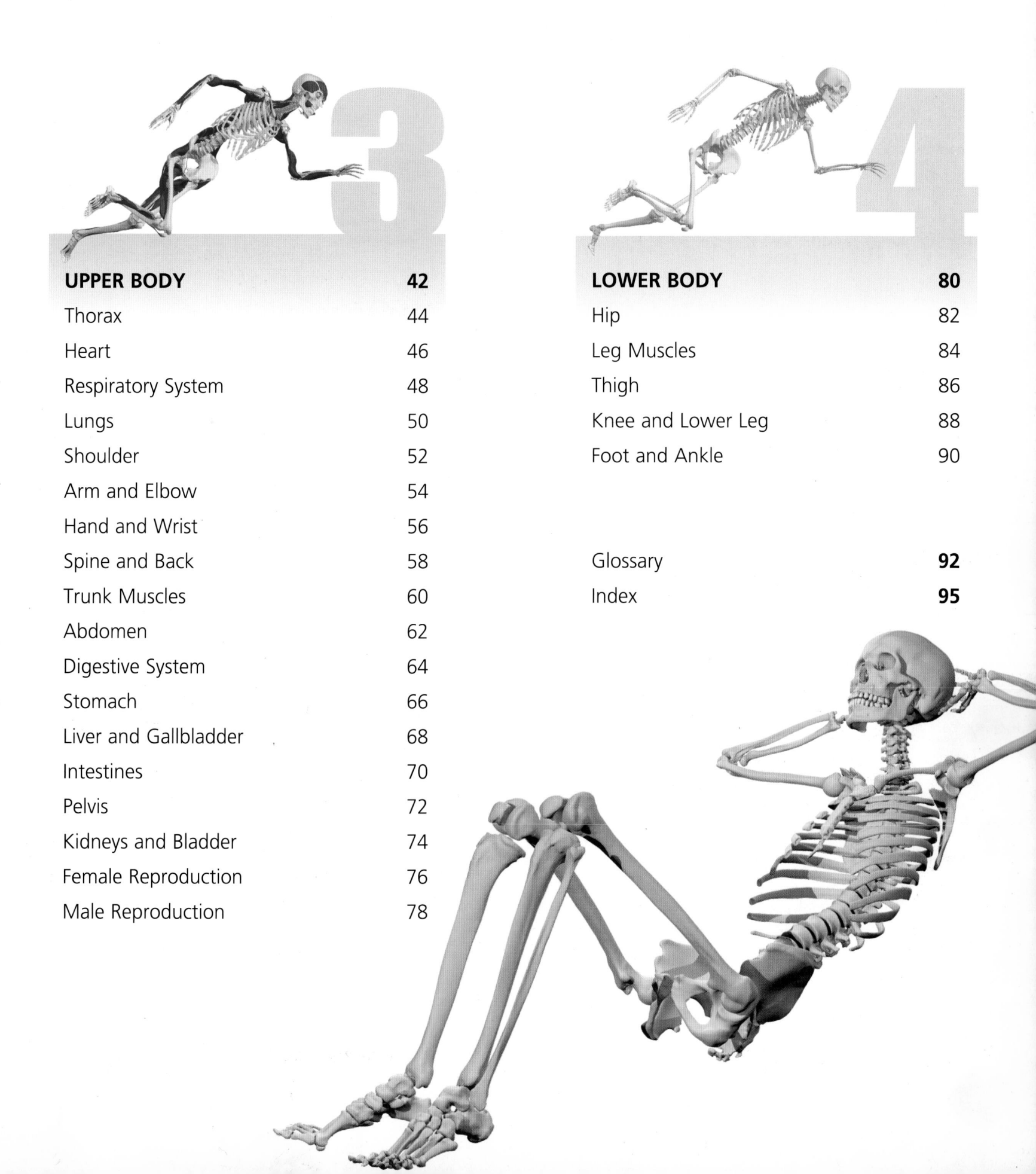

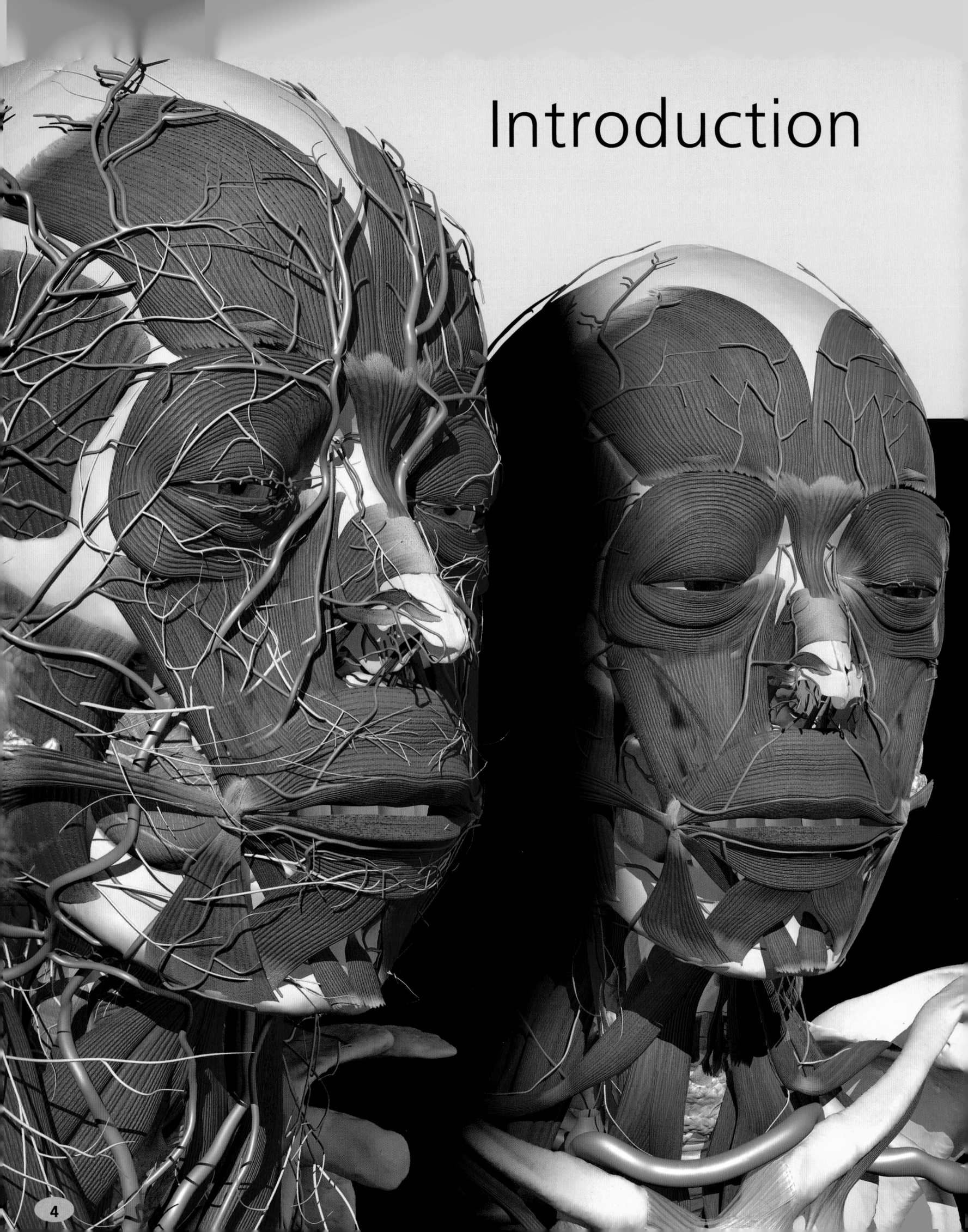

Introduction

OUR BODIES ARE REALLY JUST MACHINES. But they are more complicated and built better than any machine we can make. Our brain carries out more calculations than any computer, and, unlike any computer, can feel emotions as well as think. Our bones are made of a substance that is six times stronger than steel. Our sense of smell and vision is more sensitive and more accurate than in any apparatus we can make for ourselves. We can use different fuels for energy and can go for long periods with very little fuel. Unlike any machine, we reproduce ourselves. And unlike any machine, the body has an ability to heal itself. "Bionic" parts are sometimes used to replace damaged organs or limbs, but nothing is remotely as good as what nature has supplied.

This book shows just how complex we are—the delicate way our bones fit together, the miles of tubing that supply blood to nourish every body part, the extraordinary system we have for digesting food and waste disposal. But, though we cannot make machines as good as our bodies, we have been able to build machines that tell us more about what we look like inside than ever before. The pictures in this book are only possible because modern scanning machines, and modern computing, give the basis for these captivating images. When we look at these pictures, we should remember what a gift the body is, and that we should take care of it.

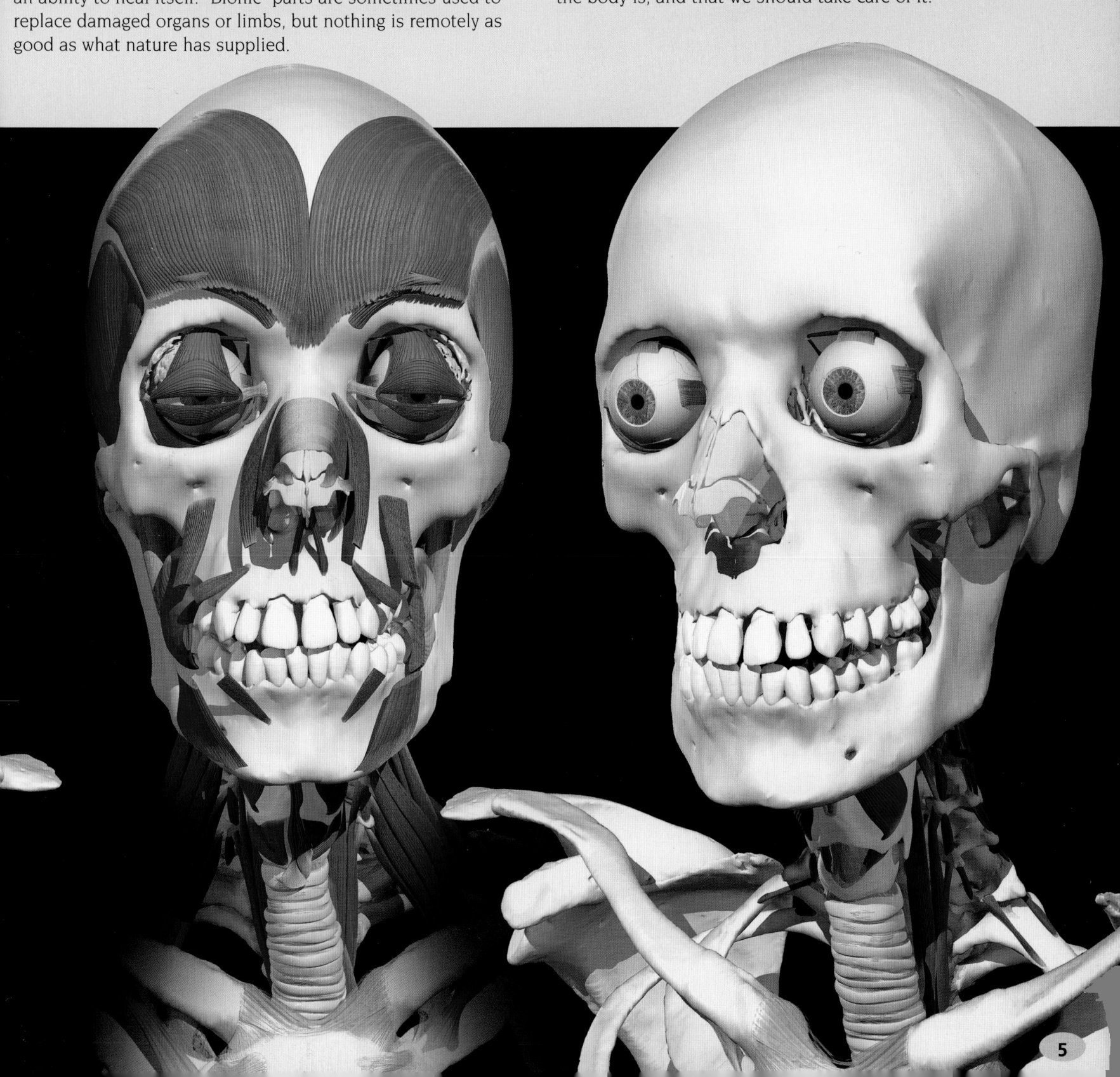

Creating the Images

LOOK THROUGH THIS BOOK and you will see some remarkable images of the human body, probably unlike any you have seen before. The three-dimensional (3-D) images you see opposite have been made using a combination of real bodies and modern technology. On a computer, this "virtual human" can be viewed from any direction and be taken apart and rebuilt, while in a book it shows body details with incredible clarity and helps us to understand more easily how the body is put together.

◀ HORIZONTAL SLICING

The first stage in creating the images is to take the donated dead body, encase it in a hardening agent, and freeze it to the very low temperature of −201°F (−94°C). The body is then sectioned horizontally across by a highly accurate cutting device to produce one-millimeter-thick sections of the body all the way down from the head to the feet. The exposed surface of each slice is photographed using a digital camera and stored in a computer.

SLICE through the head shows the brain, skull, nose, and eyeballs

LABELING

An anatomist traces the outline of an organ in a digital photo of a body slice, a process called labeling. By labeling organs from neighboring slices, the computer can build up a three-dimensional wireframe model of that organ. A computer is then used to generate and apply colors and textures to the wireframe to make the organ—in this case, the brain—look realistic.

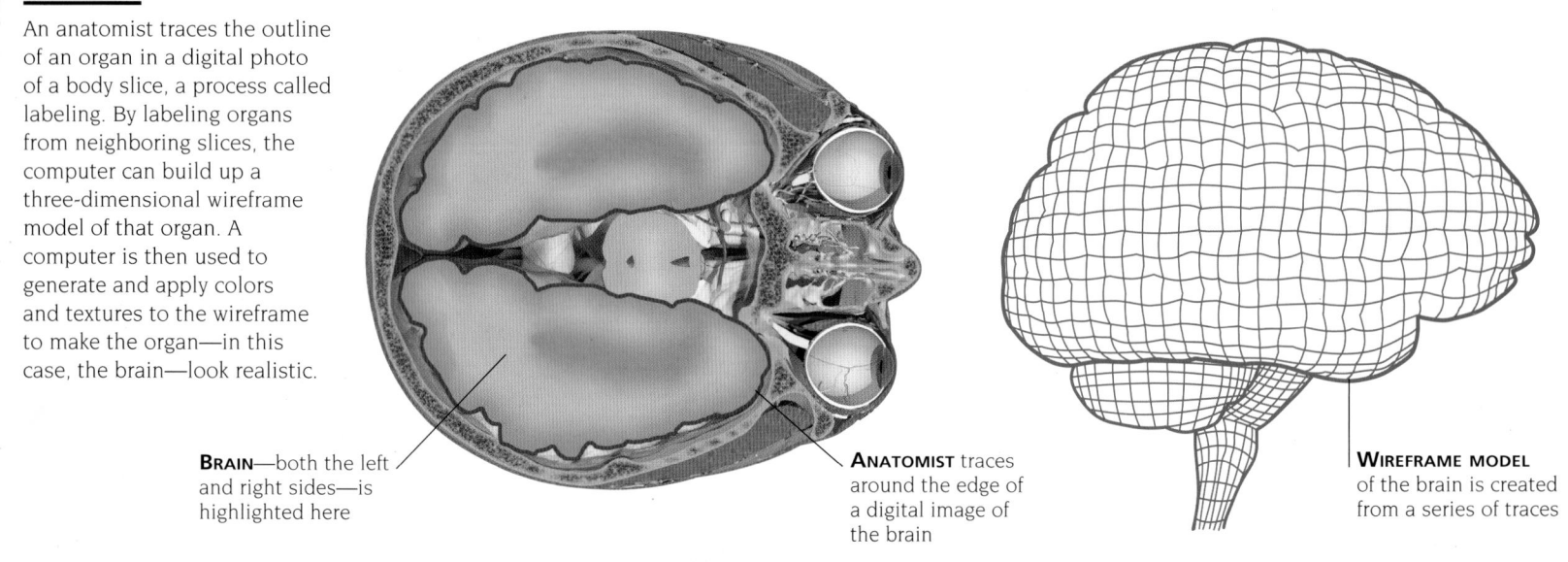

BRAIN—both the left and right sides—is highlighted here

ANATOMIST traces around the edge of a digital image of the brain

WIREFRAME MODEL of the brain is created from a series of traces

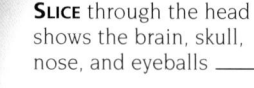

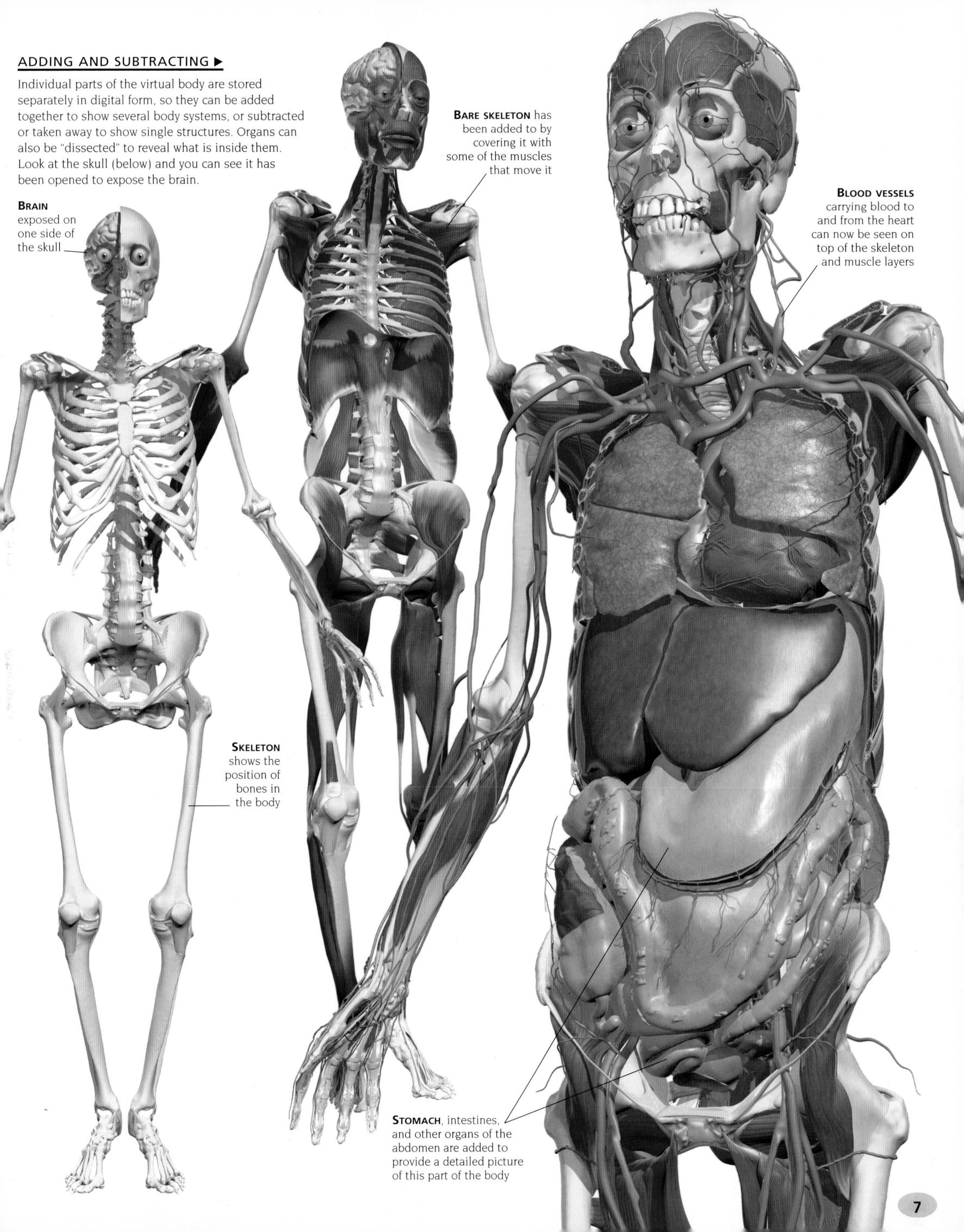

ADDING AND SUBTRACTING ▶

Individual parts of the virtual body are stored separately in digital form, so they can be added together to show several body systems, or subtracted or taken away to show single structures. Organs can also be "dissected" to reveal what is inside them. Look at the skull (below) and you can see it has been opened to expose the brain.

BRAIN exposed on one side of the skull

BARE SKELETON has been added to by covering it with some of the muscles that move it

BLOOD VESSELS carrying blood to and from the heart can now be seen on top of the skeleton and muscle layers

SKELETON shows the position of bones in the body

STOMACH, intestines, and other organs of the abdomen are added to provide a detailed picture of this part of the body

SECTION ONE: BODY SYSTEMS

Your tour of the body begins with a journey through the systems that make up a complete human being. Between them, these systems protect, support, control, and feed the body.

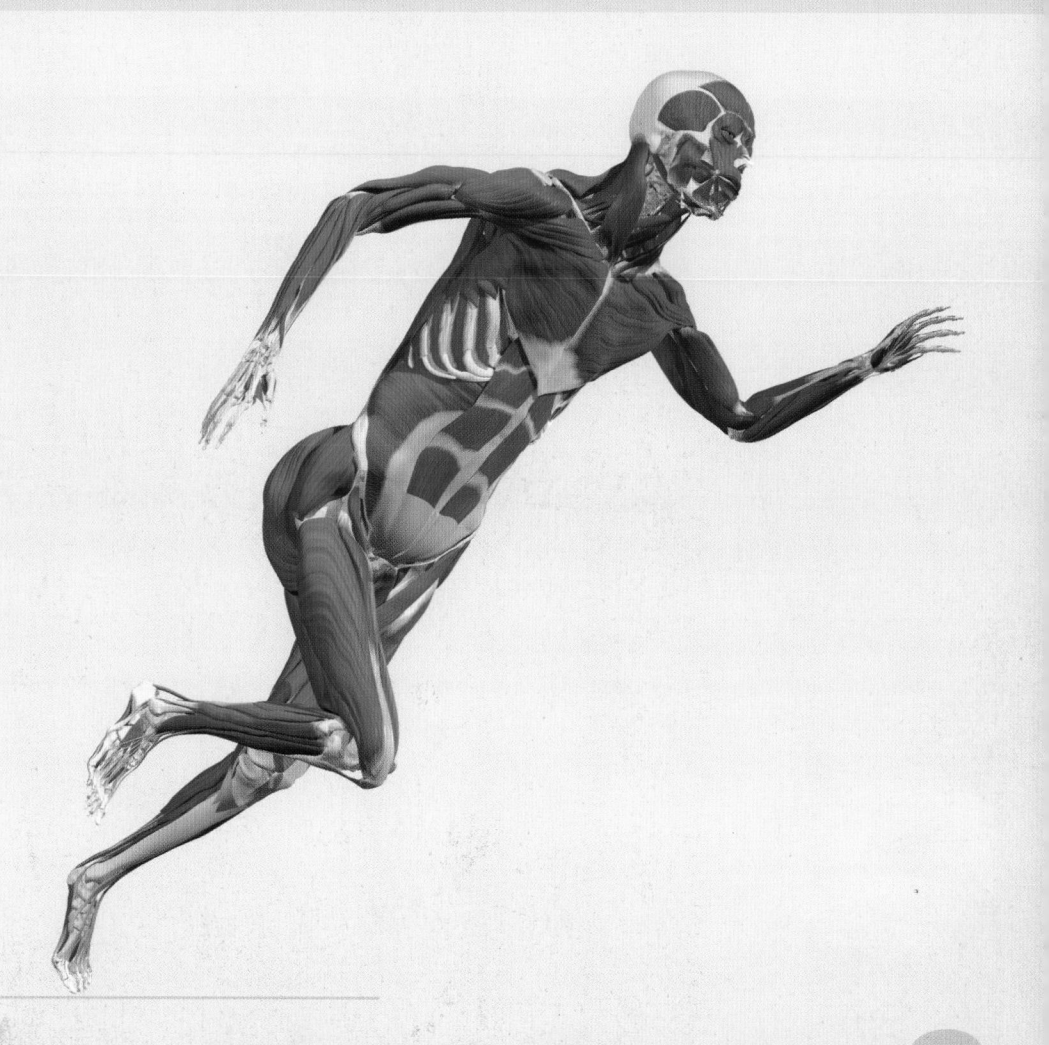

Skeletal System

WITHOUT ITS SKELETAL SYSTEM your body would be shapeless and saggy. The skeletal system, or skeleton, consists of 206 bones that form a living framework to support and shape your body. These bones are not dry and dusty, but moist living organs that are amazingly strong and, because of their inside structure, surprisingly light. Your skeleton also surrounds and protects soft, delicate organs such as your heart and brain. What's more, bones are not fixed rigidly together. Where two or more bones meet, they form a joint. Many joints are flexible, allowing bones to move.

HINGE JOINT ▼

As the name suggests, this type of joint works like a hinge, allowing bending and straightening. Hinge joints are found, for example, in the knee, ankle, and elbow.

PARTS OF A SKELETON

The skeleton can be divided into two parts. The main job of the 80 bones that make up the skull, backbone, and ribs is to support the body and protect its soft organs. The 126 bones of the arms, legs, hips, and shoulders play a key role in movement.

SKULL

RIBS

RADIUS

ULNA

HAND BONES

BACKBONE, or spinal column

THIGHBONE, or femur

SHINBONE, or tibia

FIBULA

FOOT BONES

BACK VIEW OF A SKELETON

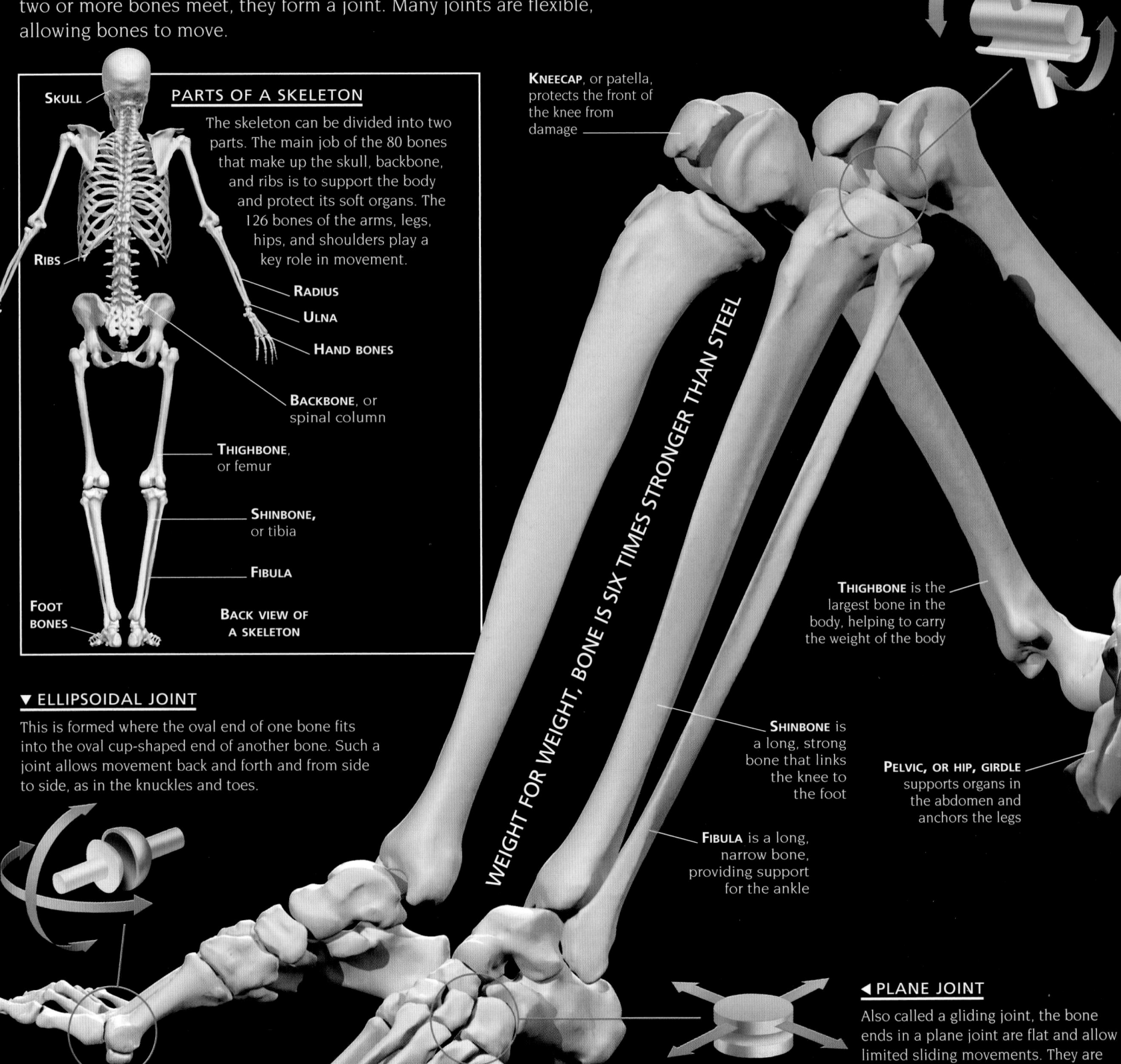

KNEECAP, or patella, protects the front of the knee from damage

WEIGHT FOR WEIGHT, BONE IS SIX TIMES STRONGER THAN STEEL

THIGHBONE is the largest bone in the body, helping to carry the weight of the body

SHINBONE is a long, strong bone that links the knee to the foot

PELVIC, OR HIP, GIRDLE supports organs in the abdomen and anchors the legs

FIBULA is a long, narrow bone, providing support for the ankle

▼ ELLIPSOIDAL JOINT

This is formed where the oval end of one bone fits into the oval cup-shaped end of another bone. Such a joint allows movement back and forth and from side to side, as in the knuckles and toes.

◄ PLANE JOINT

Also called a gliding joint, the bone ends in a plane joint are flat and allow limited sliding movements. They are found between ankle bones in the foot and wrist bones in the hand.

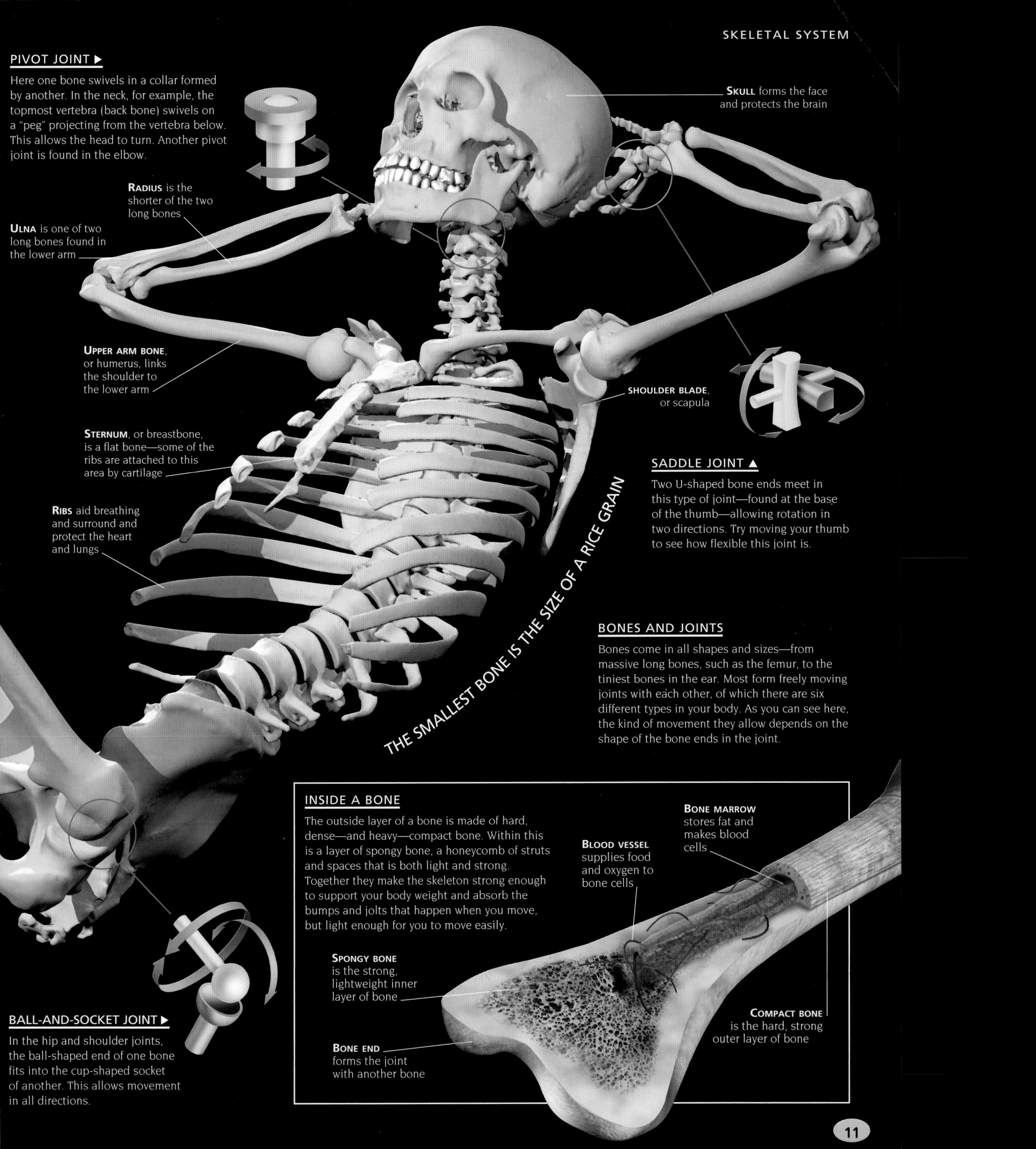

PIVOT JOINT ▶

Here one bone swivels in a collar formed by another. In the neck, for example, the topmost vertebra (back bone) swivels on a "peg" projecting from the vertebra below. This allows the head to turn. Another pivot joint is found in the elbow.

RADIUS is the shorter of the two long bones

ULNA is one of two long bones found in the lower arm

UPPER ARM BONE, or humerus, links the shoulder to the lower arm

STERNUM, or breastbone, is a flat bone—some of the ribs are attached to this area by cartilage

RIBS aid breathing and surround and protect the heart and lungs

SKULL forms the face and protects the brain

SHOULDER BLADE, or scapula

THE SMALLEST BONE IS THE SIZE OF A RICE GRAIN

SADDLE JOINT ▲

Two U-shaped bone ends meet in this type of joint—found at the base of the thumb—allowing rotation in two directions. Try moving your thumb to see how flexible this joint is.

BONES AND JOINTS

Bones come in all shapes and sizes—from massive long bones, such as the femur, to the tiniest bones in the ear. Most form freely moving joints with each other, of which there are six different types in your body. As you can see here, the kind of movement they allow depends on the shape of the bone ends in the joint.

INSIDE A BONE

The outside layer of a bone is made of hard, dense—and heavy—compact bone. Within this is a layer of spongy bone, a honeycomb of struts and spaces that is both light and strong. Together they make the skeleton strong enough to support your body weight and absorb the bumps and jolts that happen when you move, but light enough for you to move easily.

BONE MARROW stores fat and makes blood cells

BLOOD VESSEL supplies food and oxygen to bone cells

SPONGY BONE is the strong, lightweight inner layer of bone

BONE END forms the joint with another bone

COMPACT BONE is the hard, strong outer layer of bone

BALL-AND-SOCKET JOINT ▶

In the hip and shoulder joints, the ball-shaped end of one bone fits into the cup-shaped socket of another. This allows movement in all directions.

Muscular System

EVERY MOVEMENT YOU MAKE is produced by your muscular system. Muscles are made up of long cells called fibers that contract, or shorten, to move parts of your body. Most of your muscular system—up to half your body weight—consists of skeletal muscles. More than 650 skeletal muscles cover your skeleton in layers, give your body its shape, and are attached to, and pull on, your bones. By contracting they make you run, jump, or perform any one of thousands of movements. Two other muscle types work unseen inside your body: cardiac muscle powers your heartbeat, while smooth muscle moves food and other materials.

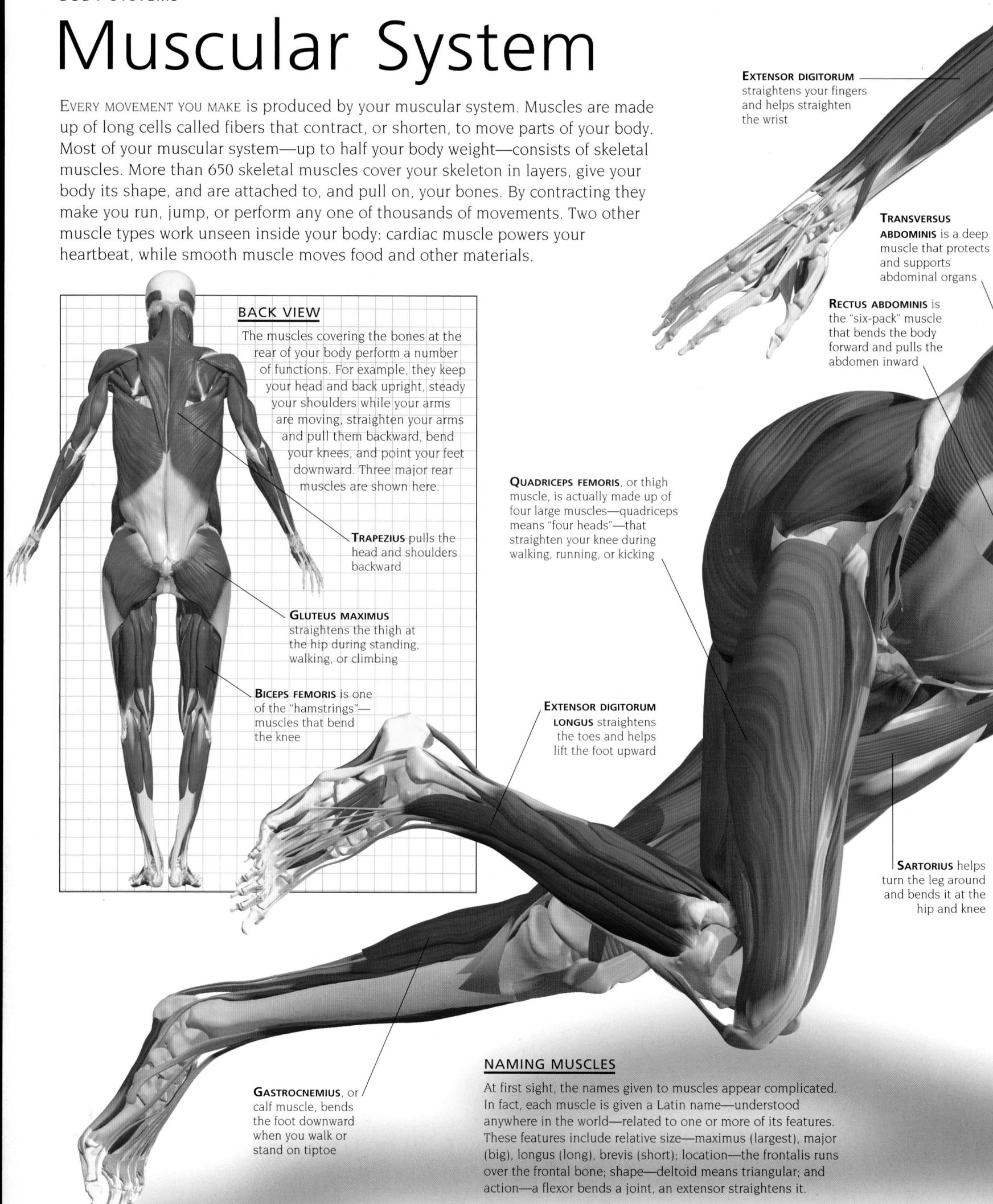

EXTENSOR DIGITORUM straightens your fingers and helps straighten the wrist

TRANSVERSUS ABDOMINIS is a deep muscle that protects and supports abdominal organs

RECTUS ABDOMINIS is the "six-pack" muscle that bends the body forward and pulls the abdomen inward

QUADRICEPS FEMORIS, or thigh muscle, is actually made up of four large muscles—quadriceps means "four heads"—that straighten your knee during walking, running, or kicking

EXTENSOR DIGITORUM LONGUS straightens the toes and helps lift the foot upward

SARTORIUS helps turn the leg around and bends it at the hip and knee

BACK VIEW

The muscles covering the bones at the rear of your body perform a number of functions. For example, they keep your head and back upright, steady your shoulders while your arms are moving, straighten your arms and pull them backward, bend your knees, and point your feet downward. Three major rear muscles are shown here.

TRAPEZIUS pulls the head and shoulders backward

GLUTEUS MAXIMUS straightens the thigh at the hip during standing, walking, or climbing

BICEPS FEMORIS is one of the "hamstrings"— muscles that bend the knee

GASTROCNEMIUS, or calf muscle, bends the foot downward when you walk or stand on tiptoe

NAMING MUSCLES

At first sight, the names given to muscles appear complicated. In fact, each muscle is given a Latin name—understood anywhere in the world—related to one or more of its features. These features include relative size—maximus (largest), major (big), longus (long), brevis (short); location—the frontalis runs over the frontal bone; shape—deltoid means triangular; and action—a flexor bends a joint, an extensor straightens it.

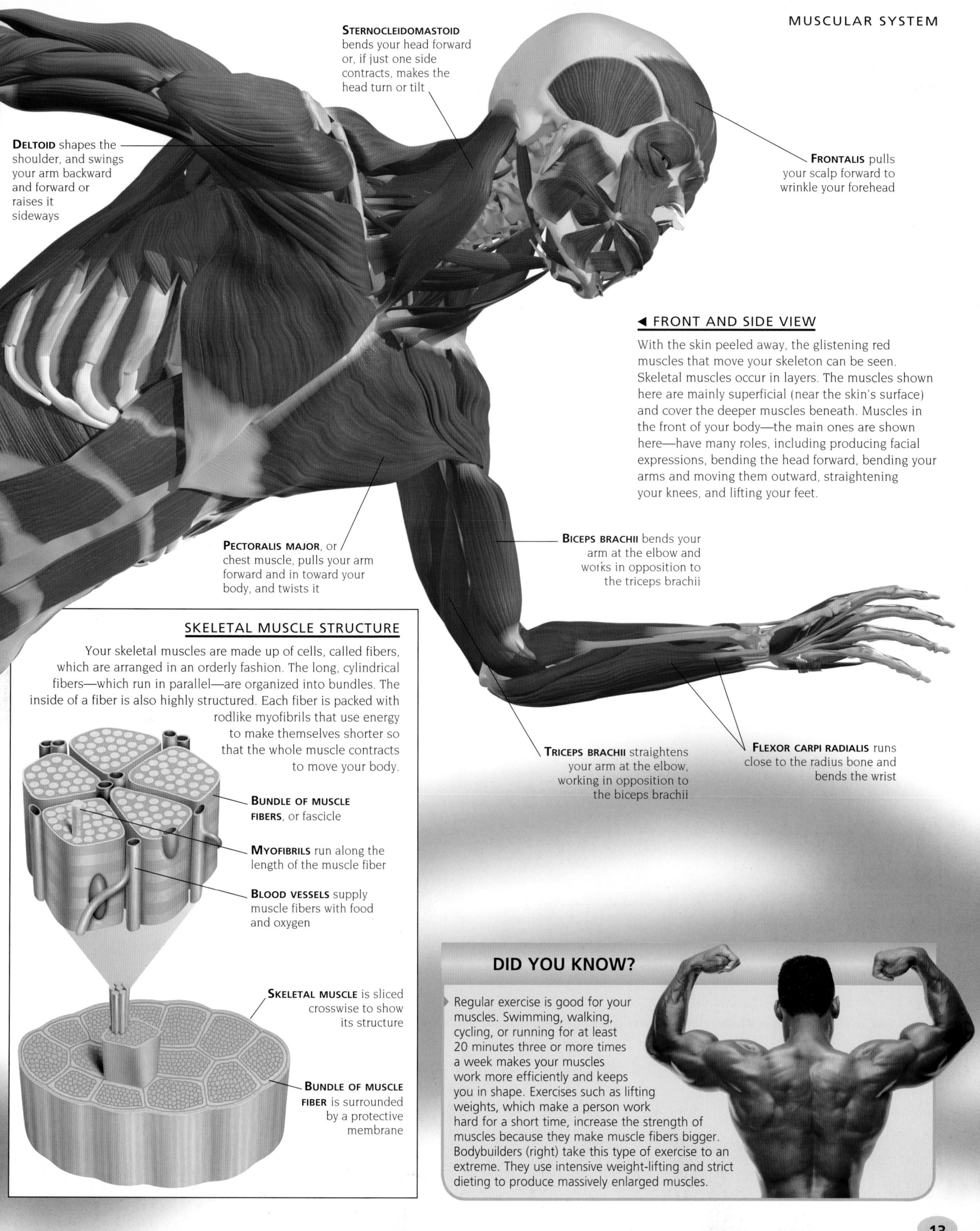

STERNOCLEIDOMASTOID bends your head forward or, if just one side contracts, makes the head turn or tilt

DELTOID shapes the shoulder, and swings your arm backward and forward or raises it sideways

FRONTALIS pulls your scalp forward to wrinkle your forehead

◄ FRONT AND SIDE VIEW

With the skin peeled away, the glistening red muscles that move your skeleton can be seen. Skeletal muscles occur in layers. The muscles shown here are mainly superficial (near the skin's surface) and cover the deeper muscles beneath. Muscles in the front of your body—the main ones are shown here—have many roles, including producing facial expressions, bending the head forward, bending your arms and moving them outward, straightening your knees, and lifting your feet.

BICEPS BRACHII bends your arm at the elbow and works in opposition to the triceps brachii

PECTORALIS MAJOR, or chest muscle, pulls your arm forward and in toward your body, and twists it

SKELETAL MUSCLE STRUCTURE

Your skeletal muscles are made up of cells, called fibers, which are arranged in an orderly fashion. The long, cylindrical fibers—which run in parallel—are organized into bundles. The inside of a fiber is also highly structured. Each fiber is packed with rodlike myofibrils that use energy to make themselves shorter so that the whole muscle contracts to move your body.

BUNDLE OF MUSCLE FIBERS, or fascicle

MYOFIBRILS run along the length of the muscle fiber

BLOOD VESSELS supply muscle fibers with food and oxygen

SKELETAL MUSCLE is sliced crosswise to show its structure

BUNDLE OF MUSCLE FIBER is surrounded by a protective membrane

TRICEPS BRACHII straightens your arm at the elbow, working in opposition to the biceps brachii

FLEXOR CARPI RADIALIS runs close to the radius bone and bends the wrist

DID YOU KNOW?

Regular exercise is good for your muscles. Swimming, walking, cycling, or running for at least 20 minutes three or more times a week makes your muscles work more efficiently and keeps you in shape. Exercises such as lifting weights, which make a person work hard for a short time, increase the strength of muscles because they make muscle fibers bigger. Bodybuilders (right) take this type of exercise to an extreme. They use intensive weight-lifting and strict dieting to produce massively enlarged muscles.

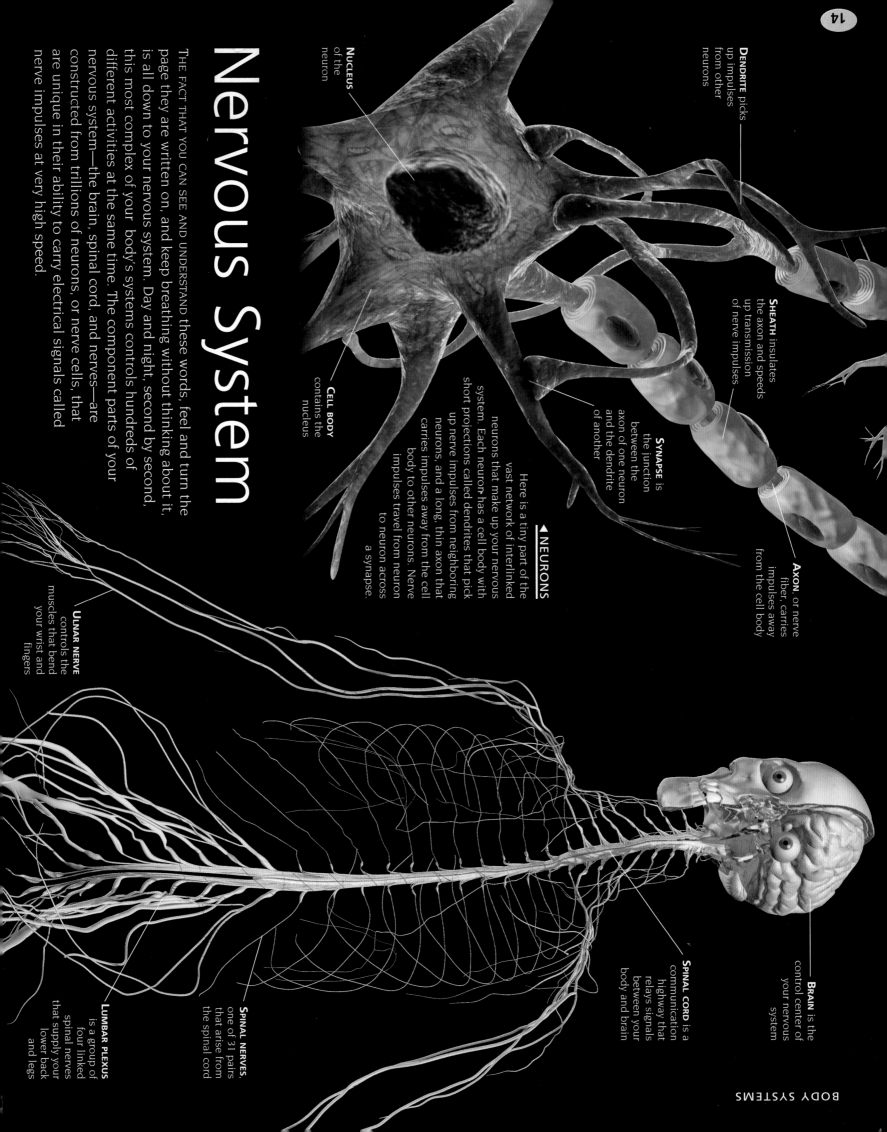

Nervous System

THE FACT THAT YOU CAN SEE AND UNDERSTAND these words, feel and turn the page they are written on, and keep breathing without thinking about it, is all down to your nervous system. Day and night, second by second, this most complex of your body's systems controls hundreds of different activities at the same time. The component parts of your nervous system—the brain, spinal cord, and nerves—are constructed from trillions of neurons, or nerve cells, that are unique in their ability to carry electrical signals called nerve impulses at very high speed.

DENDRITE picks up impulses from other neurons

NUCLEUS of the neuron

SHEATH insulates the axon and speeds up transmission of nerve impulses

SYNAPSE is the junction between the axon of one neuron and the dendrite of another

AXON, or nerve fiber, carries impulses away from the cell body

CELL BODY contains the nucleus

▲NEURONS

Here is a tiny part of the vast network of interlinked neurons that make up your nervous system. Each neuron has a cell body with short projections called dendrites that pick up nerve impulses from neighboring neurons, and a long, thin axon that carries impulses away from the cell body to other neurons. Nerve impulses travel from neuron to neuron across a synapse.

ULNAR NERVE controls the muscles that bend your wrist and fingers

LUMBAR PLEXUS is a group of four linked spinal nerves that supply your lower back and legs

SPINAL NERVES, one of 31 pairs that arise from the spinal cord

SPINAL CORD is a communication highway that relays signals between your body and brain

BRAIN is the control center of your nervous system

CRANIAL NERVES

Twelve pairs of cranial nerves fan out from the underside of your brain, as you can see below. Each pair has a name and a Roman numeral written beside it, and most control head or neck muscles, or carry messages from sense organs, such as the eye, to your brain. The vagus nerve, however, supplies your heart and other organs in your chest and abdomen.

OLFACTORY NERVE (I) carries signals from odor receptors in the nose that enable you to smell

TRIGEMINAL NERVE (V) controls your chewing muscles and carries signals from your eyes, teeth, tongue, and face

FACIAL NERVE (VII) controls facial expressions and the release of saliva and tears, and relays signals from the front of your tongue

ACCESSORY NERVE (XI) controls muscles that move your head and make you swallow

OPTIC NERVE (II) carries impulses from light detectors in the eye to the visual (image-making) part of the brain

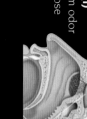

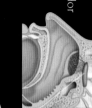

OCULOMOTOR (III), TROCHLEAR (IV), AND ABDUCENS (VI) NERVES control eye movement

VESTIBULOCOCHLEAR NERVE (VIII) relays signals from the ear that enable you to hear and balance

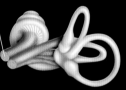

GLOSSOPHARYNGEAL (IX) AND HYPOGLOSSAL (XII) NERVES control tongue movement and relay signals about taste to your brain

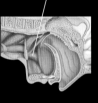

VAGUS NERVE (X) controls many vital activities including heart rate, breathing, and digestion

TIBIAL NERVE controls the calf muscles that bend your foot downward

SCIATIC NERVE supplies the thigh muscles that bend your leg

THE SYSTEM

Your nervous system can be divided into two main parts—the central nervous system (CNS) and nerves. The CNS consists of your brain and spinal cord and is in charge of operations. Trillions of neurons in the CNS receive incoming information, analyze and store it, and send out instructions. Nerves are bundles of axons (nerve fibers) that relay impulses to and from every part of your body.

COMMON PERONEAL NERVE controls the muscles that lift your foot

Cardiovascular System

TO KEEP THEMSELVES—AND YOU—ALIVE, the trillions of cells that make up your body's tissues need constant supplies of food and oxygen, and to have their waste matter removed. Delivery and removal is provided by your cardiovascular, or circulatory, system. Substances heading to or from cells are carried in a red liquid called blood. Pumped by your heart, blood circulates around the body along a network of tubes known as blood vessels. There are three types of these vessels—arteries, veins, and capillaries. Your cardiovascular system also plays a key role in protecting you from infection, and keeping your body temperature at a steady 98.6°F (37°C).

ARTERY

Arteries have thicker walls than veins or capillaries so they can withstand the high pressure produced with every heartbeat.

THICK MUSCLE layer withstands high blood pressure

ELASTIC LAYER allows the artery to expand and bounce back

CAPILLARY

By comparison, capillaries are tiny. Oxygen, food, and other materials pass through capillary walls as blood flows through the tissues.

CAPILLARY WALL is just one cell thick

VEIN

Blood inside veins is at a much lower pressure than in arteries so the walls are thinner. But with less "push," blood in veins may backflow. Valves prevent this.

VALVE inside the vein stops blood from flowing backwards

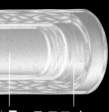

▼ BLOOD

This living liquid contains different types of cells floating in liquid plasma. Red blood cells (1) give blood its color and carry oxygen. White blood cells, including lymphocytes (2) and neutrophils (3), defend your body against disease-causing germs. Platelets (4) help blood to clot.

BLOOD VESSEL NETWORK ▶

Arteries (red) carry blood to your tissues while veins (blue) carry blood from your tissues. Not seen here are the tiny capillaries that link arteries and veins and carry blood past all tissue cells. Stretched out, your body's blood vessels would extend over an incredible 93,206 miles (150,000 km).

COMMON CAROTID ARTERY carries blood to the head and brain

HEART pumps blood along blood vessels

INFERIOR VENA CAVA is the main vein carrying blood to the heart

DESCENDING AORTA carries oxygen-rich blood to the lower body

TWO LOOPS

Blood traveling around your circulatory system follows a figure-of-eight path, with the two loops of the "eight" connected by your heart.

The shorter loop (green arrows) takes blood from your heart to your lungs, to pick up oxygen, and back to your heart. The longer loop (yellow arrows) delivers oxygen-rich blood (red) to all parts of your body, then returns oxygen-poor blood (blue) back to your heart. The journey around the two loops takes less than a minute.

PULMONARY ARTERY carries oxygen-poor blood to the lungs

RIGHT SIDE OF THE HEART pumps blood to the lungs

NETWORK OF BLOOD VESSELS inside the liver

PORTAL VEIN carries food-rich blood from the intestines to the liver

INFERIOR VENA CAVA returns blood from the lower body to the heart

NETWORK OF BLOOD VESSELS serving the lower body

NETWORK OF BLOOD VESSELS supplies the head and upper body

SUPERIOR VENA CAVA returns blood from the head and upper body to the heart

NETWORK OF BLOOD VESSELS in the left lung

AORTA is the main artery through which blood leaves the heart

PULMONARY VEIN carries oxygen-rich blood from the lungs to the heart

LEFT SIDE OF THE HEART pumps blood to all parts of the body

NETWORK OF BLOOD VESSELS serving the stomach and small intestine

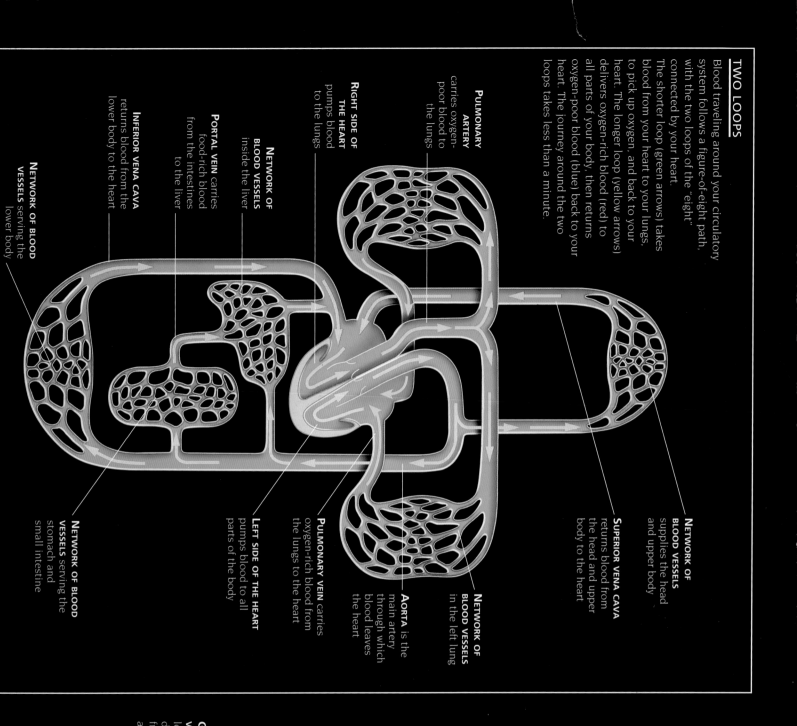

GREAT SAPHENOUS VEIN, the body's longest vein, drains blood from the foot and lower leg

FEMORAL ARTERY supplies blood to the thigh

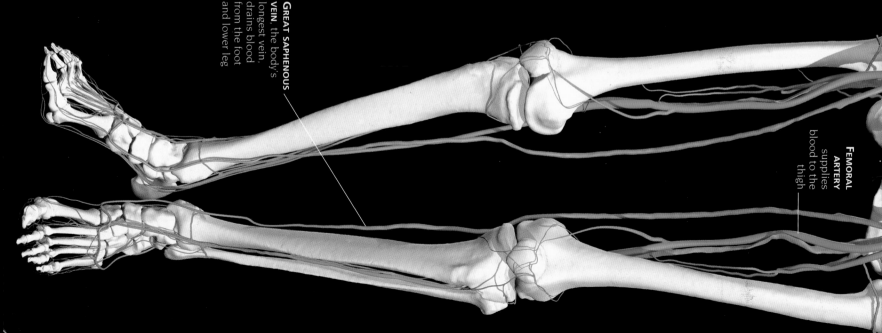

Endocrine System

TWO SYSTEMS CONTROL what happens inside your body. One is the high-speed nervous system. The other is the slower-acting endocrine, or hormonal, system, consisting of endocrine glands that release messenger chemicals called hormones into your bloodstream. Hormones target specific cells and tissues and alter their activity. Here you can see the main endocrine glands. Other organs, such as the stomach, also contain endocrine tissue.

THYROID GLAND

Wrapped around the trachea (windpipe), your thyroid gland releases the hormone thyroxine.

This targets most body cells, increasing their metabolic rate—that is, the rate at which oxygen is used to release energy from glucose—and thus their rate of cell division and growth.

THYMUS GLAND

The hormones released by this gland are essential for the development of your immune system. Under the direction of thymus hormones, cells called lymphocytes develop the ability to identify invading germs.

PINEAL GLAND

Your pineal gland sets your body's internal "clock" by releasing variable amounts of the hormone melatonin. At night, high levels of melatonin make you drowsy, while low levels released during the day leave you feeling wide awake.

HYPOTHALAMUS

Through its connection to the pituitary gland, this part of your brain provides a link between the endocrine and nervous systems. The hypothalamus makes hormones that control the release of hormones from the pituitary gland.

PITUITARY GLAND

The raisin-sized pituitary gland releases eight hormones. They control major body activities such as growth, metabolism, and reproduction, either directly or by making other glands release hormones.

PARATHYROID GLANDS

Four small glands, located on the back of the thyroid gland, release parathyroid hormone. This increases levels of calcium in your blood. Calcium is needed to make bones and teeth, and ensures that muscles and nerves work properly.

HEART releases a hormone that controls blood pressure

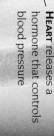

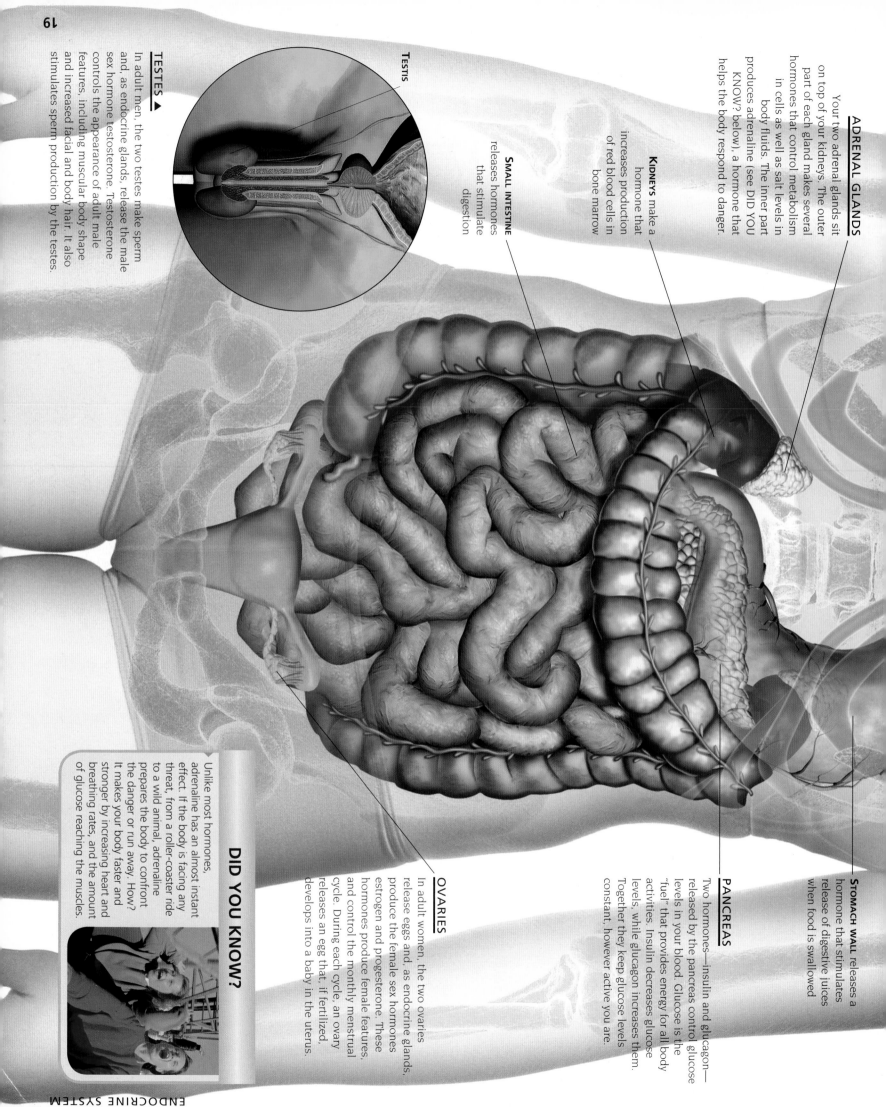

ADRENAL GLANDS

Your two adrenal glands sit on top of your kidneys. The outer part of each gland makes several hormones that control metabolism in cells as well as salt levels in body fluids. The inner part produces adrenaline (see DID YOU KNOW? below), a hormone that helps the body respond to danger.

KIDNEYS make a hormone that increases production of red blood cells in bone marrow

SMALL INTESTINE releases hormones that stimulate digestion

TESTIS

TESTES ▲

In adult men, the two testes make sperm and, as endocrine glands, release the male sex hormone testosterone. Testosterone controls the appearance of adult male features, including muscular body shape and increased facial and body hair. It also stimulates sperm production by the testes.

STOMACH WALL releases a
hormone that stimulates release of digestive juices when food is swallowed

PANCREAS

Two hormones—insulin and glucagon—released by the pancreas control glucose levels in your blood. Glucose is the "fuel" that provides energy for all body activities. Insulin decreases glucose levels, while glucagon increases them. Together they keep glucose levels constant, however active you are.

OVARIES

In adult women, the two ovaries release eggs and, as endocrine glands, produce the female sex hormones estrogen and progesterone. These hormones produce female features, and control the monthly menstrual cycle. During each cycle, an ovary releases an egg that, if fertilized, develops into a baby in the uterus.

DID YOU KNOW?

Unlike most hormones, adrenaline has an almost instant effect. If the body is facing any threat, from a roller-coaster ride to a wild animal, adrenaline prepares the body to confront the danger or run away. How? It makes your body faster and stronger by increasing heart and breathing rates, and the amount of glucose reaching the muscles.

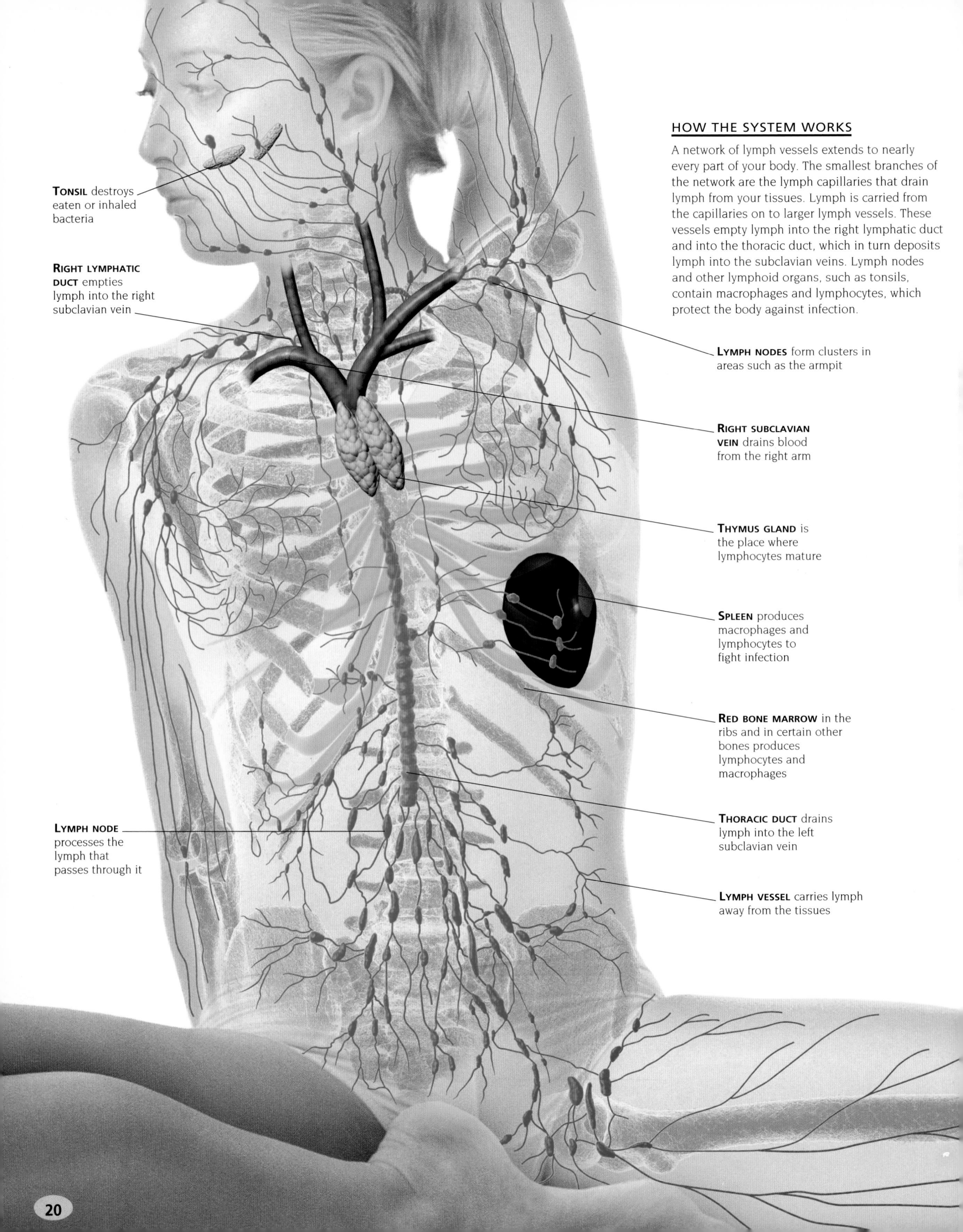

TONSIL destroys eaten or inhaled bacteria

RIGHT LYMPHATIC DUCT empties lymph into the right subclavian vein

LYMPH NODE processes the lymph that passes through it

HOW THE SYSTEM WORKS

A network of lymph vessels extends to nearly every part of your body. The smallest branches of the network are the lymph capillaries that drain lymph from your tissues. Lymph is carried from the capillaries on to larger lymph vessels. These vessels empty lymph into the right lymphatic duct and into the thoracic duct, which in turn deposits lymph into the subclavian veins. Lymph nodes and other lymphoid organs, such as tonsils, contain macrophages and lymphocytes, which protect the body against infection.

LYMPH NODES form clusters in areas such as the armpit

RIGHT SUBCLAVIAN VEIN drains blood from the right arm

THYMUS GLAND is the place where lymphocytes mature

SPLEEN produces macrophages and lymphocytes to fight infection

RED BONE MARROW in the ribs and in certain other bones produces lymphocytes and macrophages

THORACIC DUCT drains lymph into the left subclavian vein

LYMPH VESSEL carries lymph away from the tissues

Lymphatic System

YOUR LYMPHATIC SYSTEM HAS TWO important roles. First, it collects excess fluid that has passed from your blood capillaries into your tissues. This surplus fluid, called lymph, is transported along a network of vessels and returned to your bloodstream. Second, the lymphatic system helps to defend your body from disease-causing organisms called pathogens, or germs. Lymph nodes contain cells called lymphocytes and macrophages that, together with similar cells in the blood, form your body's immune system. These cells identify, target, and destroy specific pathogens that would otherwise make you ill.

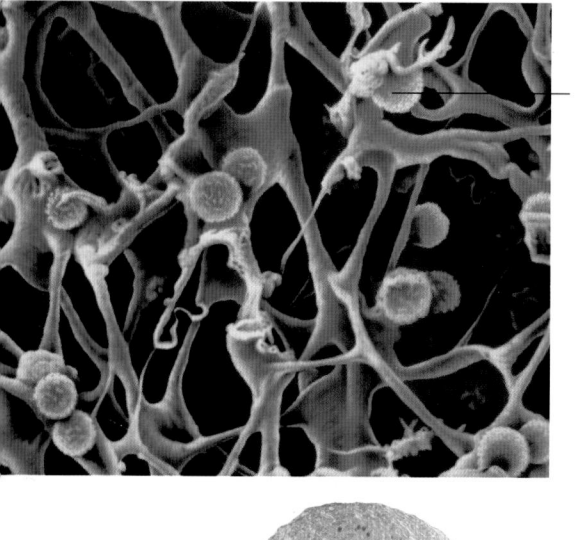

MACROPHAGE AND LYMPHOCYTE are attached to a network of fibers inside a magnified lymph node

◀ INSIDE A LYMPH NODE

The meshlike network of fibers inside a lymph node is packed with two types of white blood cells. Macrophages engulf and destroy pathogens and dead cells. Lymphocytes target pathogens, either destroying them directly or marking them for destruction by releasing chemicals called antibodies.

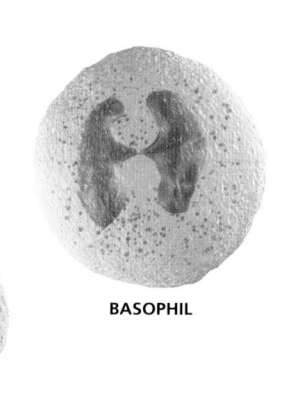

NEUTROPHIL

MONOCYTE

LYMPHOCYTE

BASOPHIL

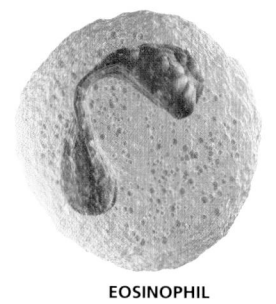

EOSINOPHIL

WHITE BLOOD CELLS ▲

Your blood contains five types of white blood cells, each with a specific role in defending your body. Two of these types of white blood cells are also found in the lymphatic system. Macrophages (the name given to monocytes when they leave the blood) are phagocytes (cell-eaters) that track down and eat pathogens. Lymphocytes target specific pathogens and launch antibodies against them.

LYMPH NODES

These bean-shaped swellings are found along the length of lymph vessels, forming clusters in the neck, armpit, and other areas. Each node is filled with a meshlike tissue, which slows the flow of lymph and supports the white blood cells that destroy pathogens. During an infection, lymph nodes may swell up and become painful, a condition that is known as "swollen glands."

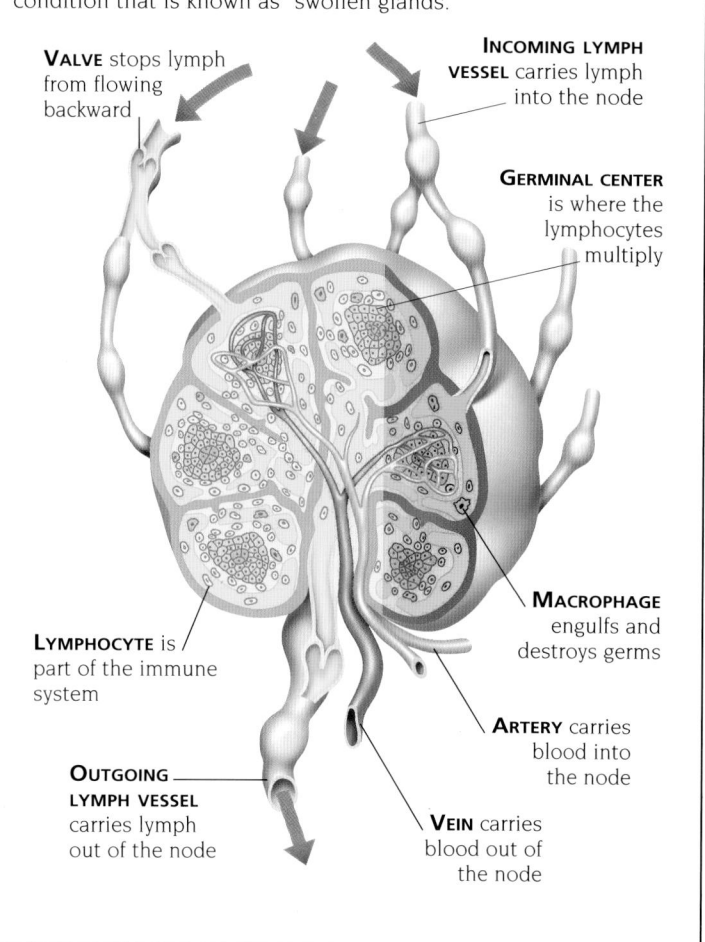

VALVE stops lymph from flowing backward

INCOMING LYMPH VESSEL carries lymph into the node

GERMINAL CENTER is where the lymphocytes multiply

MACROPHAGE engulfs and destroys germs

LYMPHOCYTE is part of the immune system

ARTERY carries blood into the node

OUTGOING LYMPH VESSEL carries lymph out of the node

VEIN carries blood out of the node

DID YOU KNOW?

This baby's thymus gland is large compared to that of the adult holding her. This is because the thymus helps the immune system to develop in the early years of life. The thymus gland releases hormones that enable lymphocytes to develop the ability to target specific disease-causing pathogens.

Skin, Hair, and Nails

WHAT WEIGHS 11 POUNDS (5 kilograms) and is your body's largest organ? It's your skin, the protective overcoat that forms a barrier between your delicate insides and the world outside. Germ-proof skin prevents disease-causing microbes from invading your body. Skin is waterproof, so you don't get waterlogged in the bathtub or when it rains. It also contains brown melanin that colors it and filters out harmful ultraviolet (UV) rays from sunlight. Skin also helps your body keep to a steady inside temperature of 98.6°F (37°C). Both hairs and nails grow out of the skin. Hair on your head protects your scalp, and elsewhere makes the skin more sensitive to light touch. Nails cover and protect the tops of your fingers and toes.

SKIN ▶

This slice through the skin makes it look quite thick but, in fact, skin varies from just 1/50 in (0.5 mm) to 1/6 in (4 mm) in thickness. Skin has two layers. The protective epidermis has an upper surface made of dead, scaly waterproof cells that are lost as skin flakes but are continually replaced. The thicker dermis contains blood vessels, hair follicles, sweat glands, and nerve endings.

HAIR

This magnified view inside skin shows one of the millions of hairs that cover almost every part of your body's surface. Hairs are long, flexible strands of dead cells that grow from pits in the skin called hair follicles. Cells in the hair bulb at the base of each follicle divide constantly to make the hair and push it upward above the skin's surface.

CUTICLE, or outer layer of hair, is covered with overlapping scales

HAIR is formed from dead cells filled with tough keratin

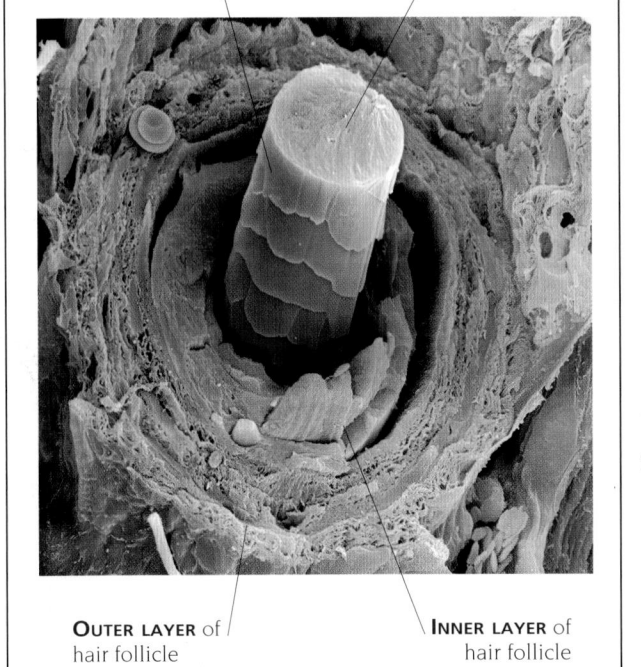

OUTER LAYER of hair follicle

INNER LAYER of hair follicle

BASE OF EPIDERMIS contains dividing cells that produce new epidermis

HAIR SHAFT is part of the hair that grows above the skin's surface

NERVE ENDINGS in skin detect touch, pressure, heat, cold, or pain

SEBACEOUS GLAND makes oily sebum, which keeps hairs and skin flexible and waterproof

HAIR ERECTOR MUSCLE pulls hair upright when you are cold

HAIR FOLLICLE is a hole in the skin from which hair grows

HAIR BULB contains cells that divide rapidly to make hairs grow

BLOOD VESSELS change in width to increase or decrease heat loss from the body

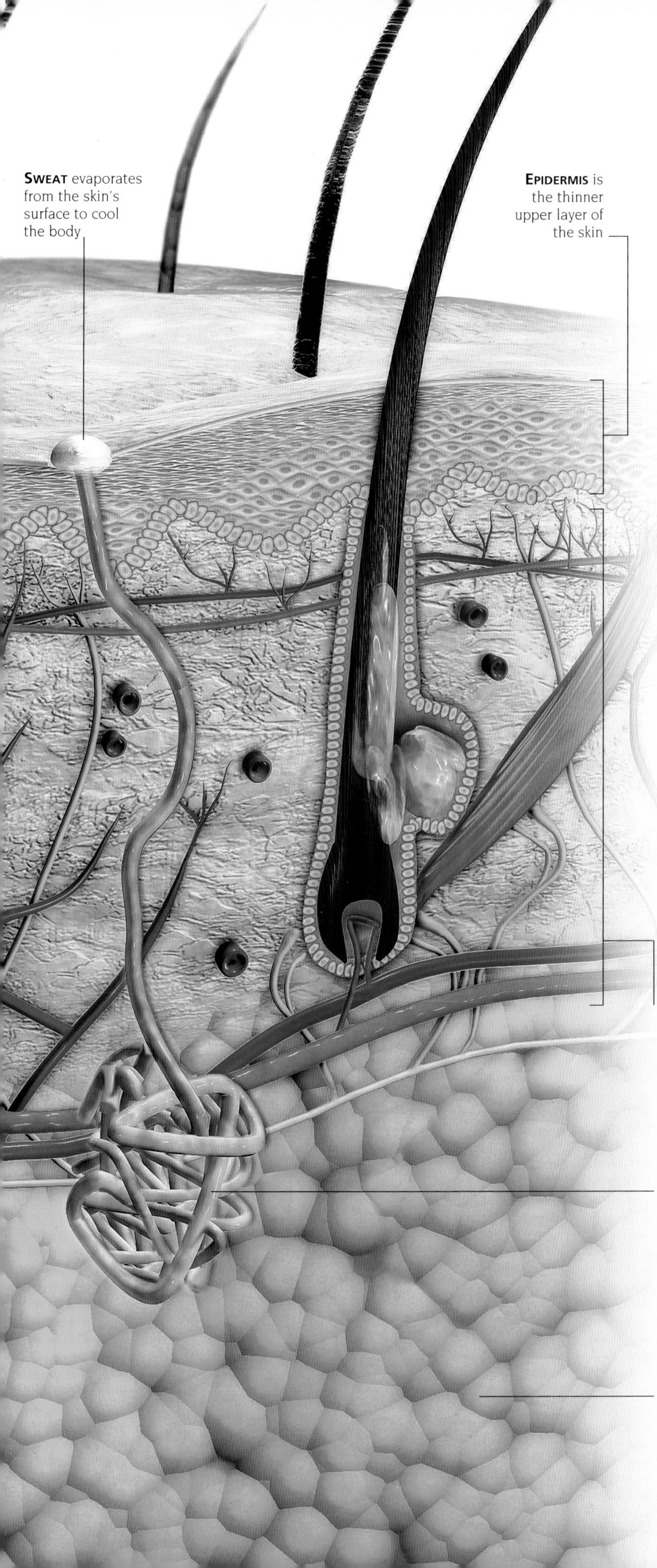

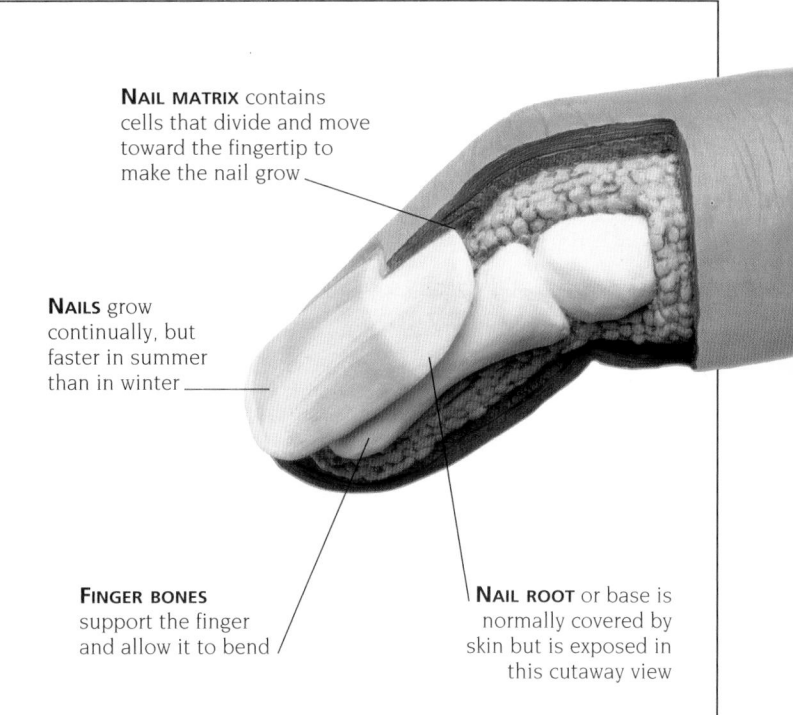

SWEAT evaporates from the skin's surface to cool the body

EPIDERMIS is the thinner upper layer of the skin

NAIL MATRIX contains cells that divide and move toward the fingertip to make the nail grow

NAILS grow continually, but faster in summer than in winter

FINGER BONES support the finger and allow it to bend

NAIL ROOT or base is normally covered by skin but is exposed in this cutaway view

NAILS

Your nails are very useful. As well as covering and protecting the ends of your fingers and toes, they let you scratch itches and help you pick up small objects. Nails are hard outgrowths of the epidermis that grow from cells in the nail matrix behind the nail's root. As these cells move forward, they harden and die. That's why it does not hurt when you cut your nails.

DERMIS is the thicker lower layer of the skin that contains blood vessels and nerves

SWEAT GLAND makes watery sweat that is carried along a tube to the skin's surface

FAT LAYER under the dermis helps to keep you warm

DID YOU KNOW?

Scientists can now grow skin artificially in the laboratory. Here you can see a thin sheet of newly grown skin being lifted from a culture dish. It was grown from a small piece of healthy epidermis taken from a hospital patient. The patient had suffered life-threatening burns that had severely damaged regions of his skin. But this lab-grown version of his own skin will be laid on top of the damaged areas to speed up healing and repair.

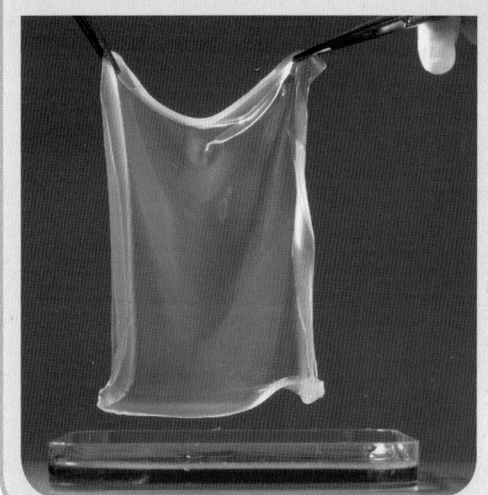

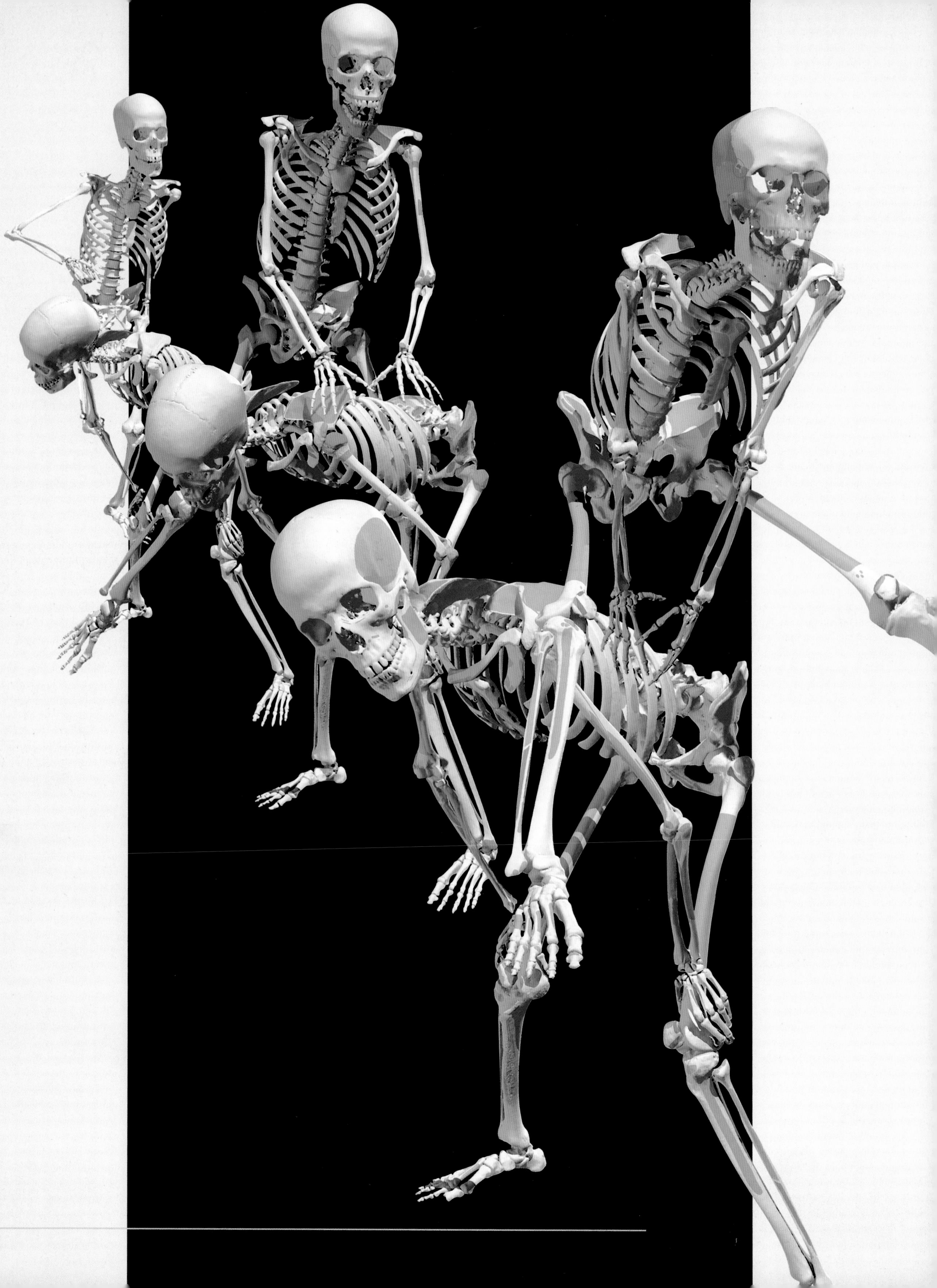

SECTION TWO: HEAD

By looking inside the head, this section lets you explore the skull and brain, eyes and ears, and mouth and nose. See as well, those versatile muscles that shape your smiles and frowns.

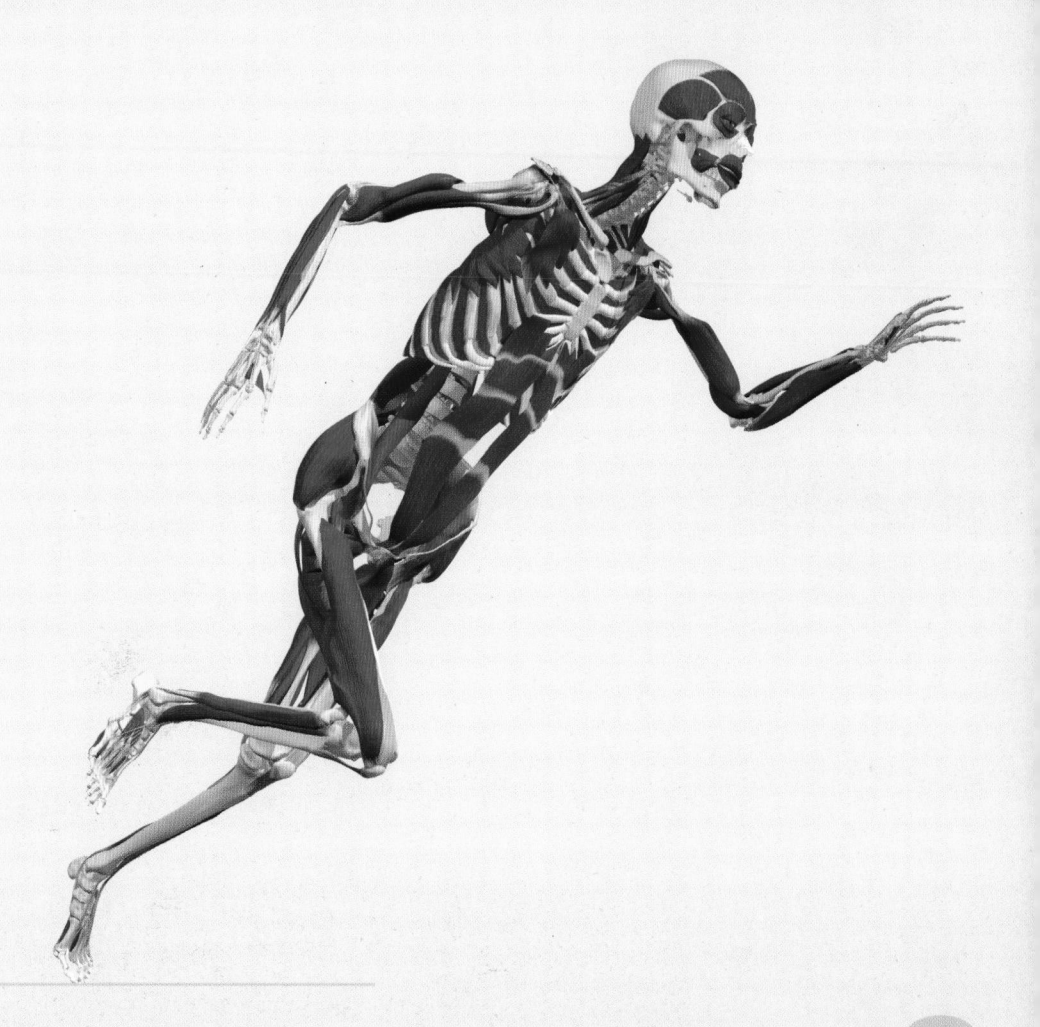

Head and Neck

THIS REMARKABLE IMAGE shows the head and neck with skin and muscle removed. On the right-hand side, the bones of the skull are in place. On the left-hand side, they have been removed to expose the wrinkled surface of the brain. On both sides, you can see the intricate and complex network of blood vessels and nerves.

BRAIN is the control center of the body, enabling you to think, learn, feel, and move

IRIS is the colored part of the eye that controls the size of the pupil

PUPIL controls the amount of light entering the eye by getting wider or narrower

AURICULAR NERVE gives sensation to the outer ear.

BRAINSTEM is the lower part of the brain that controls vital unconscious body activities such as breathing

FACIAL VEIN drains blood from the face

FRONTAL BONE forms the forehead and is connected by rigid joints to the other skull bones, which provide a protective casing around the brain

TEMPORAL VEIN drains blood from the scalp

NASAL BONE forms the upper part, or bridge, of the nose

TEMPORAL ARTERY supplies blood to the scalp

EYE SOCKET, or orbit, surrounds and protects most of the eyeball

TEMPORAL BONE forms part of the side of the skull

EYEBALL contains sensors that detect light and enable you to see

FACIAL NERVE BRANCHES transmit nerve signals to facial muscles and also bring sensation to the face

CHEEKBONE or zygomatic bone forms the cheek and part of the eye socket

FACIAL ARTERY supplies blood to the face

LATERAL NASAL ARTERIES supply blood to the nose

NASAL CAVITY contains sensors that detect smells in the air

UPPER JAWBONE, or maxilla, works with the lower jaw to bite and chew

HEAD

THE HEAD

Your head contains your brain and four major sense organs—eyes, ears, tongue, and nose. Its framework is formed by the skull bones that encase and protect your delicate brain as well as shaping your face. The mouth opens to allow food, water, and—with the nose—air to enter your body.

LABIAL ARTERY supplies blood to the lips

BUCCAL (CHEEK) NERVE gives sensation to skin over the fleshy part of the cheek

BRANCH OF FACIAL NERVE allows you to feel through your lower lip

DENTAL ARTERY supplies blood to the teeth and gums

VERTEBRAL ARTERY

SPINAL CORD is a bundle of nerve cells that extends down the back from the brainstem and relays messages between your brain and the rest of your body

EXTERNAL JUGULAR VEIN drains blood from the scalp and the face

ANTERIOR (RIGHT) JUGULAR VEIN drains blood from the neck

SUBCLAVIAN ARTERY supplies the arm with blood

BRACHIAL PLEXUS is a nerve network that relays nerve messages to and from your arm and hand

SUBCLAVIAN VEIN carries blood from the arm toward the heart

BRACHIOCEPHALIC TRUNK carries blood toward the right-hand side of the head and neck

THYROID VEIN drains the thyroid gland

BRACHIOCEPHALIC VEIN

TEETH anchored in the jawbones cut and crush food during chewing

LOWER JAWBONE, or mandible, moves to allow your mouth to open or close

INTERNAL JUGULAR VEIN drains blood from the brain and from the deeper parts of the face and neck

FIRST INTERCOSTAL NERVE supplies the muscles between the first and second ribs

COMMON CAROTID ARTERY carries blood to the head and brain

AORTA is your body's main artery. It carries oxygen-rich blood away from the heart

THE NECK

As well as supporting your head and allowing it to move, your neck is also the communication channel between your head and the rest of your body. Through it passes the spinal cord that links brain to body as well as the blood vessels that carry blood to and from your head.

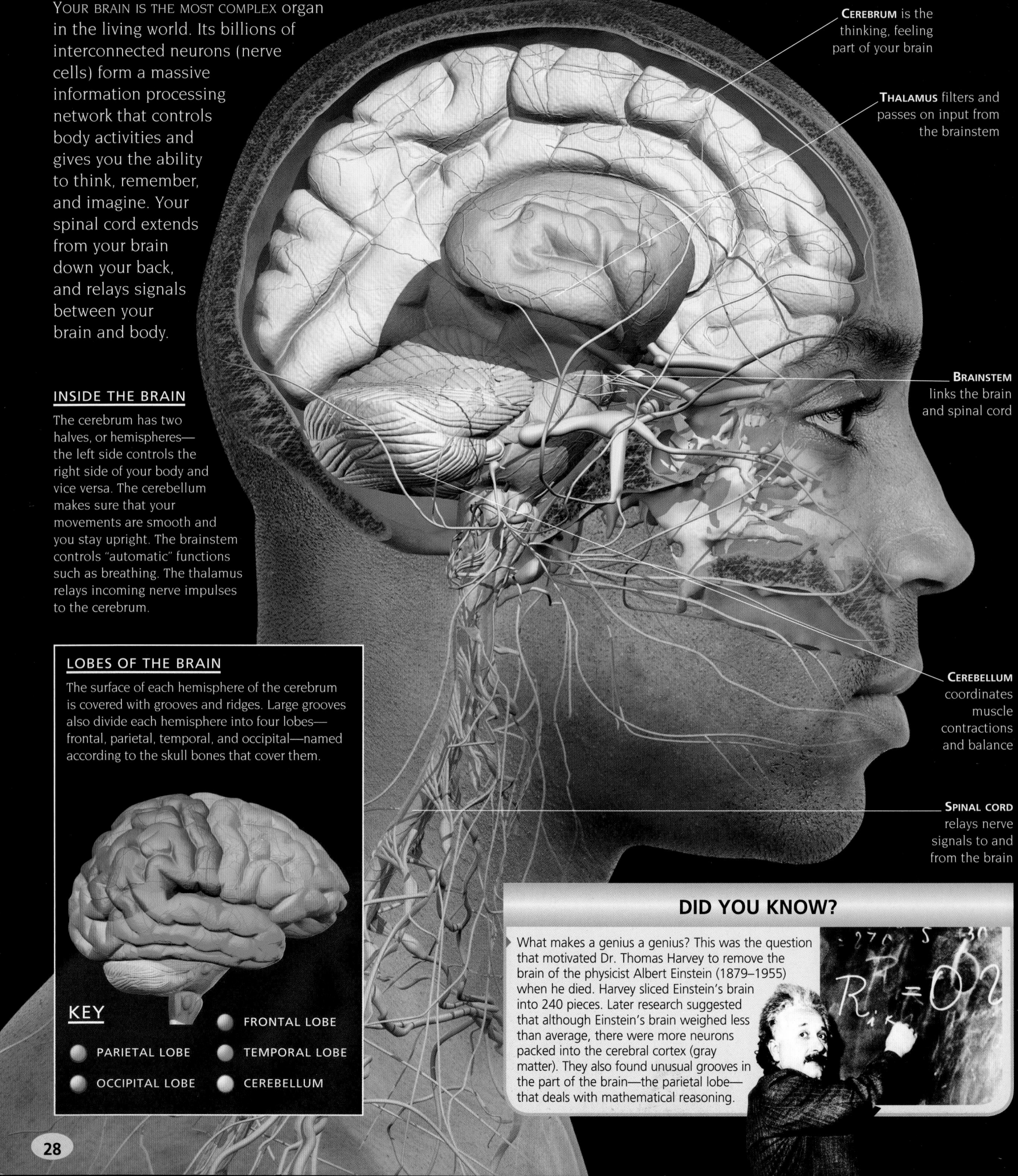

YOUR BRAIN IS THE MOST COMPLEX organ in the living world. Its billions of interconnected neurons (nerve cells) form a massive information processing network that controls body activities and gives you the ability to think, remember, and imagine. Your spinal cord extends from your brain down your back, and relays signals between your brain and body.

INSIDE THE BRAIN

The cerebrum has two halves, or hemispheres—the left side controls the right side of your body and vice versa. The cerebellum makes sure that your movements are smooth and you stay upright. The brainstem controls "automatic" functions such as breathing. The thalamus relays incoming nerve impulses to the cerebrum.

CEREBRUM is the thinking, feeling part of your brain

THALAMUS filters and passes on input from the brainstem

BRAINSTEM links the brain and spinal cord

CEREBELLUM coordinates muscle contractions and balance

SPINAL CORD relays nerve signals to and from the brain

LOBES OF THE BRAIN

The surface of each hemisphere of the cerebrum is covered with grooves and ridges. Large grooves also divide each hemisphere into four lobes—frontal, parietal, temporal, and occipital—named according to the skull bones that cover them.

KEY

- PARIETAL LOBE
- OCCIPITAL LOBE
- FRONTAL LOBE
- TEMPORAL LOBE
- CEREBELLUM

DID YOU KNOW?

What makes a genius a genius? This was the question that motivated Dr. Thomas Harvey to remove the brain of the physicist Albert Einstein (1879–1955) when he died. Harvey sliced Einstein's brain into 240 pieces. Later research suggested that although Einstein's brain weighed less than average, there were more neurons packed into the cerebral cortex (gray matter). They also found unusual grooves in the part of the brain—the parietal lobe—that deals with mathematical reasoning.

THE CEREBRUM

Your cerebrum makes up about 85 percent of your brain. The thin outer layer of each of its hemispheres forms the cerebral cortex. This allows you to think, feel, speak, move, and have consciousness or self-awareness. The surface of the cortex is massively folded, enabling more of it to be packed into the small space inside your skull.

PREFRONTAL CORTEX deals with thinking, learning, imagination, personality, and behavior

BROCA'S AREA produces speech

YOUR BRAIN IS MORE COMPLEX THAN ANY COMPUTER

PREMOTOR CORTEX coordinates complex movements such as playing a musical instrument

PRIMARY MOTOR CORTEX sends signals to muscles to move the body

PRIMARY SENSORY CORTEX receives signals from sensors in skin and muscles

SENSORY ASSOCIATION area interprets skin sensations and stores them in memory

VISUAL ASSOCIATION area analyzes input from the primary visual cortex to form images

WERNICKE'S AREA helps to interpret both written and spoken language

PRIMARY VISUAL CORTEX receives signals from the eye

AUDITORY ASSOCIATION CORTEX detects and memorizes sound patterns such as words or tunes

PRIMARY AUDITORY CORTEX detects sound

CRANIAL NERVES arise from the underside of the brain and serve mainly the face, neck, and ear

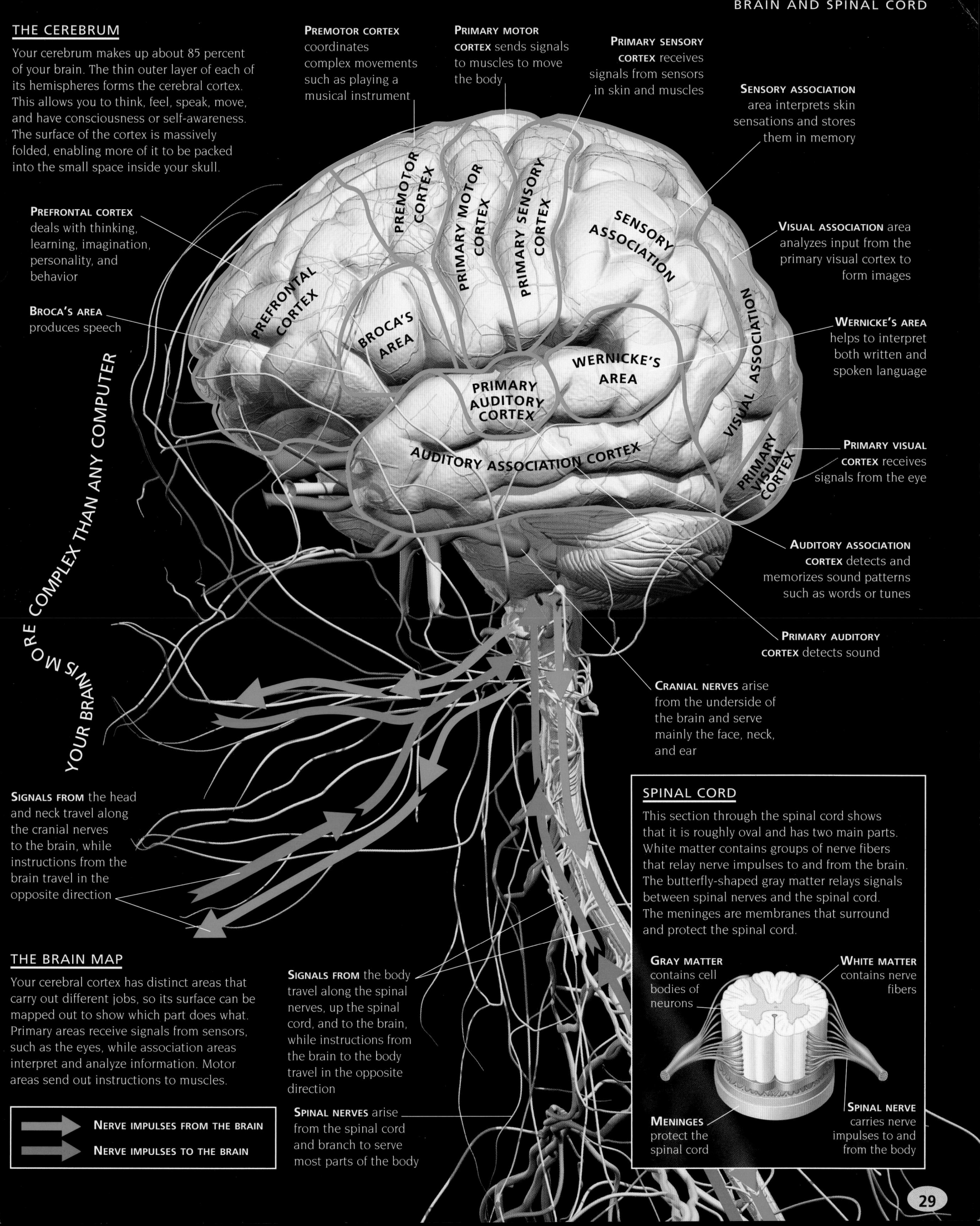

(Brain labels within illustration: PREMOTOR CORTEX, PRIMARY MOTOR CORTEX, PRIMARY SENSORY CORTEX, SENSORY ASSOCIATION, PREFRONTAL CORTEX, BROCA'S AREA, PRIMARY AUDITORY CORTEX, WERNICKE'S AREA, AUDITORY ASSOCIATION CORTEX, VISUAL ASSOCIATION, PRIMARY VISUAL CORTEX)

SIGNALS FROM the head and neck travel along the cranial nerves to the brain, while instructions from the brain travel in the opposite direction

THE BRAIN MAP

Your cerebral cortex has distinct areas that carry out different jobs, so its surface can be mapped out to show which part does what. Primary areas receive signals from sensors, such as the eyes, while association areas interpret and analyze information. Motor areas send out instructions to muscles.

➤ **NERVE IMPULSES FROM THE BRAIN**

➤ **NERVE IMPULSES TO THE BRAIN**

SIGNALS FROM the body travel along the spinal nerves, up the spinal cord, and to the brain, while instructions from the brain to the body travel in the opposite direction

SPINAL NERVES arise from the spinal cord and branch to serve most parts of the body

SPINAL CORD

This section through the spinal cord shows that it is roughly oval and has two main parts. White matter contains groups of nerve fibers that relay nerve impulses to and from the brain. The butterfly-shaped gray matter relays signals between spinal nerves and the spinal cord. The meninges are membranes that surround and protect the spinal cord.

GRAY MATTER contains cell bodies of neurons

WHITE MATTER contains nerve fibers

MENINGES protect the spinal cord

SPINAL NERVE carries nerve impulses to and from the body

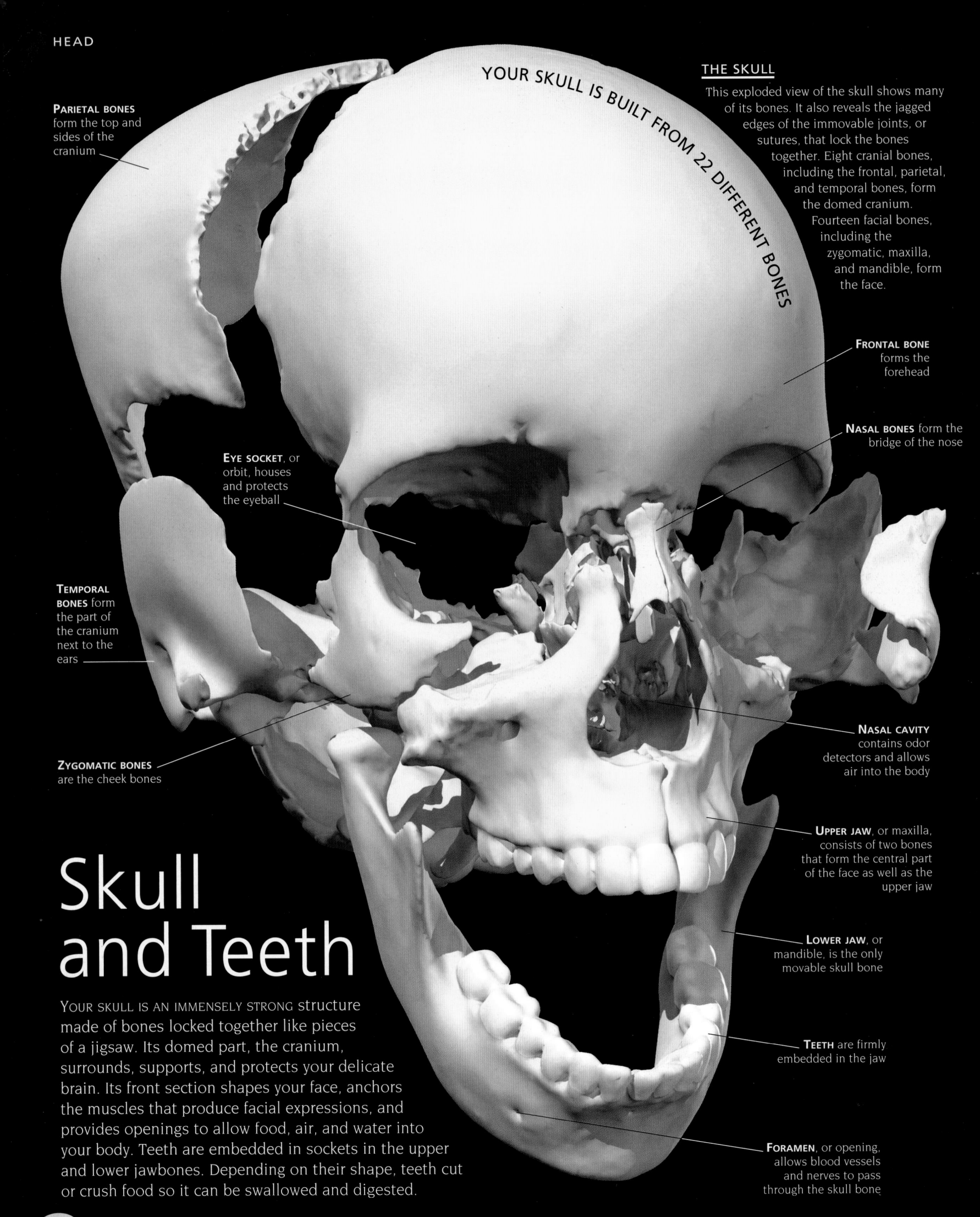

PARIETAL BONES form the top and sides of the cranium

THE SKULL
This exploded view of the skull shows many of its bones. It also reveals the jagged edges of the immovable joints, or sutures, that lock the bones together. Eight cranial bones, including the frontal, parietal, and temporal bones, form the domed cranium. Fourteen facial bones, including the zygomatic, maxilla, and mandible, form the face.

FRONTAL BONE forms the forehead

NASAL BONES form the bridge of the nose

EYE SOCKET, or orbit, houses and protects the eyeball

TEMPORAL BONES form the part of the cranium next to the ears

NASAL CAVITY contains odor detectors and allows air into the body

ZYGOMATIC BONES are the cheek bones

UPPER JAW, or maxilla, consists of two bones that form the central part of the face as well as the upper jaw

LOWER JAW, or mandible, is the only movable skull bone

Skull and Teeth

YOUR SKULL IS AN IMMENSELY STRONG structure made of bones locked together like pieces of a jigsaw. Its domed part, the cranium, surrounds, supports, and protects your delicate brain. Its front section shapes your face, anchors the muscles that produce facial expressions, and provides openings to allow food, air, and water into your body. Teeth are embedded in sockets in the upper and lower jawbones. Depending on their shape, teeth cut or crush food so it can be swallowed and digested.

TEETH are firmly embedded in the jaw

FORAMEN, or opening, allows blood vessels and nerves to pass through the skull bone

TOOTH ENAMEL IS THE HARDEST SUBSTANCE IN YOUR BODY

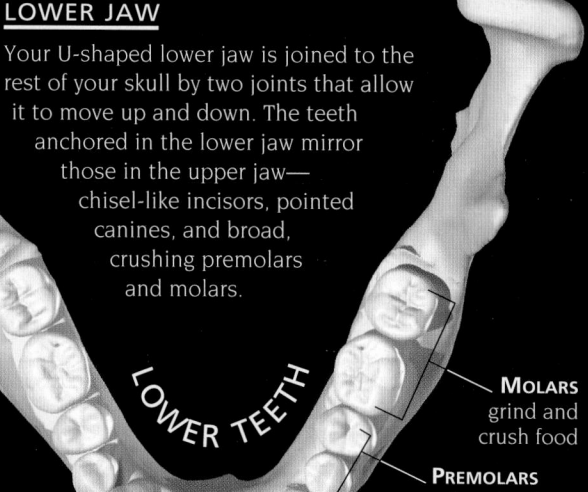

LOWER JAW

Your U-shaped lower jaw is joined to the rest of your skull by two joints that allow it to move up and down. The teeth anchored in the lower jaw mirror those in the upper jaw— chisel-like incisors, pointed canines, and broad, crushing premolars and molars.

LOWER TEETH

MOLARS grind and crush food

PREMOLARS chew food

CANINES grip and tear food

INCISORS cut and slice food

OCCIPITAL BONE forms the back and base of the cranium

EXTERNAL AUDITORY MEATUS is the opening through which sounds enter the ears

FORAMEN MAGNUM is the large opening through which the brain connects to the spinal cord

SPHENOID BONE forms part of the base of the cranium

PALATINE BONES, with maxilla, forms the hard palate (roof of the mouth)

MOLAR

MAXILLA

PREMOLAR

CANINE

UPPER TEETH

INCISORS

◀ SKULL FROM BELOW

As well as the bones forming the skull's underside, you can see here the teeth anchored in the upper jawbones. In each jaw, a full set of adult teeth contains four incisors, two canines, four premolars, and six molars—a total of 32 (2 x 16) in all. Some adults, like this one, are missing their back molar, or wisdom, teeth.

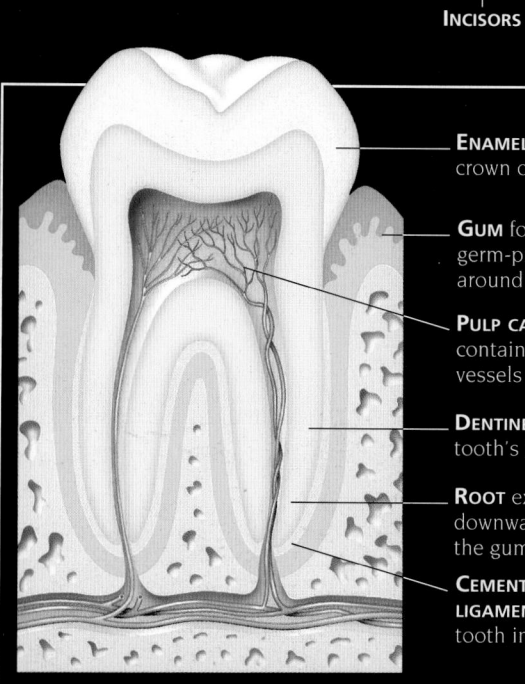

ENAMEL forms the crown of the tooth

GUM forms germ-proof collar around the tooth

PULP CAVITY contains blood vessels and nerves

DENTINE forms the tooth's framework

ROOT extends downward from the gum

CEMENT AND LIGAMENTS fix the tooth in socket

CROSS SECTION OF A TOOTH

The crown, or top, of a tooth is made of hard, white enamel and is usually all you see of a tooth unless one falls out. But most of a tooth's structure lies hidden in the jaw, as shown in this section. Beneath the enamel is a framework of bonelike dentine that shapes the tooth. Dentine extends downward into the root of the tooth, which is firmly fixed into its socket in the jawbone. A cavity within dentine contains soft pulp, which has blood vessels, nerves, and nerve endings that detect heat, cold, pain, and pressure.

DID YOU KNOW?

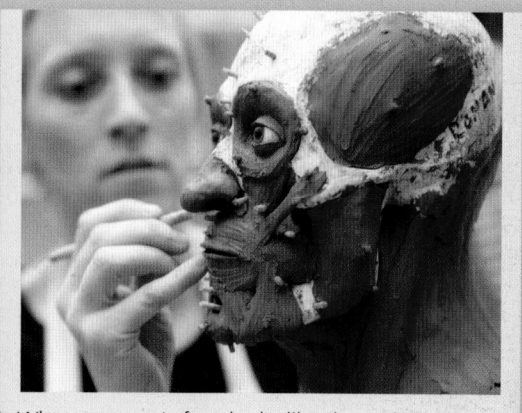

▶ What a person's face looks like depends on the shape of their skull and its muscles. Forensic sculptors use this information to rebuild someone's face long after they have died. Why? To help police identify murder victims or help archaeologists bring people "back to life." How? Using a copy of the skull, this forensic sculptor is covering "bones" with "muscles" made from clay. These muscles are then covered with "skin" to recreate the face.

Head Muscles

FACIAL EXPRESSIONS MEAN THE SAME THROUGHOUT THE WORLD

WHETHER YOU ARE HAPPY OR SAD, angry or frightened, disgusted or surprised, it is obvious how you feel from the expression on your face. Each expression is shaped by facial muscles that are connected to your skull bones at one end but, unusually, attached to skin at the other. When they contract, they tug at small areas of the face to produce the galaxy of facial expressions that communicate your feelings.

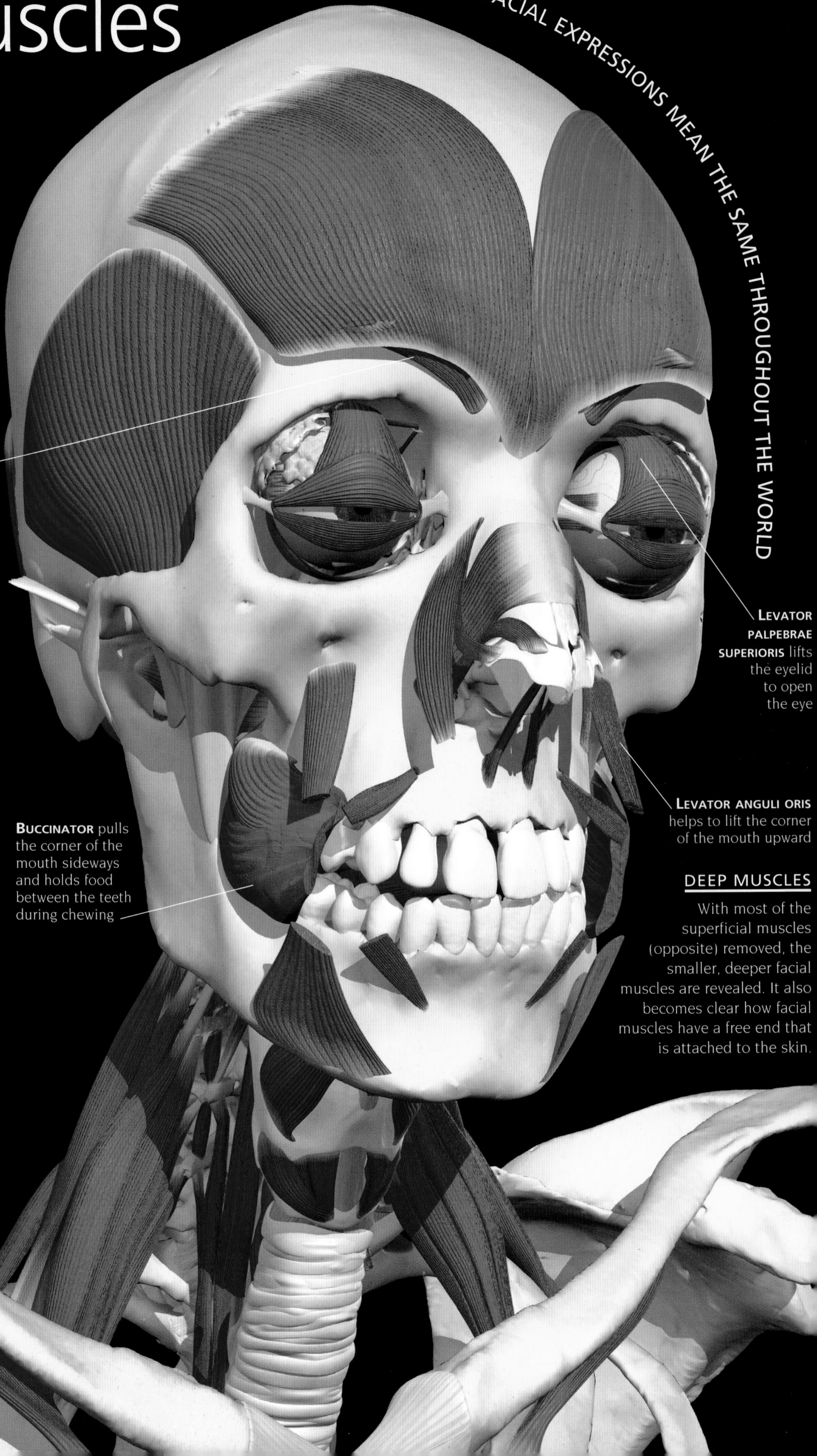
CORRUGATOR SUPERCILII draws the eyebrows together during frowning
LEVATOR PALPEBRAE SUPERIORIS lifts the eyelid to open the eye
BUCCINATOR pulls the corner of the mouth sideways and holds food between the teeth during chewing
LEVATOR ANGULI ORIS helps to lift the corner of the mouth upward

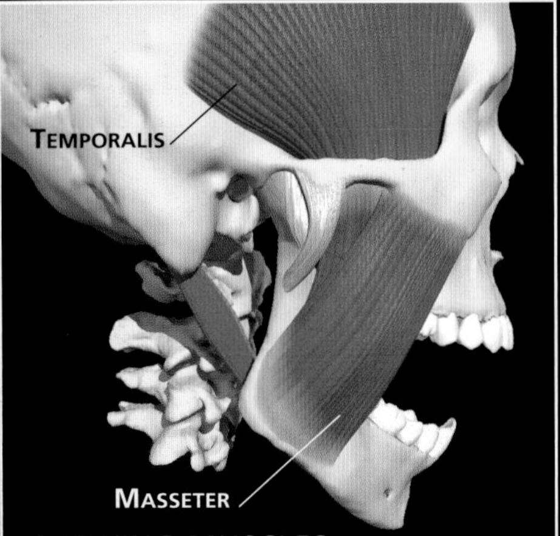
TEMPORALIS
MASSETER

CHEWING MUSCLES

To feel your powerful chewing muscles—the masseter and temporalis—in action, put your fingertips on the sides of your head, then clench and unclench your teeth. Chewing muscles pull your lower jaw upward, creating the enormous force needed to crush food between your back teeth.

DEEP MUSCLES

With most of the superficial muscles (opposite) removed, the smaller, deeper facial muscles are revealed. It also becomes clear how facial muscles have a free end that is attached to the skin.

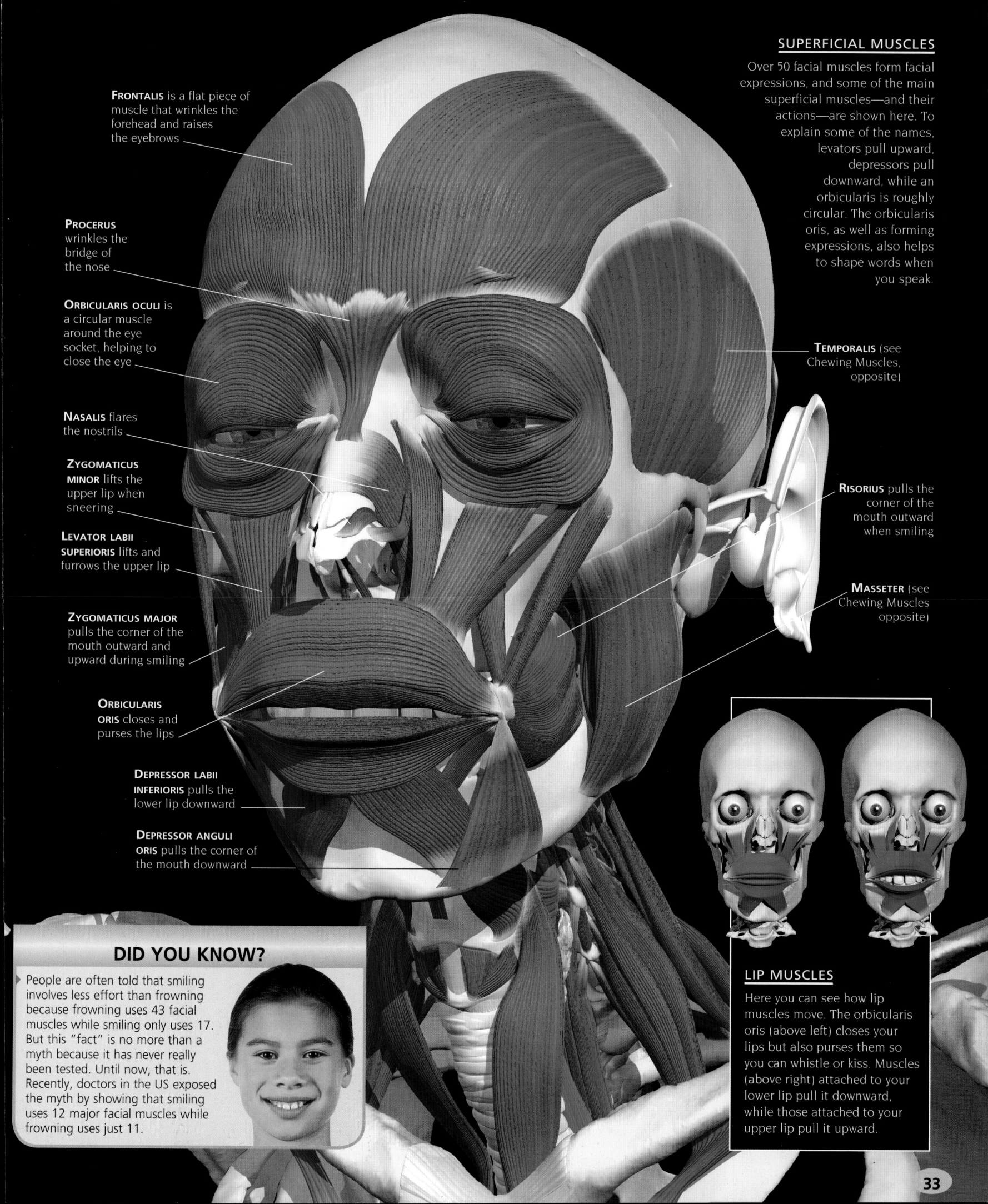

FRONTALIS is a flat piece of muscle that wrinkles the forehead and raises the eyebrows

PROCERUS wrinkles the bridge of the nose

ORBICULARIS OCULI is a circular muscle around the eye socket, helping to close the eye

NASALIS flares the nostrils

ZYGOMATICUS MINOR lifts the upper lip when sneering

LEVATOR LABII SUPERIORIS lifts and furrows the upper lip

ZYGOMATICUS MAJOR pulls the corner of the mouth outward and upward during smiling

ORBICULARIS ORIS closes and purses the lips

DEPRESSOR LABII INFERIORIS pulls the lower lip downward

DEPRESSOR ANGULI ORIS pulls the corner of the mouth downward

SUPERFICIAL MUSCLES

Over 50 facial muscles form facial expressions, and some of the main superficial muscles—and their actions—are shown here. To explain some of the names, levators pull upward, depressors pull downward, while an orbicularis is roughly circular. The orbicularis oris, as well as forming expressions, also helps to shape words when you speak.

TEMPORALIS (see Chewing Muscles, opposite)

RISORIUS pulls the corner of the mouth outward when smiling

MASSETER (see Chewing Muscles opposite)

LIP MUSCLES

Here you can see how lip muscles move. The orbicularis oris (above left) closes your lips but also purses them so you can whistle or kiss. Muscles (above right) attached to your lower lip pull it downward, while those attached to your upper lip pull it upward.

DID YOU KNOW?

People are often told that smiling involves less effort than frowning because frowning uses 43 facial muscles while smiling only uses 17. But this "fact" is no more than a myth because it has never really been tested. Until now, that is. Recently, doctors in the US exposed the myth by showing that smiling uses 12 major facial muscles while frowning uses just 11.

Tongue and Nose

WHEN YOU CHEW, AND YOUR TONGUE MIXES food with saliva, taste molecules from the food dissolve in saliva and are detected by tiny taste buds. When you breathe in, air swirls through your nose and any odor (smell) molecules are picked up by odor detectors. Together, the senses of taste and smell allow you to experience flavors such as chocolate or cheese. But smell is much more sensitive than taste. That is why food tastes so bland when you have a stuffed-up nose. Your tongue and nose also warn you about potential dangers, such as the taste of poison or the smell of smoke.

THE TONGUE AND TASTE

There are about 10,000 taste-detecting buds in your tongue. They detect just four basic tastes—sweet, sour, salty, and bitter. As this taste map shows, taste buds in different parts of your tongue are sensitive to different tastes. Each is detected by a specific area of the tongue.

OLFACTORY BULB carries nerve impulses to smell centers in the brain where they are interpreted as smells

OLFACTORY NERVE FIBERS carry nerve signals from odor receptors to the olfactory bulb through tiny holes in the skull

ODOR DETECTORS, when triggered by specific odor molecules, send nerve impulses to your brain

NASAL CAVITY, which has odor receptors, channels air from your nostrils to the throat

NASAL CARTILAGES support the external part of the nose

HARD PALATE, or roof of the mouth, separates the nasal cavity from the mouth cavity

YOUR NOSE CAN DETECT MORE THAN 10,000 SMELLS

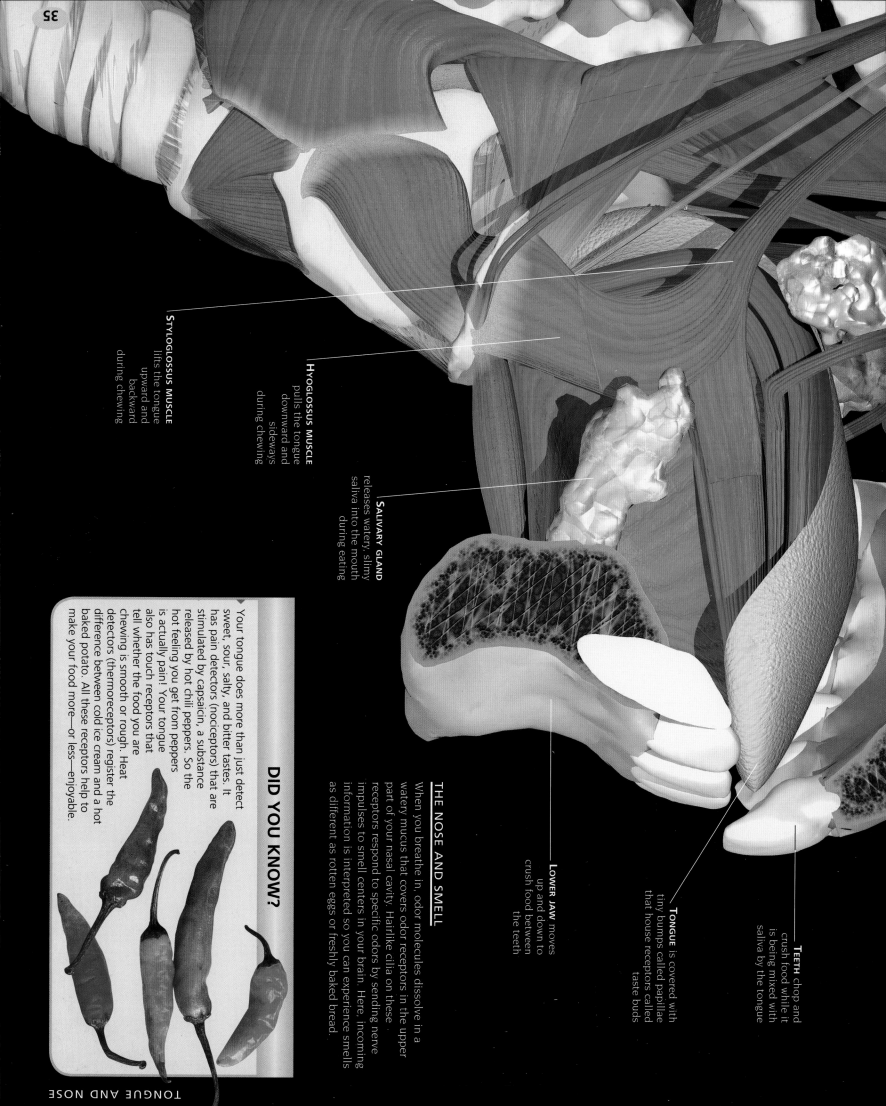

STYLOGLOSSUS MUSCLE lifts the tongue upward and backward during chewing

HYOGLOSSUS MUSCLE pulls the tongue downward and sideways during chewing

SALIVARY GLAND releases watery, slimy saliva into the mouth during eating

TEETH chop and crush food while it is being mixed with saliva by the tongue

TONGUE is covered with tiny bumps called papillae that house receptors called taste buds

LOWER JAW moves up and down to crush food between the teeth

THE NOSE AND SMELL

When you breathe in, odor molecules dissolve in a watery mucus that covers odor receptors in the upper part of your nasal cavity. Hairlike cilia on these receptors respond to specific odors by sending nerve impulses to smell centers in your brain. Here, incoming information is interpreted so you can experience smells as different as rotten eggs or freshly baked bread.

DID YOU KNOW?

Your tongue does more than just detect sweet, sour, salty, and bitter tastes. It has pain detectors (nociceptors) that are stimulated by capsaicin, a substance released by hot chili peppers. So the hot feeling you get from peppers is actually pain! Your tongue also has touch receptors that tell whether the food you are chewing is smooth or rough. Heat detectors (thermoreceptors) register the difference between cold ice cream and a hot baked potato. All these receptors help to make your food more—or less—enjoyable.

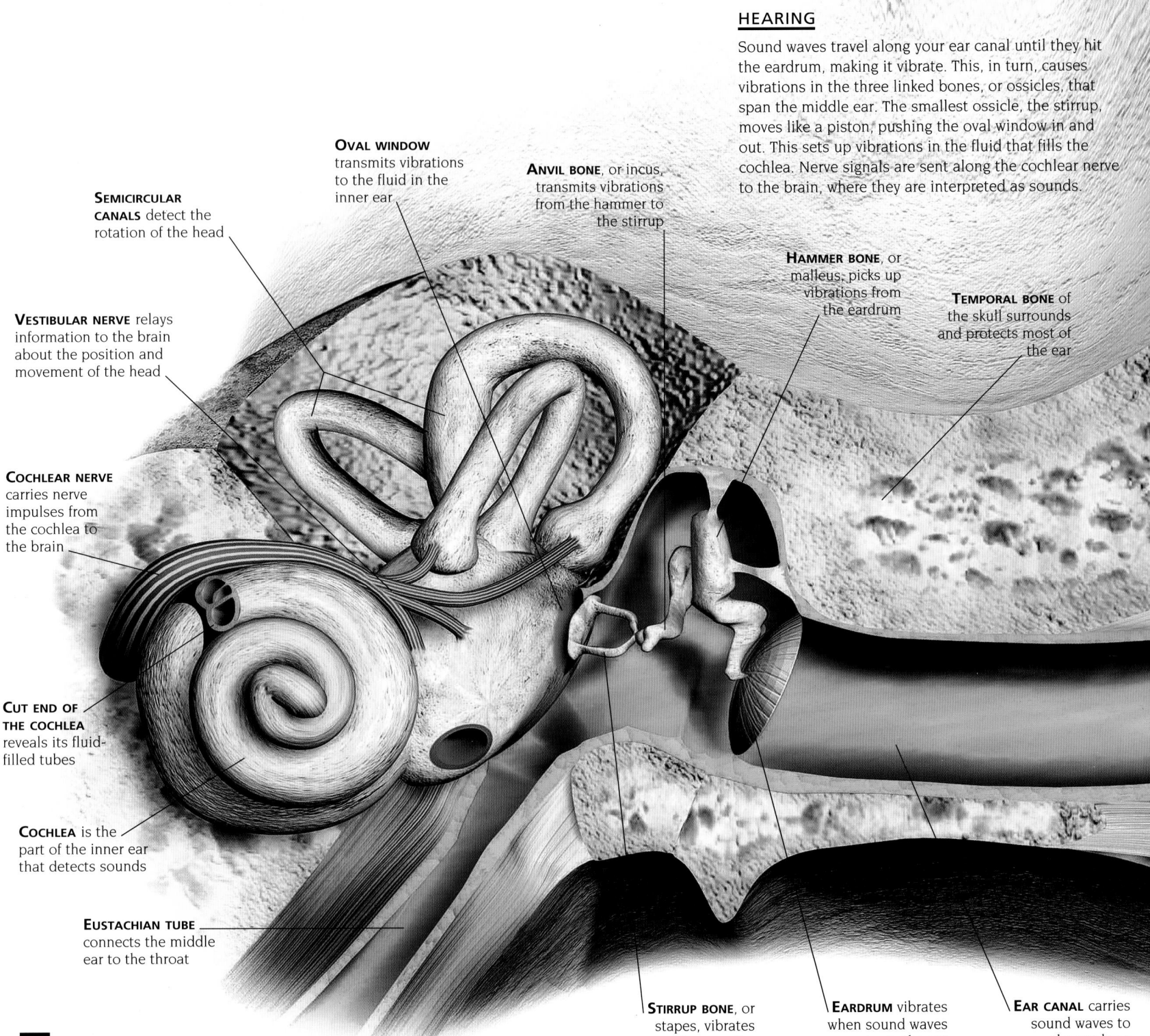

HEARING

Sound waves travel along your ear canal until they hit the eardrum, making it vibrate. This, in turn, causes vibrations in the three linked bones, or ossicles, that span the middle ear. The smallest ossicle, the stirrup, moves like a piston, pushing the oval window in and out. This sets up vibrations in the fluid that fills the cochlea. Nerve signals are sent along the cochlear nerve to the brain, where they are interpreted as sounds.

SEMICIRCULAR CANALS detect the rotation of the head

OVAL WINDOW transmits vibrations to the fluid in the inner ear

ANVIL BONE, or incus, transmits vibrations from the hammer to the stirrup

HAMMER BONE, or malleus, picks up vibrations from the eardrum

TEMPORAL BONE of the skull surrounds and protects most of the ear

VESTIBULAR NERVE relays information to the brain about the position and movement of the head

COCHLEAR NERVE carries nerve impulses from the cochlea to the brain

CUT END OF THE COCHLEA reveals its fluid-filled tubes

COCHLEA is the part of the inner ear that detects sounds

EUSTACHIAN TUBE connects the middle ear to the throat

STIRRUP BONE, or stapes, vibrates and moves the oval window

EARDRUM vibrates when sound waves arrive in the ear

EAR CANAL carries sound waves to the eardrum

Ear

FROM THE FAINT, HIGH-PITCHED WHINE of a mosquito to the earth-shaking roar of a passenger jet, your ears can detect a vast array of sounds. Sensors in the ear send nerve impulses to the hearing centers of the brain, which determine what you are listening to and where it is coming from. Most of the ear lies hidden inside the temporal bone of the skull. An outer ear canal is separated from the air-filled middle ear by the eardrum. Three tiny bones—the hammer, anvil, and stirrup—link the eardrum to the oval window, the entrance to the fluid-filled inner ear, which contains the sound-detecting cochlea. Your ears also help your body to maintain its balance and posture. Balance sensors are located in the inner ear.

DID YOU KNOW?

Cochlear implants (CI) can help people who are profoundly deaf and unable to use normal hearing aids. Here, CI patient Gemma Heath laughs with amazement as she hears sounds for the first time. During the operation to install her CI, tiny wires were inserted into her cochlea and a microphone was fixed to her skull above the ear. When the microphone picks up sounds, it sends electrical signals to the wires in the cochlea. This stimulates the cochlear nerve and sends impulses to the brain, enabling Gemma to detect sound patterns.

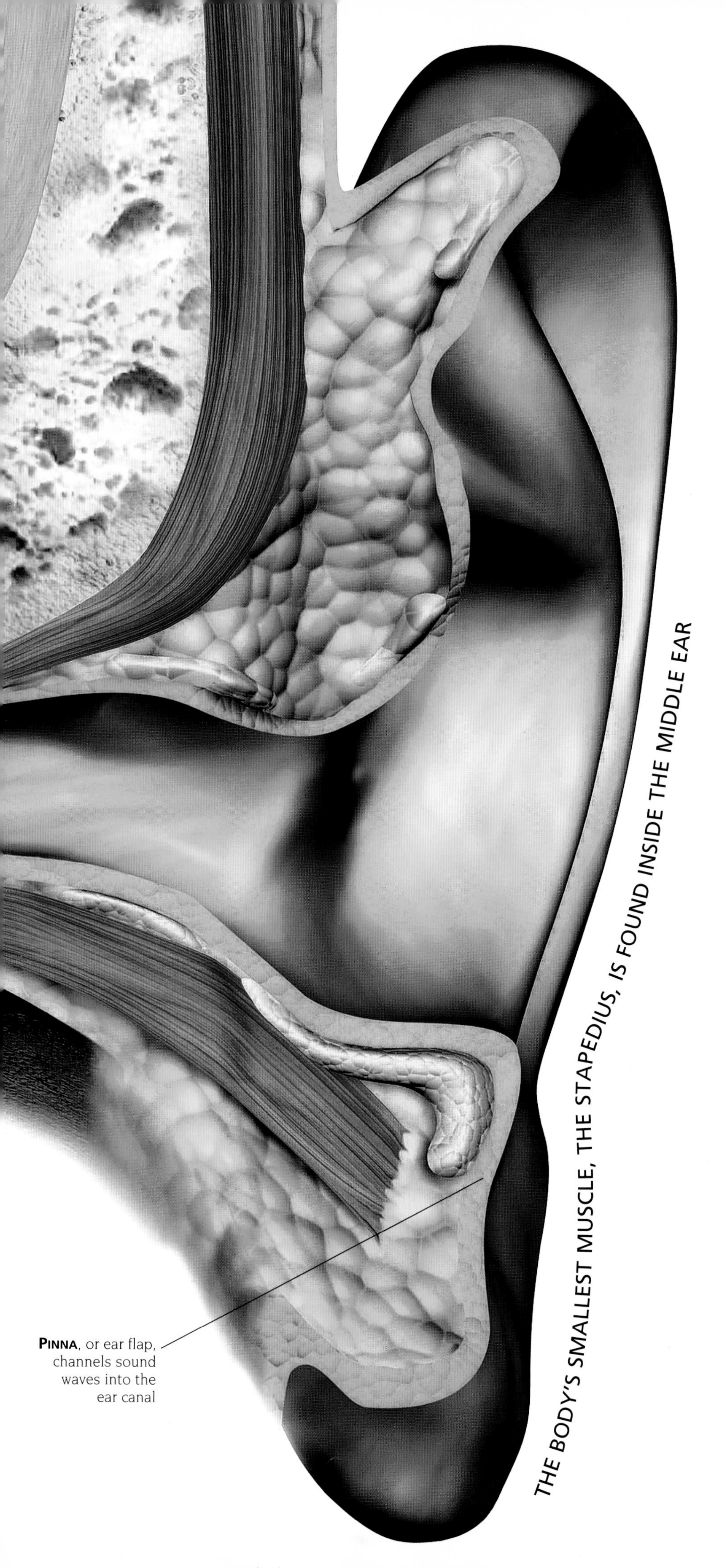

SENSE OF BALANCE

To keep you upright and balanced, your brain receives a constant stream of nerve signals from balance organs in your ears, as well as from your eyes, muscles, and joints. Inside your inner ear, there are two distinct balance organs. Three fluid-filled, semicircular canals contain sensors that detect movement. The utricle and saccule contain sensors that detect both the pull of gravity and acceleration.

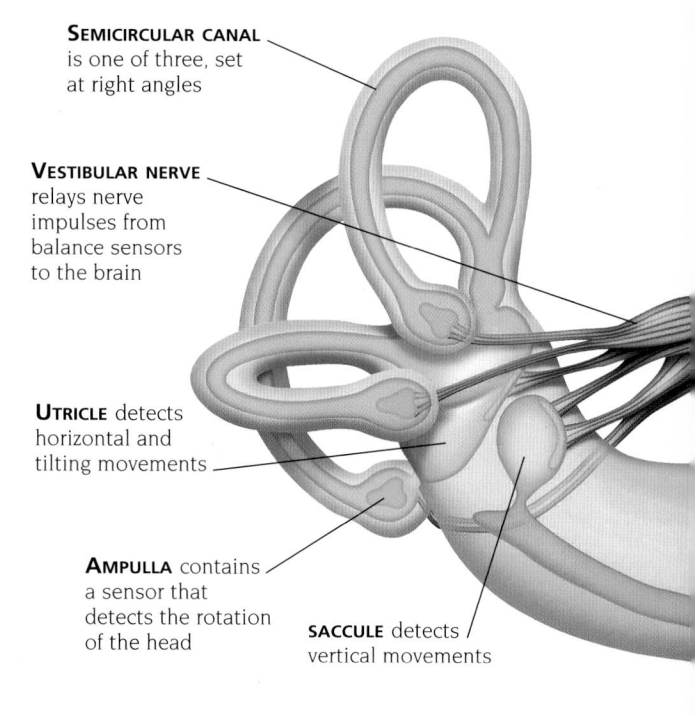

SEMICIRCULAR CANAL is one of three, set at right angles

VESTIBULAR NERVE relays nerve impulses from balance sensors to the brain

UTRICLE detects horizontal and tilting movements

AMPULLA contains a sensor that detects the rotation of the head

SACCULE detects vertical movements

HEAD MOVEMENTS

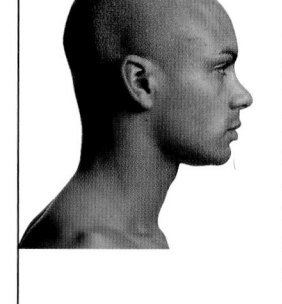

Balance sensors in the ear track the movement and position of your head. Your utricle and saccule detect linear (straight-line) movements, such as when a car speeds up or an elevator rises. The semicircular canals detect rotational movement in any direction.

LINEAR MOVEMENT

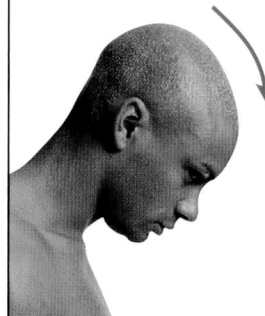

If you tilt your head forward, the sensor in your utricle slides forward slightly with the force of gravity and sends signals to your brain to indicate that your head has moved. Acceleration of the body (and head) forward or backward in a straight line would produce the same effect.

ROTATIONAL MOVEMENT

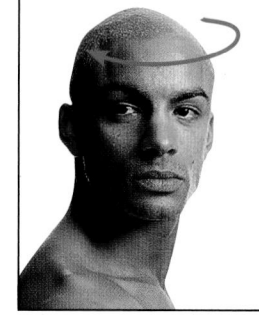

The three semicircular canals work together to detect how fast and in which direction your head is turning. When your head rotates, fluid in the canals moves and triggers sensors to send signals to your brain. By interpreting the signals arriving from each of the three canals, your brain can work out the direction of the rotation.

PINNA, or ear flap, channels sound waves into the ear canal

THE BODY'S SMALLEST MUSCLE, THE STAPEDIUS, IS FOUND INSIDE THE MIDDLE EAR

Eye

YOUR EYES PROVIDE YOUR BRAIN with a vast amount of information about what is happening around you, making vision your body's dominant sense. Like surveillance cameras, your eyes are constantly on the move, scanning everything in view. Your eyes automatically adjust the amount of light entering them, so they are not dazzled by bright light, yet still work in dim conditions. Without you having to think about it, the lens of each eye changes shape to focus light rays from close or distant objects onto a bank of light-sensitive photoreceptors. Signals from these light sensors are turned into three-dimensional images by your brain.

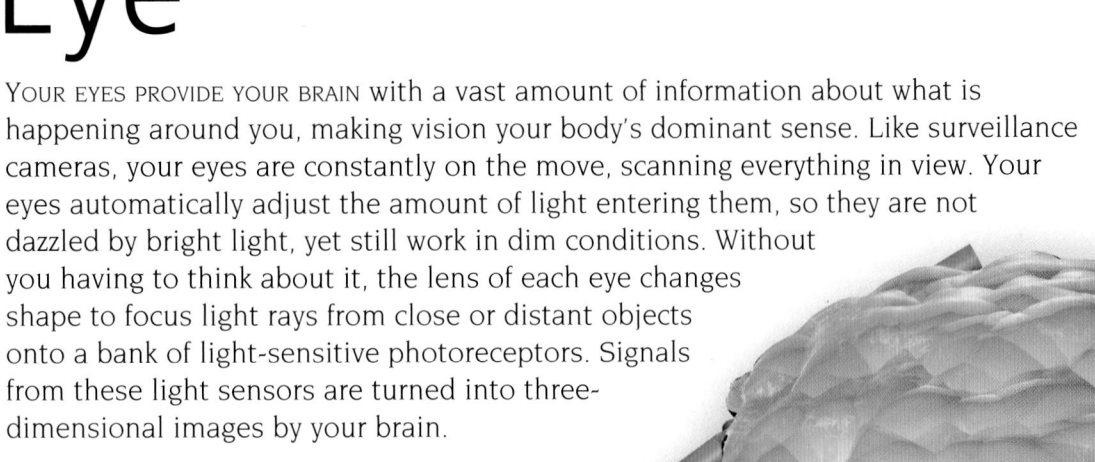

TEAR GLAND releases tears to moisten and clean the front of the eye

SUPERIOR RECTUS MUSCLE makes the eyeball look upward

SCLERA is the tough coat covering most of the eyeball

OUTSIDE VIEW

Here you can see a top view of the left eyeball. A tough sclera—the white of the eye—provides protection, while the clear cornea allows light into the front of the eye. Normally, only the front of the eyeball is visible. The rest is hidden inside the bony eye socket.

CORNEA is the clear zone at the front of the eyeball

OPTIC NERVE carries nerve impulses from the eye to the brain

MEDIAL RECTUS MUSCLE

TENDON OF SUPERIOR OBLIQUE MUSCLE turns as it passes through cartilage "pulley"

LOOKING IN AND OUT

These images of the right eye show the three pairs of muscles that move it. Rectus muscles are straight and oblique muscles are angled.

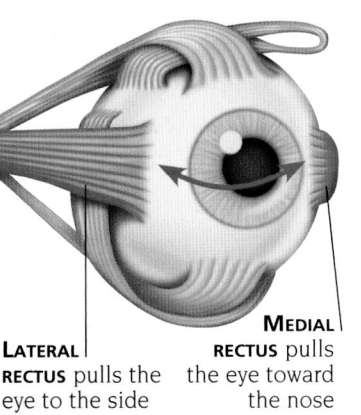

LATERAL RECTUS pulls the eye to the side

MEDIAL RECTUS pulls the eye toward the nose

LOOKING UP AND DOWN

Eye muscles are attached to the sclera of the eye at one end and the bony eye socket at the other.

SUPERIOR RECTUS pulls the eye upward

INFERIOR RECTUS pulls the eye downward

LOOKING AROUND

Your eyes are constantly on the move, smoothly following moving objects, and jerkily scanning static ones.

SUPERIOR OBLIQUE pulls the eye upward and to the side

INFERIOR OBLIQUE pulls the eye downward and toward the side of the head

DID YOU KNOW?

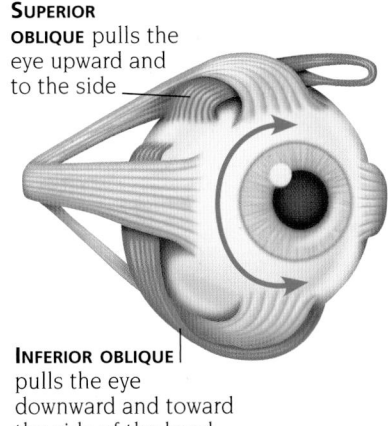

The colored patterns of your irises are as unique to you as your fingerprints. This uniqueness can be used to identify people during security checks. The iris is scanned by a computer, which maps (above) and stores the pattern. To check a person's identity, a new scan of their iris is compared with the stored version.

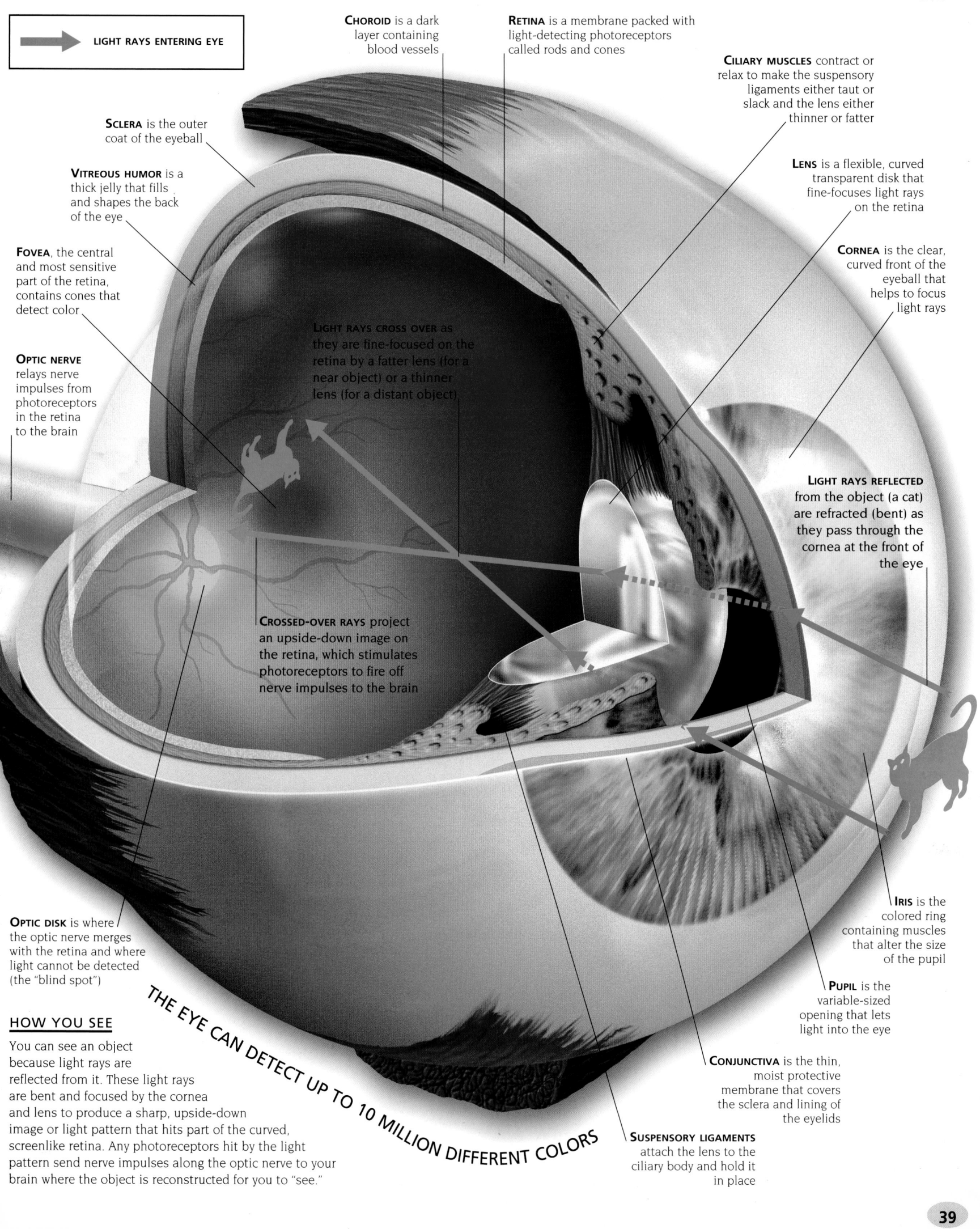

LIGHT RAYS ENTERING EYE

CHOROID is a dark layer containing blood vessels

RETINA is a membrane packed with light-detecting photoreceptors called rods and cones

CILIARY MUSCLES contract or relax to make the suspensory ligaments either taut or slack and the lens either thinner or fatter

SCLERA is the outer coat of the eyeball

VITREOUS HUMOR is a thick jelly that fills and shapes the back of the eye

LENS is a flexible, curved transparent disk that fine-focuses light rays on the retina

FOVEA, the central and most sensitive part of the retina, contains cones that detect color

CORNEA is the clear, curved front of the eyeball that helps to focus light rays

LIGHT RAYS CROSS OVER as they are fine-focused on the retina by a fatter lens (for a near object) or a thinner lens (for a distant object)

OPTIC NERVE relays nerve impulses from photoreceptors in the retina to the brain

LIGHT RAYS REFLECTED from the object (a cat) are refracted (bent) as they pass through the cornea at the front of the eye

CROSSED-OVER RAYS project an upside-down image on the retina, which stimulates photoreceptors to fire off nerve impulses to the brain

OPTIC DISK is where the optic nerve merges with the retina and where light cannot be detected (the "blind spot")

IRIS is the colored ring containing muscles that alter the size of the pupil

PUPIL is the variable-sized opening that lets light into the eye

CONJUNCTIVA is the thin, moist protective membrane that covers the sclera and lining of the eyelids

SUSPENSORY LIGAMENTS attach the lens to the ciliary body and hold it in place

HOW YOU SEE

You can see an object because light rays are reflected from it. These light rays are bent and focused by the cornea and lens to produce a sharp, upside-down image or light pattern that hits part of the curved, screenlike retina. Any photoreceptors hit by the light pattern send nerve impulses along the optic nerve to your brain where the object is reconstructed for you to "see."

THE EYE CAN DETECT UP TO 10 MILLION DIFFERENT COLORS

Mouth and Throat

IMAGINE IF YOU COULDN'T OPEN YOUR MOUTH. Eating and drinking would be impossible, as would speaking and panting after running fast. Fortunately, your mouth does open to allow food and drink into your digestive system. It also provides a passage that carries air, and shapes sound waves produced in the larynx into speech. The inside of your mouth is wet and slimy, due to the release of saliva, which moistens and cleans your mouth. Your throat, or pharynx, is a muscular tube that runs from the back of your nasal cavity to about halfway down your neck. Its job is to carry air and food farther toward their final destinations. This section through a head shows the inside of the mouth (tongue removed) and throat.

THE MOUTH

Your mouth is bounded by your lips at the front, by the hard and soft palates (roof of the mouth), by the cheeks at the side, and by your tongue. The space inside is called the oral cavity. At its rear, the oral cavity opens into the throat. This opening is guarded by tonsils, which destroy harmful bacteria carried into your mouth by food and air.

NASOPHARYNX, or upper throat

SOFT PALATE is a muscular flap that stops food from going into the nasal cavity during swallowing

NASAL CAVITY is a hollow space behind the nose through which air flows to and from your throat

FRONTAL SINUS is one of several air spaces in the skull that reduces its overall weight

HARD PALATE forms most of the roof of the oral cavity

SALIVARY GLANDS POUR ABOUT 1 QUART (1 LITER) OF SALIVA INTO YOUR MOUTH DAILY

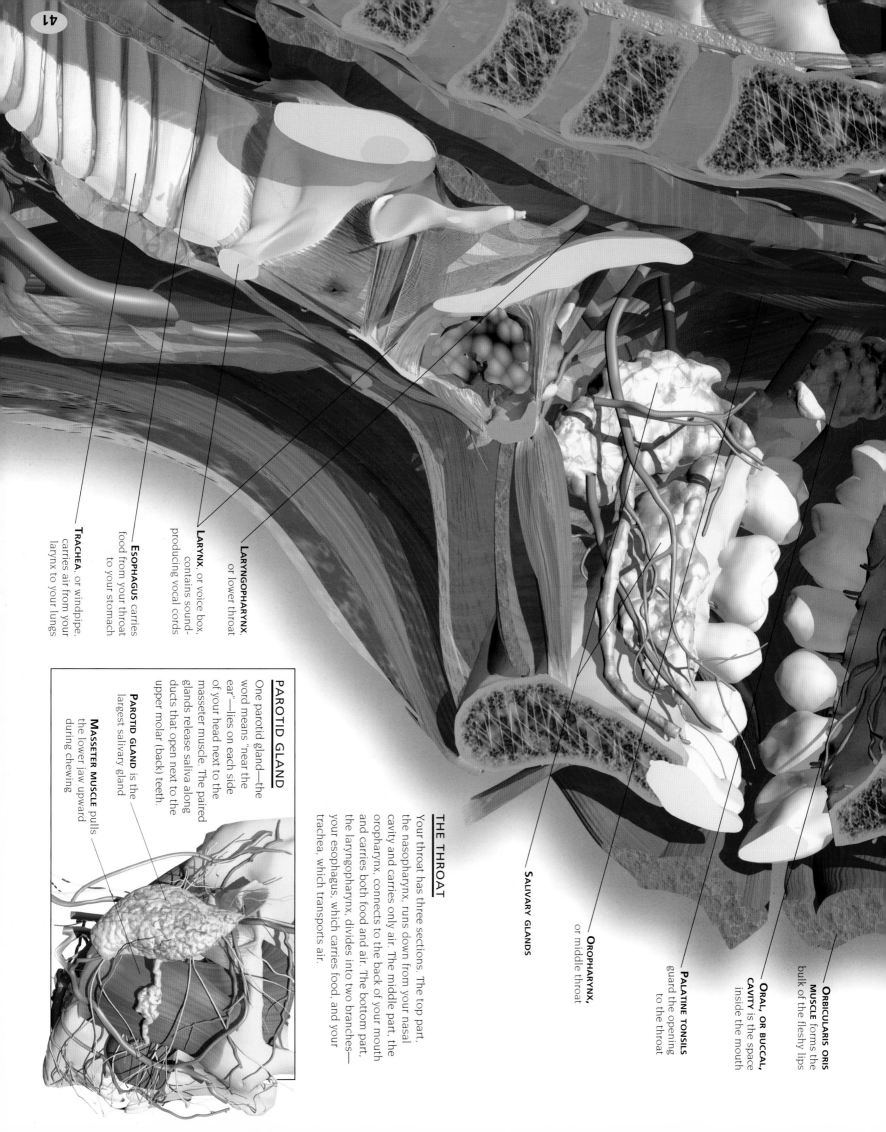

TRACHEA, or windpipe, carries air from your larynx to your lungs

ESOPHAGUS carries food from your throat to your stomach

LARYNX, or voice box, contains sound-producing vocal cords

LARYNGOPHARYNX, or lower throat

PAROTID GLAND

One parotid gland—the word means "near the ear"—lies on each side of your head next to the masseter muscle. The paired glands release saliva along ducts that open next to the upper molar (back) teeth.

PAROTID GLAND is the largest salivary gland

MASSETER MUSCLE pulls the lower jaw upward during chewing

THE THROAT

Your throat has three sections. The top part, the nasopharynx, runs down from your nasal cavity and carries only air. The middle part, the oropharynx, connects to the back of your mouth and carries both food and air. The bottom part, the laryngopharynx, divides into two branches— your esophagus, which carries food, and your trachea, which transports air.

SALIVARY GLANDS

OROPHARYNX, or middle throat

PALATINE TONSILS guard the opening to the throat

ORAL, OR BUCCAL, CAVITY is the space inside the mouth

ORBICULARIS ORIS MUSCLE forms the bulk of the fleshy lips

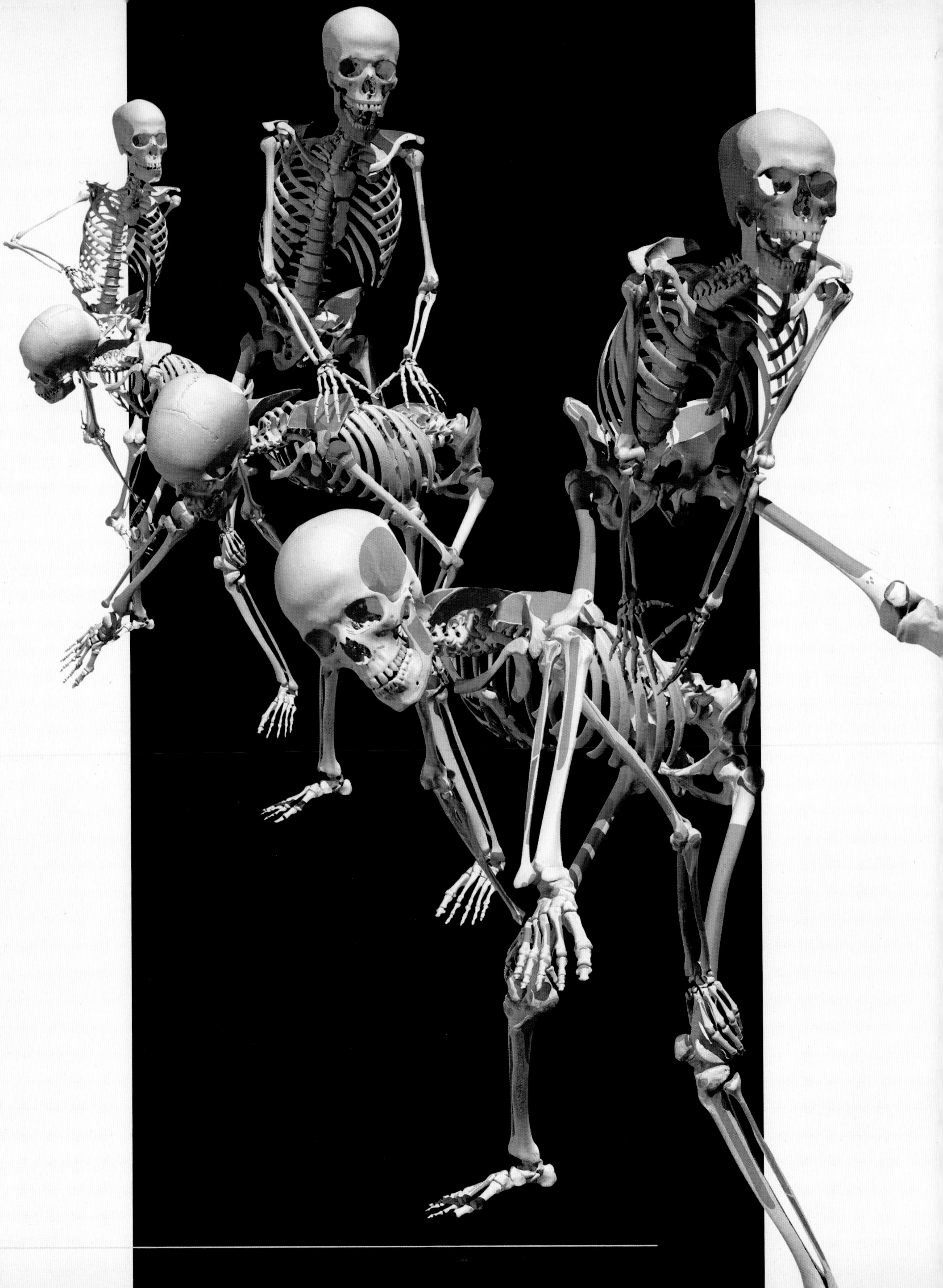

SECTION THREE: UPPER BODY

In this exploration of the upper body, you will visit the heart, lungs, stomach, and much more. Discover, too, how the arms and hands work, and why they are so important for our survival.

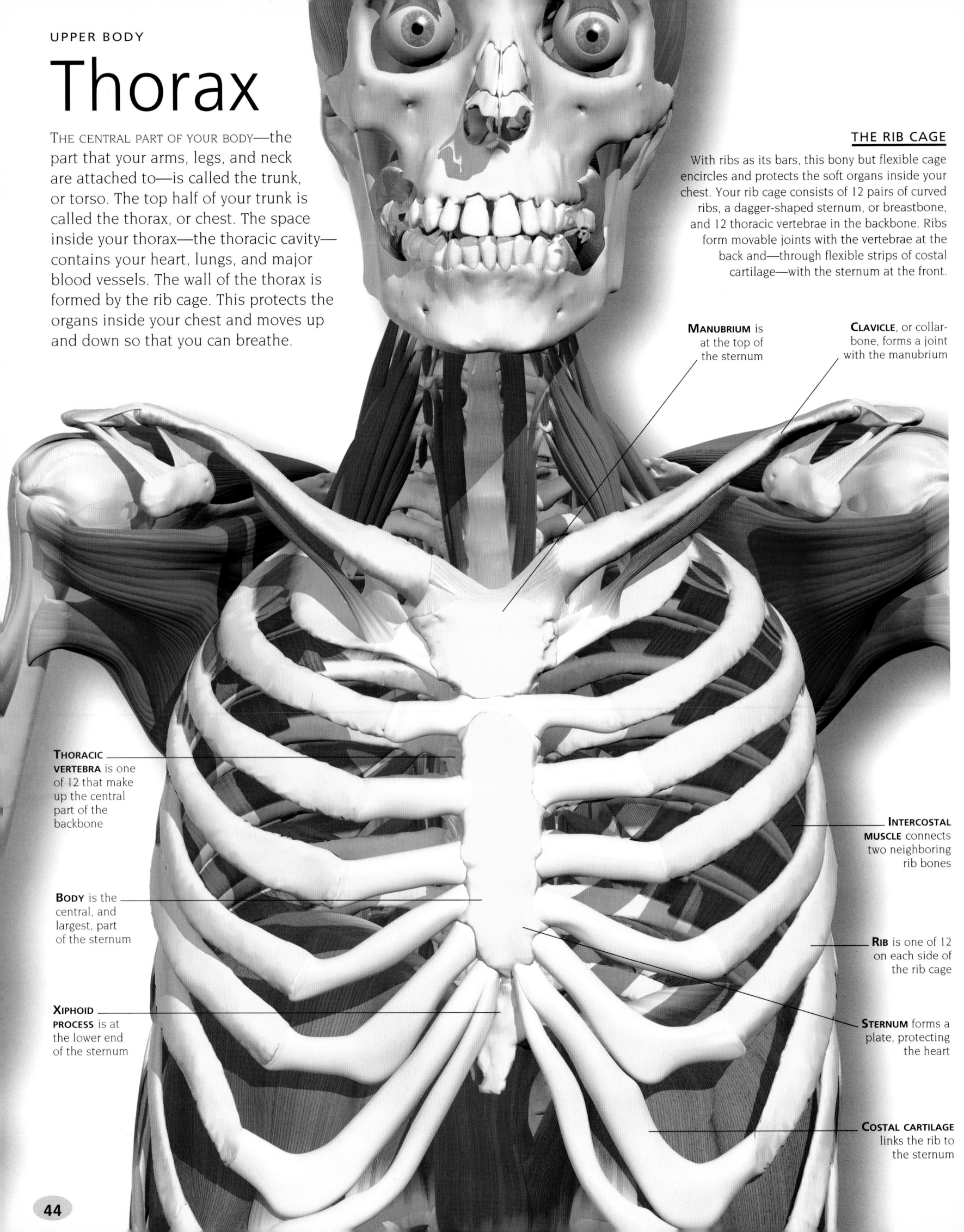

Thorax

THE CENTRAL PART OF YOUR BODY—the part that your arms, legs, and neck are attached to—is called the trunk, or torso. The top half of your trunk is called the thorax, or chest. The space inside your thorax—the thoracic cavity—contains your heart, lungs, and major blood vessels. The wall of the thorax is formed by the rib cage. This protects the organs inside your chest and moves up and down so that you can breathe.

THE RIB CAGE

With ribs as its bars, this bony but flexible cage encircles and protects the soft organs inside your chest. Your rib cage consists of 12 pairs of curved ribs, a dagger-shaped sternum, or breastbone, and 12 thoracic vertebrae in the backbone. Ribs form movable joints with the vertebrae at the back and—through flexible strips of costal cartilage—with the sternum at the front.

MANUBRIUM is at the top of the sternum

CLAVICLE, or collarbone, forms a joint with the manubrium

THORACIC VERTEBRA is one of 12 that make up the central part of the backbone

INTERCOSTAL MUSCLE connects two neighboring rib bones

BODY is the central, and largest, part of the sternum

RIB is one of 12 on each side of the rib cage

STERNUM forms a plate, protecting the heart

XIPHOID PROCESS is at the lower end of the sternum

COSTAL CARTILAGE links the rib to the sternum

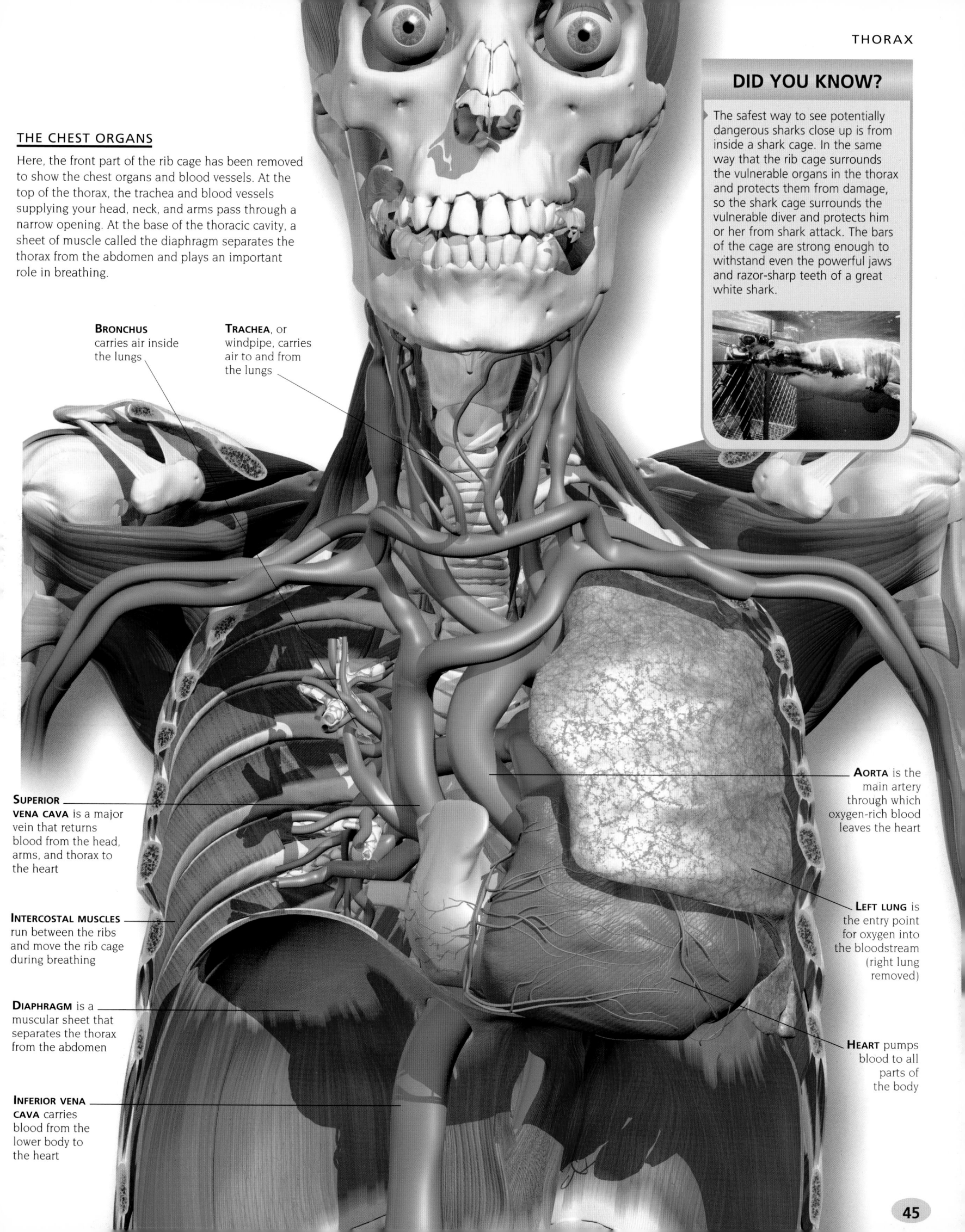

THE CHEST ORGANS

Here, the front part of the rib cage has been removed to show the chest organs and blood vessels. At the top of the thorax, the trachea and blood vessels supplying your head, neck, and arms pass through a narrow opening. At the base of the thoracic cavity, a sheet of muscle called the diaphragm separates the thorax from the abdomen and plays an important role in breathing.

DID YOU KNOW?

The safest way to see potentially dangerous sharks close up is from inside a shark cage. In the same way that the rib cage surrounds the vulnerable organs in the thorax and protects them from damage, so the shark cage surrounds the vulnerable diver and protects him or her from shark attack. The bars of the cage are strong enough to withstand even the powerful jaws and razor-sharp teeth of a great white shark.

BRONCHUS carries air inside the lungs

TRACHEA, or windpipe, carries air to and from the lungs

SUPERIOR VENA CAVA is a major vein that returns blood from the head, arms, and thorax to the heart

INTERCOSTAL MUSCLES run between the ribs and move the rib cage during breathing

DIAPHRAGM is a muscular sheet that separates the thorax from the abdomen

INFERIOR VENA CAVA carries blood from the lower body to the heart

AORTA is the main artery through which oxygen-rich blood leaves the heart

LEFT LUNG is the entry point for oxygen into the bloodstream (right lung removed)

HEART pumps blood to all parts of the body

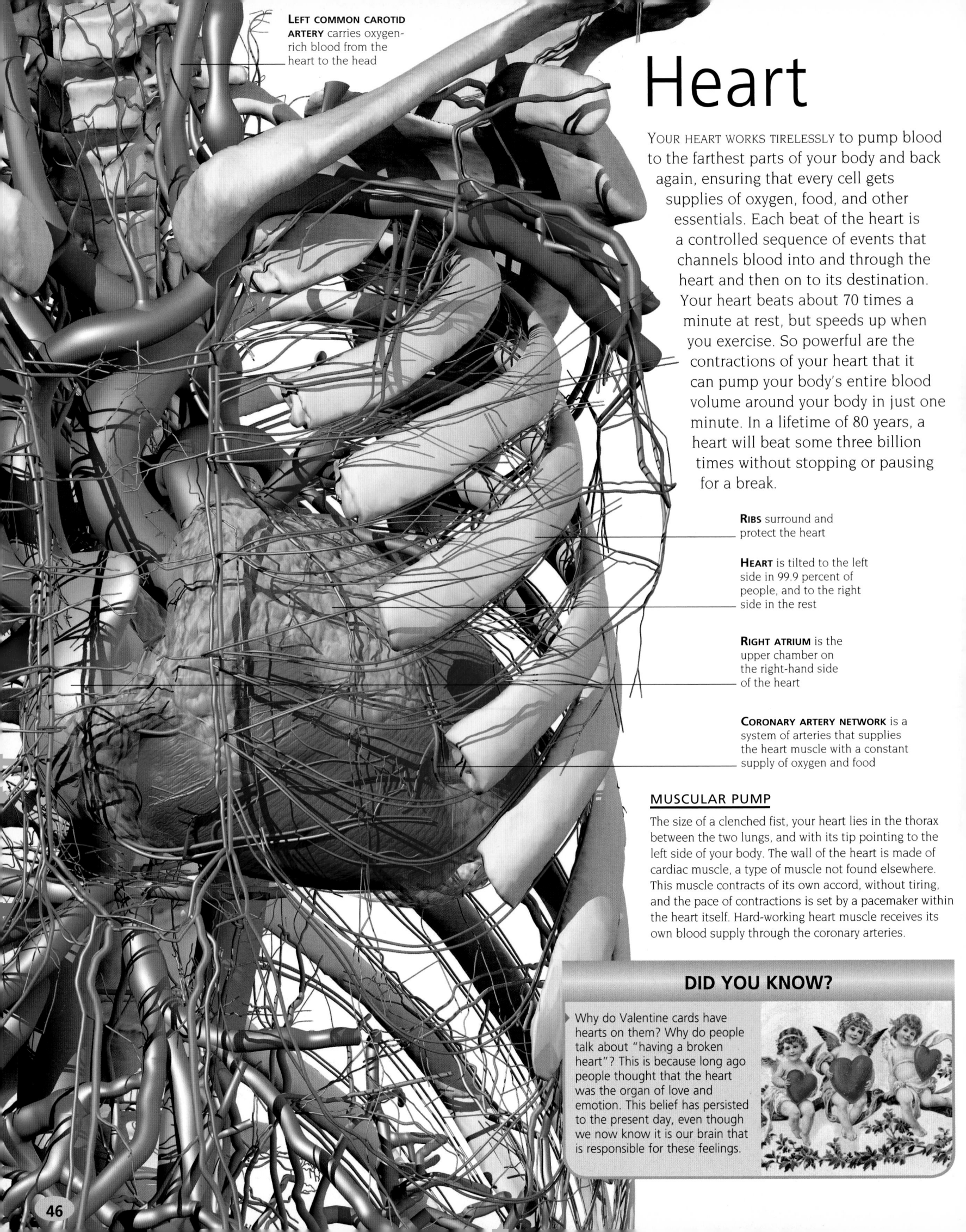

LEFT COMMON CAROTID
ARTERY carries oxygen-
rich blood from the
heart to the head

Heart

YOUR HEART WORKS TIRELESSLY to pump blood
to the farthest parts of your body and back
again, ensuring that every cell gets
supplies of oxygen, food, and other
essentials. Each beat of the heart is
a controlled sequence of events that
channels blood into and through the
heart and then on to its destination.
Your heart beats about 70 times a
minute at rest, but speeds up when
you exercise. So powerful are the
contractions of your heart that it
can pump your body's entire blood
volume around your body in just one
minute. In a lifetime of 80 years, a
heart will beat some three billion
times without stopping or pausing
for a break.

RIBS surround and
protect the heart

HEART is tilted to the left
side in 99.9 percent of
people, and to the right
side in the rest

RIGHT ATRIUM is the
upper chamber on
the right-hand side
of the heart

CORONARY ARTERY NETWORK is a
system of arteries that supplies
the heart muscle with a constant
supply of oxygen and food

MUSCULAR PUMP

The size of a clenched fist, your heart lies in the thorax
between the two lungs, and with its tip pointing to the
left side of your body. The wall of the heart is made of
cardiac muscle, a type of muscle not found elsewhere.
This muscle contracts of its own accord, without tiring,
and the pace of contractions is set by a pacemaker within
the heart itself. Hard-working heart muscle receives its
own blood supply through the coronary arteries.

DID YOU KNOW?

Why do Valentine cards have
hearts on them? Why do people
talk about "having a broken
heart"? This is because long ago
people thought that the heart
was the organ of love and
emotion. This belief has persisted
to the present day, even though
we now know it is our brain that
is responsible for these feelings.

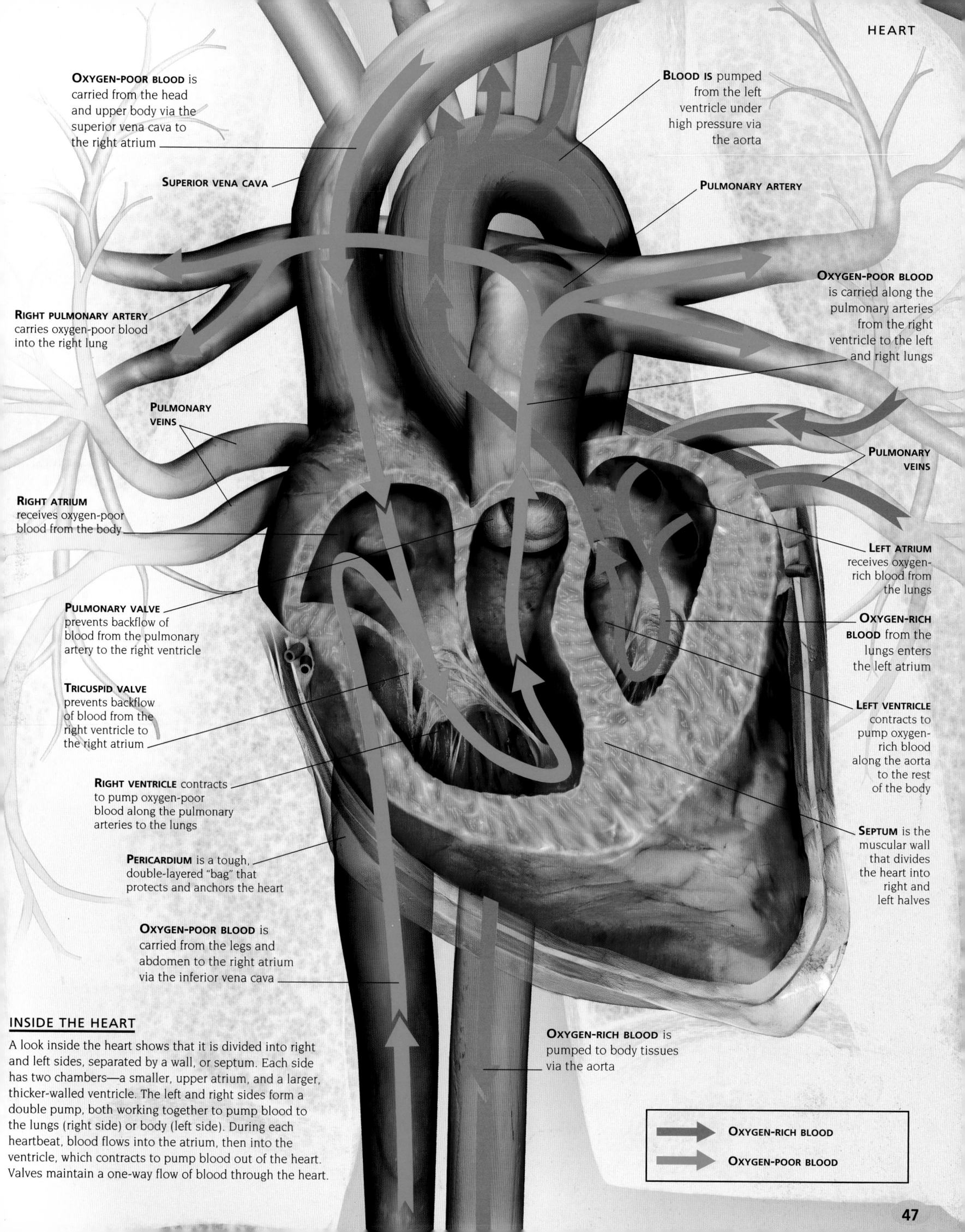

OXYGEN-POOR BLOOD is carried from the head and upper body via the superior vena cava to the right atrium

SUPERIOR VENA CAVA

RIGHT PULMONARY ARTERY carries oxygen-poor blood into the right lung

PULMONARY VEINS

RIGHT ATRIUM receives oxygen-poor blood from the body

PULMONARY VALVE prevents backflow of blood from the pulmonary artery to the right ventricle

TRICUSPID VALVE prevents backflow of blood from the right ventricle to the right atrium

RIGHT VENTRICLE contracts to pump oxygen-poor blood along the pulmonary arteries to the lungs

PERICARDIUM is a tough, double-layered "bag" that protects and anchors the heart

OXYGEN-POOR BLOOD is carried from the legs and abdomen to the right atrium via the inferior vena cava

BLOOD IS pumped from the left ventricle under high pressure via the aorta

PULMONARY ARTERY

OXYGEN-POOR BLOOD is carried along the pulmonary arteries from the right ventricle to the left and right lungs

PULMONARY VEINS

LEFT ATRIUM receives oxygen-rich blood from the lungs

OXYGEN-RICH BLOOD from the lungs enters the left atrium

LEFT VENTRICLE contracts to pump oxygen-rich blood along the aorta to the rest of the body

SEPTUM is the muscular wall that divides the heart into right and left halves

OXYGEN-RICH BLOOD is pumped to body tissues via the aorta

INSIDE THE HEART

A look inside the heart shows that it is divided into right and left sides, separated by a wall, or septum. Each side has two chambers—a smaller, upper atrium, and a larger, thicker-walled ventricle. The left and right sides form a double pump, both working together to pump blood to the lungs (right side) or body (left side). During each heartbeat, blood flows into the atrium, then into the ventricle, which contracts to pump blood out of the heart. Valves maintain a one-way flow of blood through the heart.

→ **OXYGEN-RICH BLOOD**

→ **OXYGEN-POOR BLOOD**

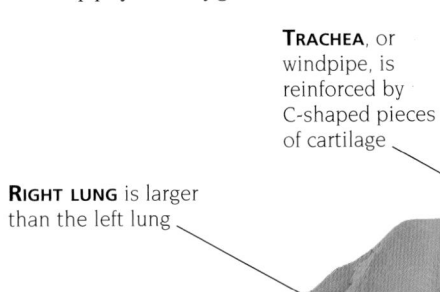

Respiratory System

YOUR RESPIRATORY, OR BREATHING, SYSTEM draws oxygen into your body and removes carbon dioxide. Your body cells use oxygen to release the energy they need to live. Energy is released by a process called cell respiration. This process also releases waste carbon dioxide, which has to be removed before it poisons your body. The respiratory system consists of the lungs and the air passages that carry air to and from the lungs. It works by drawing "fresh" air containing oxygen into your body and pushing out "stale" air containing carbon dioxide. You can never take a break from breathing—you breathe around 20,000 times a day—because your cells need a constant supply of oxygen.

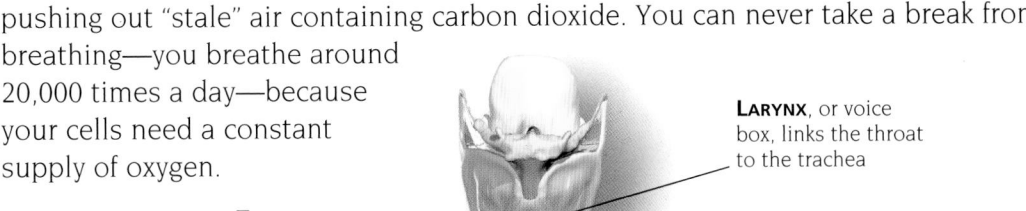

LARYNX, or voice box, links the throat to the trachea

TRACHEA, or windpipe, is reinforced by C-shaped pieces of cartilage

RIGHT LUNG is larger than the left lung

LEFT LUNG is smaller because it shares chest space with the heart

RIGHT BRONCHUS is a branch of the trachea that carries air to the right lung

LUNGS AND AIRWAYS

When you breathe in, air flows toward the lungs along a series of airways—the nose, mouth, throat (not shown here), larynx, and trachea. At its lower end, the trachea divides into two branches called bronchi. Each bronchus enters a lung, where it divides repeatedly. Oxygen enters your bloodstream deep inside your lungs.

DID YOU KNOW?

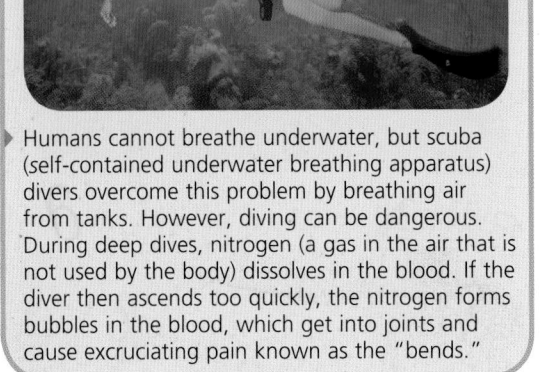

Humans cannot breathe underwater, but scuba (self-contained underwater breathing apparatus) divers overcome this problem by breathing air from tanks. However, diving can be dangerous. During deep dives, nitrogen (a gas in the air that is not used by the body) dissolves in the blood. If the diver then ascends too quickly, the nitrogen forms bubbles in the blood, which get into joints and cause excruciating pain known as the "bends."

THE LARYNX

Your larynx links your throat to your trachea. The larynx is a funnel-shaped "box," made of plates of cartilage. The uppermost cartilage is a leaflike flap called the epiglottis. When you swallow food, the epiglottis blocks the entrance to the larynx and stops food from going into your lungs. Stretched across the larynx are two membranes called vocal cords. Sounds are produced when air breathed out from the lungs passes through the vocal cords. These sounds are shaped by your lips and tongue to produce speech.

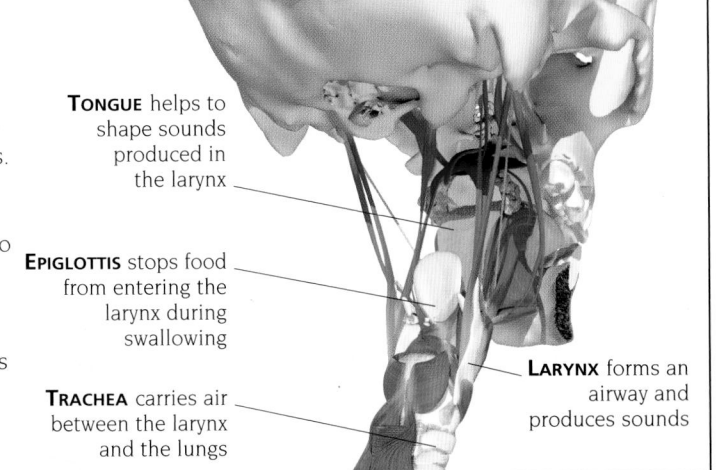

TONGUE helps to shape sounds produced in the larynx

EPIGLOTTIS stops food from entering the larynx during swallowing

TRACHEA carries air between the larynx and the lungs

LARYNX forms an airway and produces sounds

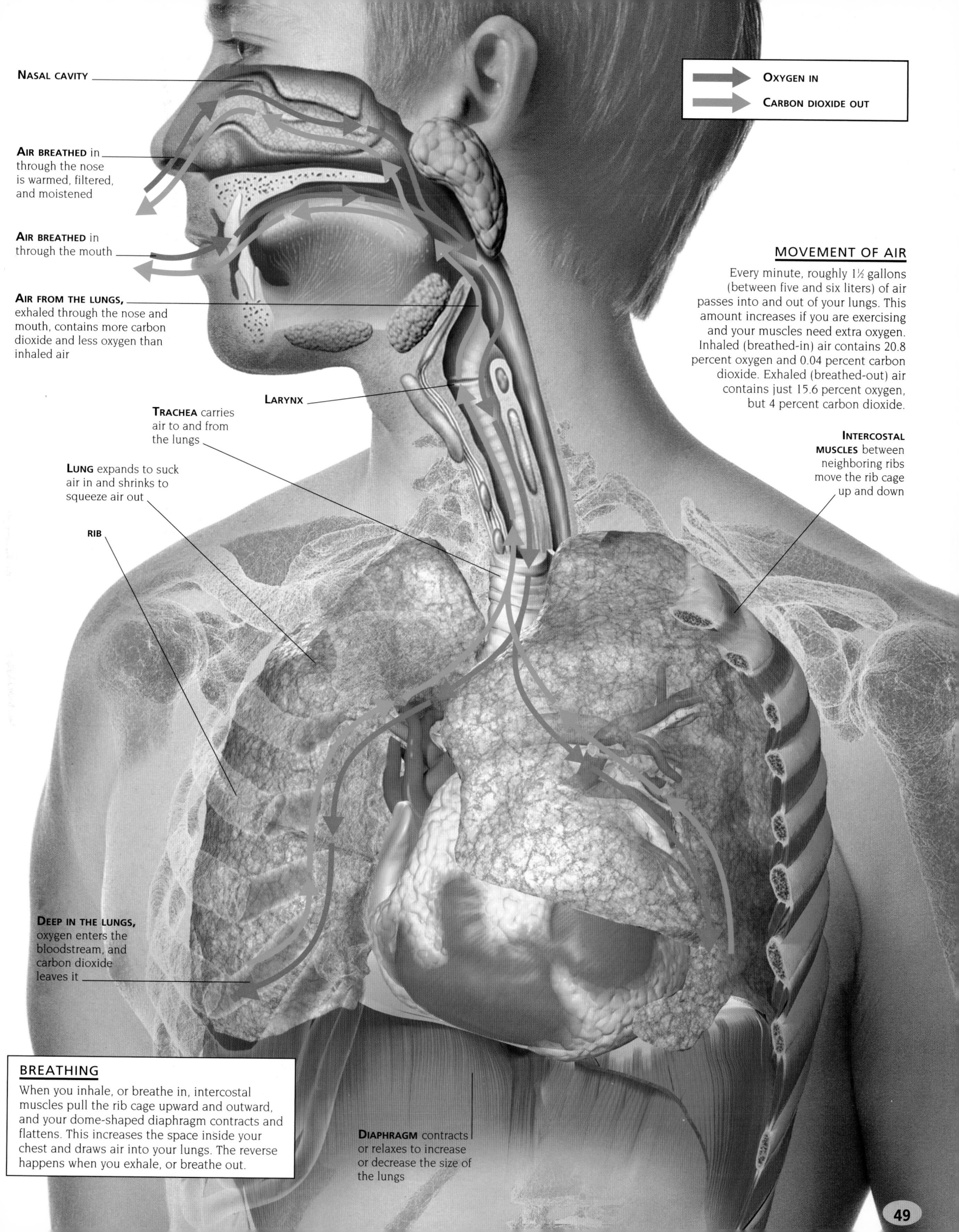

NASAL CAVITY

AIR BREATHED in through the nose is warmed, filtered, and moistened

AIR BREATHED in through the mouth

AIR FROM THE LUNGS, exhaled through the nose and mouth, contains more carbon dioxide and less oxygen than inhaled air

LARYNX

TRACHEA carries air to and from the lungs

LUNG expands to suck air in and shrinks to squeeze air out

RIB

DEEP IN THE LUNGS, oxygen enters the bloodstream, and carbon dioxide leaves it

OXYGEN IN

CARBON DIOXIDE OUT

MOVEMENT OF AIR

Every minute, roughly 1½ gallons (between five and six liters) of air passes into and out of your lungs. This amount increases if you are exercising and your muscles need extra oxygen. Inhaled (breathed-in) air contains 20.8 percent oxygen and 0.04 percent carbon dioxide. Exhaled (breathed-out) air contains just 15.6 percent oxygen, but 4 percent carbon dioxide.

INTERCOSTAL MUSCLES between neighboring ribs move the rib cage up and down

BREATHING

When you inhale, or breathe in, intercostal muscles pull the rib cage upward and outward, and your dome-shaped diaphragm contracts and flattens. This increases the space inside your chest and draws air into your lungs. The reverse happens when you exhale, or breathe out.

DIAPHRAGM contracts or relaxes to increase or decrease the size of the lungs

Lungs

INSIDE YOUR TWO LUNGS, oxygen from the air enters your bloodstream, and waste carbon dioxide leaves your bloodstream to be breathed out. Your cone-shaped lungs surround your heart. The tips of the lungs reach above your clavicles (collarbones) and their bases rest on your diaphragm. Lungs are pink in color because of the large number of blood vessels inside them. They contain a vast, branching network of air passages that end in the millions of air sacs through which oxygen is exchanged for carbon dioxide. Lungs are also elastic, allowing them to expand or shrink as they follow the movements of the rib cage and diaphragm during breathing.

TRACHEA, or windpipe, is the "trunk" of the bronchial tree

PRIMARY BRONCHUS branches off from the trachea and enters the lung

SECONDARY BRONCHUS is one of the branches of the primary bronchus

BRONCHIOLE is the final, smallest branch of the lung's air passages

THE BRONCHIAL TREE

This is a resin cast of the network of air passages in the two lungs. Each lung is served by a branch of the trachea, called a primary bronchus. The primary bronchus divides into smaller bronchi, which branch repeatedly to form tiny tubes called bronchioles. This network is often called the bronchial tree. Turn the page upside down to see its trunk, branches, and twigs.

TERMINAL BRONCHIOLE is no wider than a hair

BRANCH OF THE PULMONARY VEIN carries oxygen-rich blood to the heart

BRANCH OF THE PULMONARY ARTERY carries oxygen-poor blood

DID YOU KNOW?

Opera singers require years of training to produce high-quality singing. The muscles of the chest and diaphragm are trained to produce a highly controlled output of air through the larynx (voice box), so that notes can be sustained without fading. Singers must also be able to control their vocal cords to produce sounds of precise volume and quality.

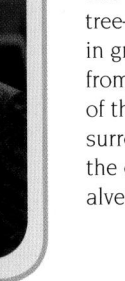

THE AIR SACS ▶

The tiniest branches of the bronchial tree—the 30,000 terminal bronchioles – end in grapelike air sacs called alveoli. Oxygen from the air passes through the thin walls of the alveoli and into the capillaries surrounding them. Carbon dioxide moves in the opposite direction. There are 300 million alveoli packed into your two lungs.

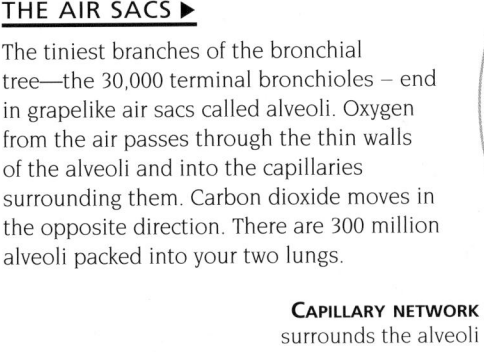

CAPILLARY NETWORK surrounds the alveoli

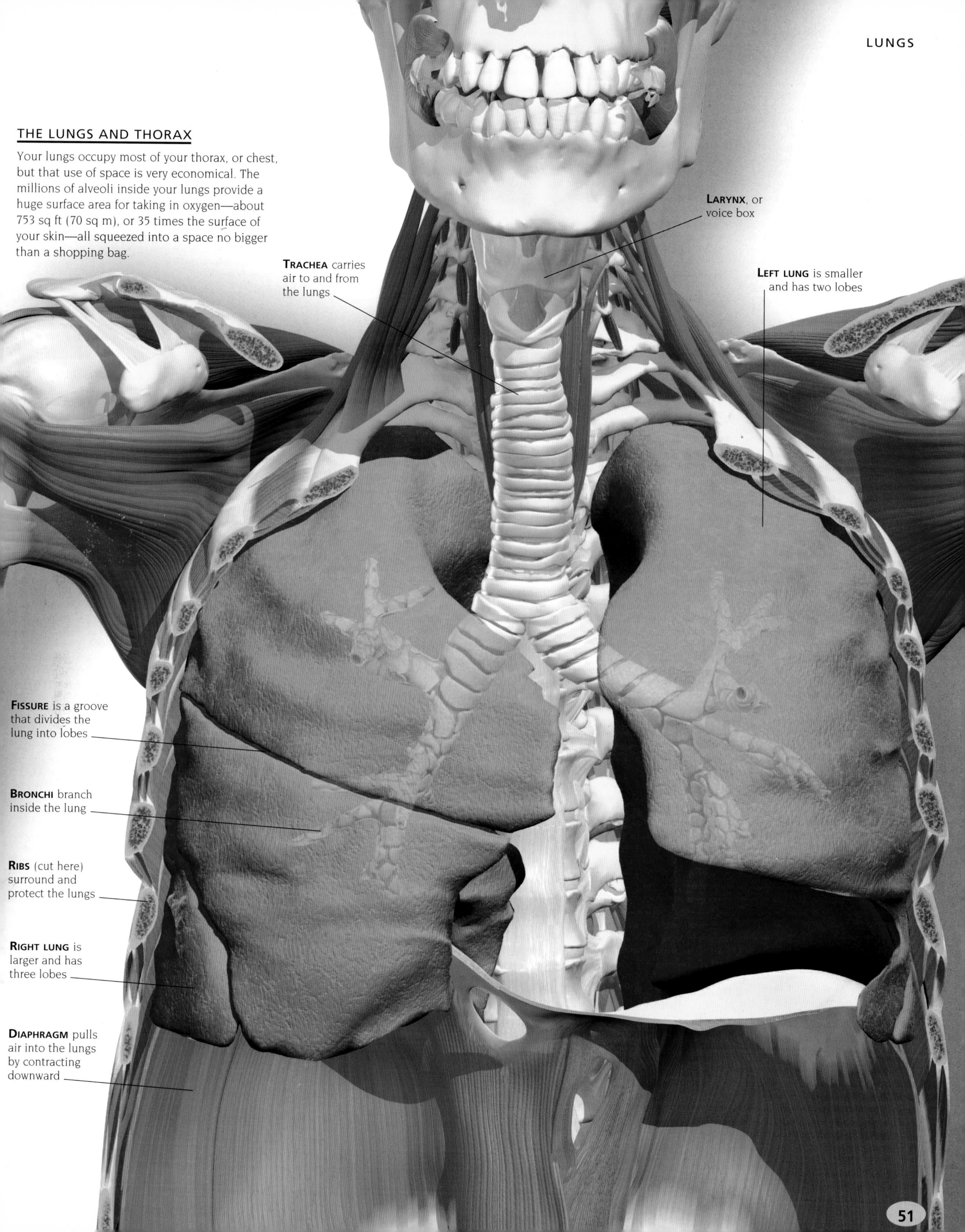

THE LUNGS AND THORAX

Your lungs occupy most of your thorax, or chest, but that use of space is very economical. The millions of alveoli inside your lungs provide a huge surface area for taking in oxygen—about 753 sq ft (70 sq m), or 35 times the surface of your skin—all squeezed into a space no bigger than a shopping bag.

LARYNX, or voice box

TRACHEA carries air to and from the lungs

LEFT LUNG is smaller and has two lobes

FISSURE is a groove that divides the lung into lobes

BRONCHI branch inside the lung

RIBS (cut here) surround and protect the lungs

RIGHT LUNG is larger and has three lobes

DIAPHRAGM pulls air into the lungs by contracting downward

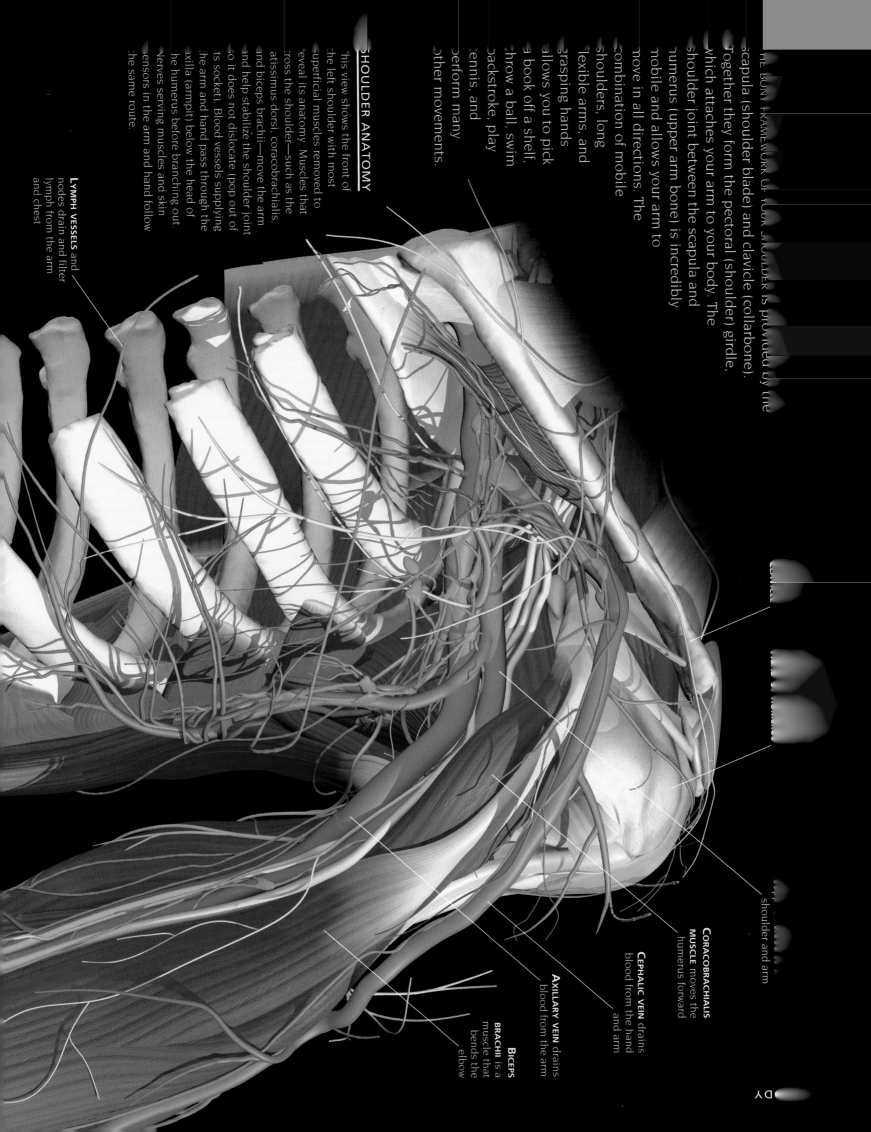

scapula (shoulder blade) and clavicle (collarbone).
Together they form the pectoral (shoulder) girdle,
which attaches your arm to your body. The
shoulder joint between the scapula and
humerus (upper arm bone) is incredibly
mobile and allows your arm to
move in all directions. The
combination of mobile
shoulders, long
flexible arms, and
grasping hands
allows you to pick
a book off a shelf,
throw a ball, swim
backstroke, play
tennis, and
perform many
other movements.

SHOULDER ANATOMY

This view shows the front of
the left shoulder with most
superficial muscles removed to
reveal its anatomy. Muscles that
cross the shoulder—such as the
latissimus dorsi, coracobrachialis,
and biceps brachii—move the arm
and help stabilize the shoulder joint
so it does not dislocate (pop out of
its socket). Blood vessels supplying
the arm and hand pass through the
axilla (armpit) below the head of
the humerus before branching out.
Nerves serving muscles and skin
sensors in the arm and hand follow
the same route.

LYMPH VESSELS and
nodes drain and filter
lymph from the arm
and chest

**CORACOBRACHIALIS
MUSCLE** moves the
humerus forward

shoulder and arm

CEPHALIC VEIN drains
blood from the hand
and arm

AXILLARY VEIN drains
blood from the arm

**BICEPS
BRACHII** is a
muscle that
bends the
elbow

This very flexible ball-and-socket joint is formed where the head of the humerus fits into the scapula's shallow glenoid cavity. The joint is held together mainly by tendons of muscles that cross the shoulder joint, especially the biceps brachii.

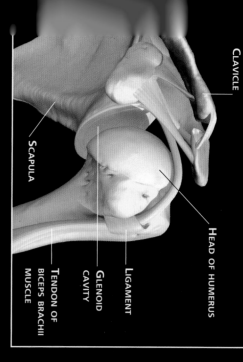

CLAVICLE

SCAPULA

HEAD OF HUMERUS

LIGAMENT

GLENOID CAVITY

TENDON OF BICEPS BRACHII MUSCLE

SIXTH RIB

SERRATUS ANTERIOR MUSCLE raises the arm

LATISSIMUS DORSI pulls the arm downward, backward, and inward

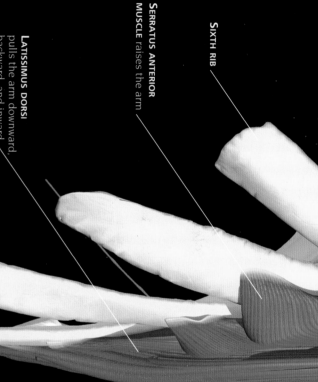

MEDIAN NERVE controls some of the muscles that bend the wrist and fingers

BRACHIALIS MUSCLE bends the arm at the elbow

YOUR SHOULDER JOINT IS THE MOST FLEXIBLE JOINT IN YOUR ENTIRE BODY

THROWING A BALL

This sequence shows the chest, arm, and shoulder muscles used for throwing a ball. Muscles contract (green) to straighten the arm and pull it back, lift it up and forward, then pull it downward and backward in a power stroke during which the ball is released.

DID YOU KNOW?

Having flexible shoulders is something we humans share with our close ape relatives, such as this orangutan. Humans and apes evolved from a tree-living ancestor who lived millions of years ago. This ancestor had evolved long arms that could swing all the way around. It could also reach up above its head, pull itself up trees, and swing from branch to branch—as could its descendants. Modern humans have kept their flexible shoulders because they allow us to perform a vast array of useful movements.

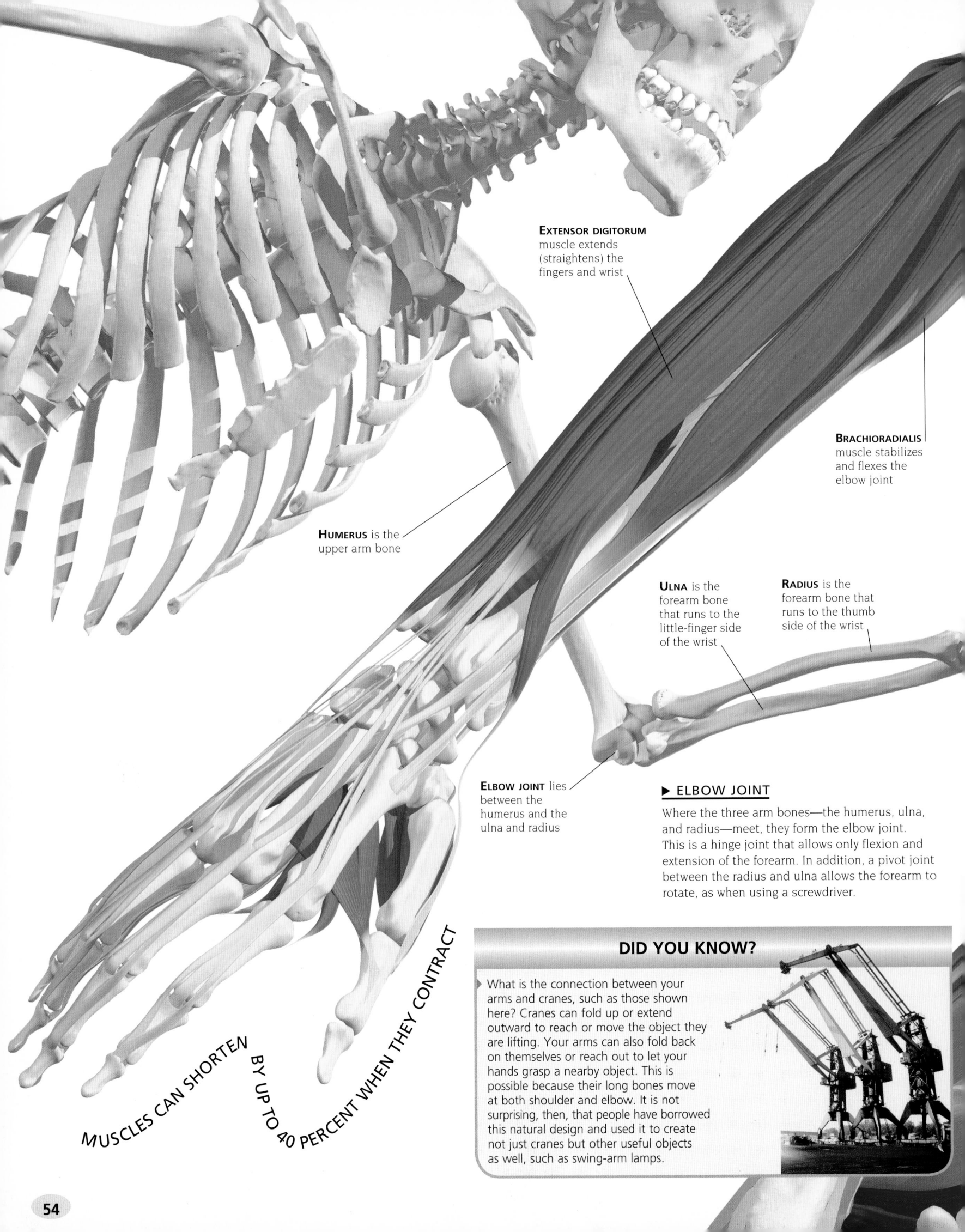

EXTENSOR DIGITORUM muscle extends (straightens) the fingers and wrist

BRACHIORADIALIS muscle stabilizes and flexes the elbow joint

HUMERUS is the upper arm bone

ULNA is the forearm bone that runs to the little-finger side of the wrist

RADIUS is the forearm bone that runs to the thumb side of the wrist

ELBOW JOINT lies between the humerus and the ulna and radius

▶ ELBOW JOINT

Where the three arm bones—the humerus, ulna, and radius—meet, they form the elbow joint. This is a hinge joint that allows only flexion and extension of the forearm. In addition, a pivot joint between the radius and ulna allows the forearm to rotate, as when using a screwdriver.

DID YOU KNOW?

What is the connection between your arms and cranes, such as those shown here? Cranes can fold up or extend outward to reach or move the object they are lifting. Your arms can also fold back on themselves or reach out to let your hands grasp a nearby object. This is possible because their long bones move at both shoulder and elbow. It is not surprising, then, that people have borrowed this natural design and used it to create not just cranes but other useful objects as well, such as swing-arm lamps.

MUSCLES CAN SHORTEN BY UP TO 40 PERCENT WHEN THEY CONTRACT

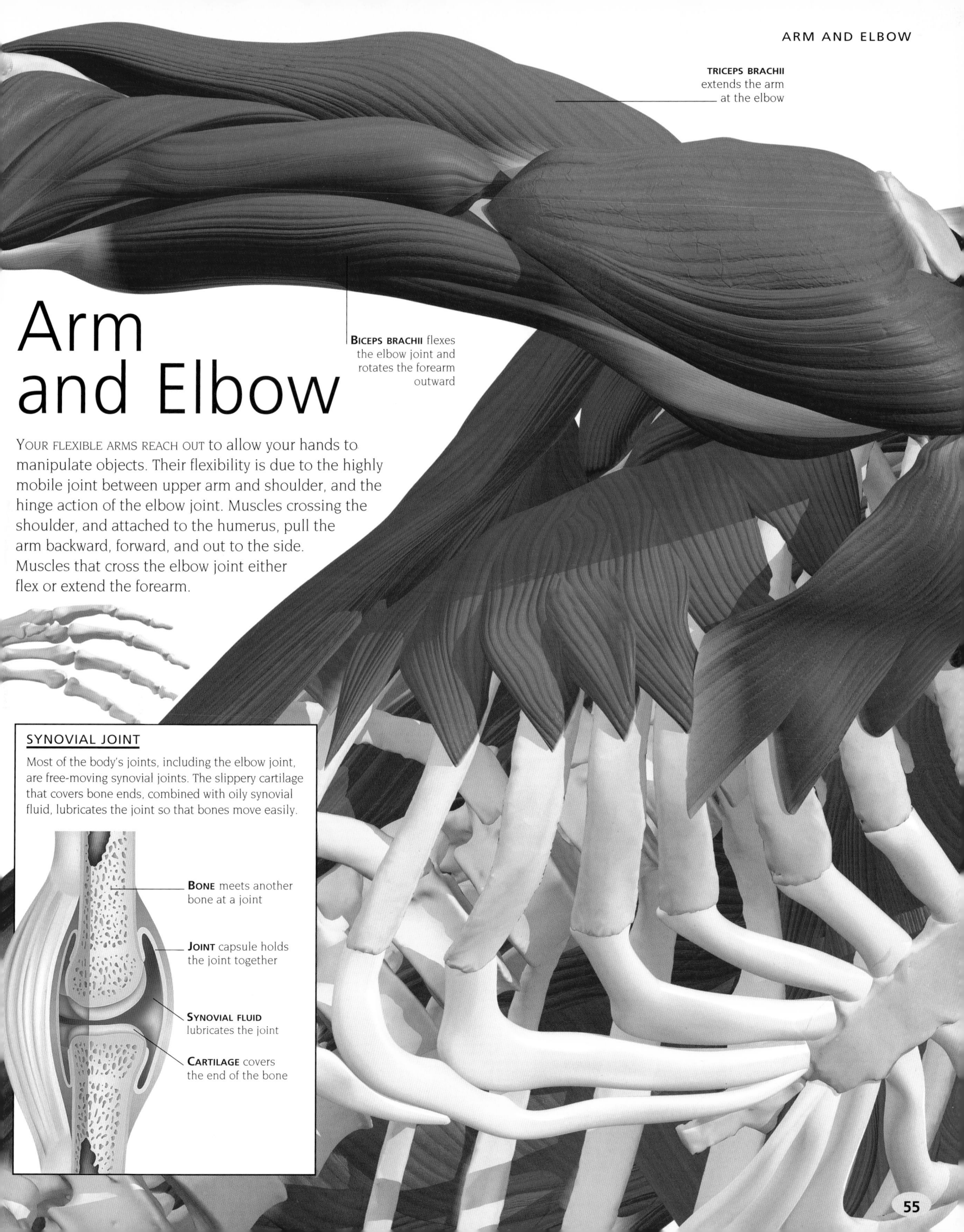

TRICEPS BRACHII
extends the arm
at the elbow

BICEPS BRACHII flexes
the elbow joint and
rotates the forearm
outward

Arm and Elbow

YOUR FLEXIBLE ARMS REACH OUT to allow your hands to
manipulate objects. Their flexibility is due to the highly
mobile joint between upper arm and shoulder, and the
hinge action of the elbow joint. Muscles crossing the
shoulder, and attached to the humerus, pull the
arm backward, forward, and out to the side.
Muscles that cross the elbow joint either
flex or extend the forearm.

SYNOVIAL JOINT

Most of the body's joints, including the elbow joint,
are free-moving synovial joints. The slippery cartilage
that covers bone ends, combined with oily synovial
fluid, lubricates the joint so that bones move easily.

BONE meets another
bone at a joint

JOINT capsule holds
the joint together

SYNOVIAL FLUID
lubricates the joint

CARTILAGE covers
the end of the bone

Hand and Wrist

WALKING ON TWO LEGS leaves your hands and wrists free to perform many tasks that play an important part in your life—such as eating, carrying, writing, or expressing thoughts through gestures. Your hands and wrists owe their versatility to their flexible bony framework—especially your long finger bones and highly mobile thumb—and the muscles and tendons in your forearm and hand that move the bones.

COMMON PALMAR DIGITAL ARTERY carries blood to the finger

TENDON OF FLEXOR DIGITORUM pulls the finger bones to bend the finger

FIRST LUMBRICAL MUSCLE helps point the index finger

FLEXOR POLLICIS BREVIS MUSCLE bends the thumb across the palm

SUPERFICIAL PALMAR VENOUS ARCH drains blood from the digital veins

SUPERFICIAL PALMAR ARTERIAL ARCH splits into branches that supply the fingers

COMMON FLEXOR TENDON SHEATH wraps around the tendons and reduces friction when they move

ABDUCTOR POLLICIS BREVIS MUSCLE pulls the thumb away from the index finger

FLEXOR RETINACULUM holds flexor tendons in place as they cross from the forearm to the hand

RADIAL ARTERY supplies blood to the wrist, thumb, and index finger

RADIAL VEIN drains blood from the fingers and palm

COMMON PALMAR DIGITAL VEIN drains blood from the finger

FLEXOR DIGITI MINIMI BREVIS bends the little finger

PROPER PALMAR DIGITAL NERVE controls the muscles that bend the fingers

ABDUCTOR DIGITI MINIMI MUSCLE pulls the little finger out to the side

PALMARIS BREVIS MUSCLE aids grip by wrinkling the skin on this side of the palm

ULNAR ARTERY supplies blood to the palm and some of the fingers

ULNAR NERVE controls some of the muscles that flex the wrist and fingers

ULNAR VEIN drains blood from the fingers and palm

PALMAR (FRONT) VIEW OF THE HAND

PALMAR DIGITAL VEIN drains blood from the finger

FLEXOR TENDON SHEATH surrounds and lubricates the tendon

DISTAL PHALANX (last bone) of the second digit (index finger)

YOU USE SEVEN DIFFERENT MUSCLES TO MOVE YOUR INDEX FINGER

OVER THE ENTIRE HAND, THERE ARE ABOUT 17,000 TOUCH RECEPTORS

YOUR FINGERNAILS GROW ABOUT $\frac{1}{8}$ IN (3 MM) PER MONTH

DISTAL PHALANX (last bone) of the fifth digit (little finger)

FIBROUS SHEATH attaches the flexor tendon sheaths to the finger bones

PALMAR DIGITAL NERVE gives sensation to the finger

PALMAR DIGITAL ARTERY supplies blood to the finger

DID YOU KNOW?

Primates are the only mammals with a thumb that can move across the palm to press against—or oppose—each of the fingers. Apes in particular have highly mobile, opposable thumbs. This makes apes' hands as versatile as human hands, which can perform hundreds of tasks, from holding a pencil to turning the pages of this book.

Middle phalanx

Metacarpals (palm bones)

Distal (far) phalanx (finger bone)

Proximal (near) phalanx

Carpals (wrist bones)

BONES ▲

The hand is made up of 27 bones. There are five metacarpals, or palm bones, 14 phalanges, or finger bones, and eight small carpals, or wrist bones, which form a flexible wrist joint with the forearm bones.

Digital vein

Lymph vessel

Metacarpal artery

Cephalic vein

Digital nerve

NERVES AND BLOOD VESSELS ▲

A network of nerves controls your finger muscles and carries nerve signals from sensors in the skin to your brain. Arteries and veins deliver blood to (and remove blood from) your muscles, tendons, skin, and other parts of your hands.

Tendon attachment to the bone

Connection between tendons

Dorsal interosseus muscle

Extensor tendons

TENDONS AND MUSCLES ▲

The tendons crossing the back of the hand straighten your fingers, while those crossing the palm of your hand bend your fingers. Small muscles in the hand produce a variety of finger movements.

Spine and Back

YOUR BACK IS THE REAR PART of your trunk—
the central part of your body—that
extends downward from your neck to
your hips. Its main axis is the spine,
also called the backbone or vertebral
column, which is a chain of small
but tough bones. The spine, along
with other bones and muscles,
provides strong support for your
trunk but at the same time
allows the back to flex, extend,
and turn so that the body
can perform a wide
range of bending and
turning movements.

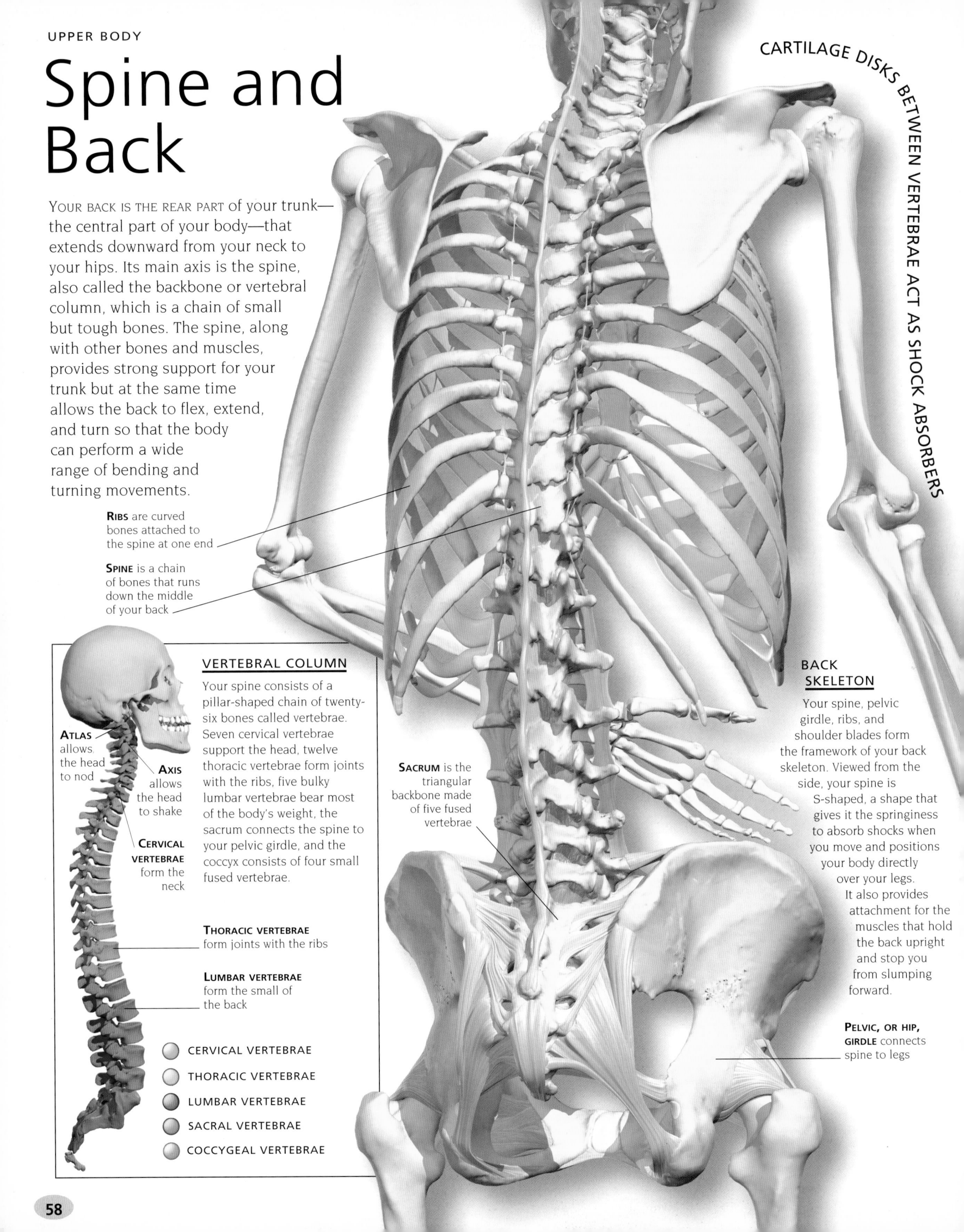

RIBS are curved
bones attached to
the spine at one end

SPINE is a chain
of bones that runs
down the middle
of your back

CARTILAGE DISKS BETWEEN VERTEBRAE ACT AS SHOCK ABSORBERS

VERTEBRAL COLUMN

Your spine consists of a
pillar-shaped chain of twenty-
six bones called vertebrae.
Seven cervical vertebrae
support the head, twelve
thoracic vertebrae form joints
with the ribs, five bulky
lumbar vertebrae bear most
of the body's weight, the
sacrum connects the spine to
your pelvic girdle, and the
coccyx consists of four small
fused vertebrae.

ATLAS
allows
the head
to nod

AXIS
allows
the head
to shake

**CERVICAL
VERTEBRAE**
form the
neck

THORACIC VERTEBRAE
form joints with the ribs

LUMBAR VERTEBRAE
form the small of
the back

- CERVICAL VERTEBRAE
- THORACIC VERTEBRAE
- LUMBAR VERTEBRAE
- SACRAL VERTEBRAE
- COCCYGEAL VERTEBRAE

SACRUM is the
triangular
backbone made
of five fused
vertebrae

BACK SKELETON

Your spine, pelvic
girdle, ribs, and
shoulder blades form
the framework of your back
skeleton. Viewed from the
side, your spine is
S-shaped, a shape that
gives it the springiness
to absorb shocks when
you move and positions
your body directly
over your legs.
It also provides
attachment for the
muscles that hold
the back upright
and stop you
from slumping
forward.

**PELVIC, OR HIP,
GIRDLE** connects
spine to legs

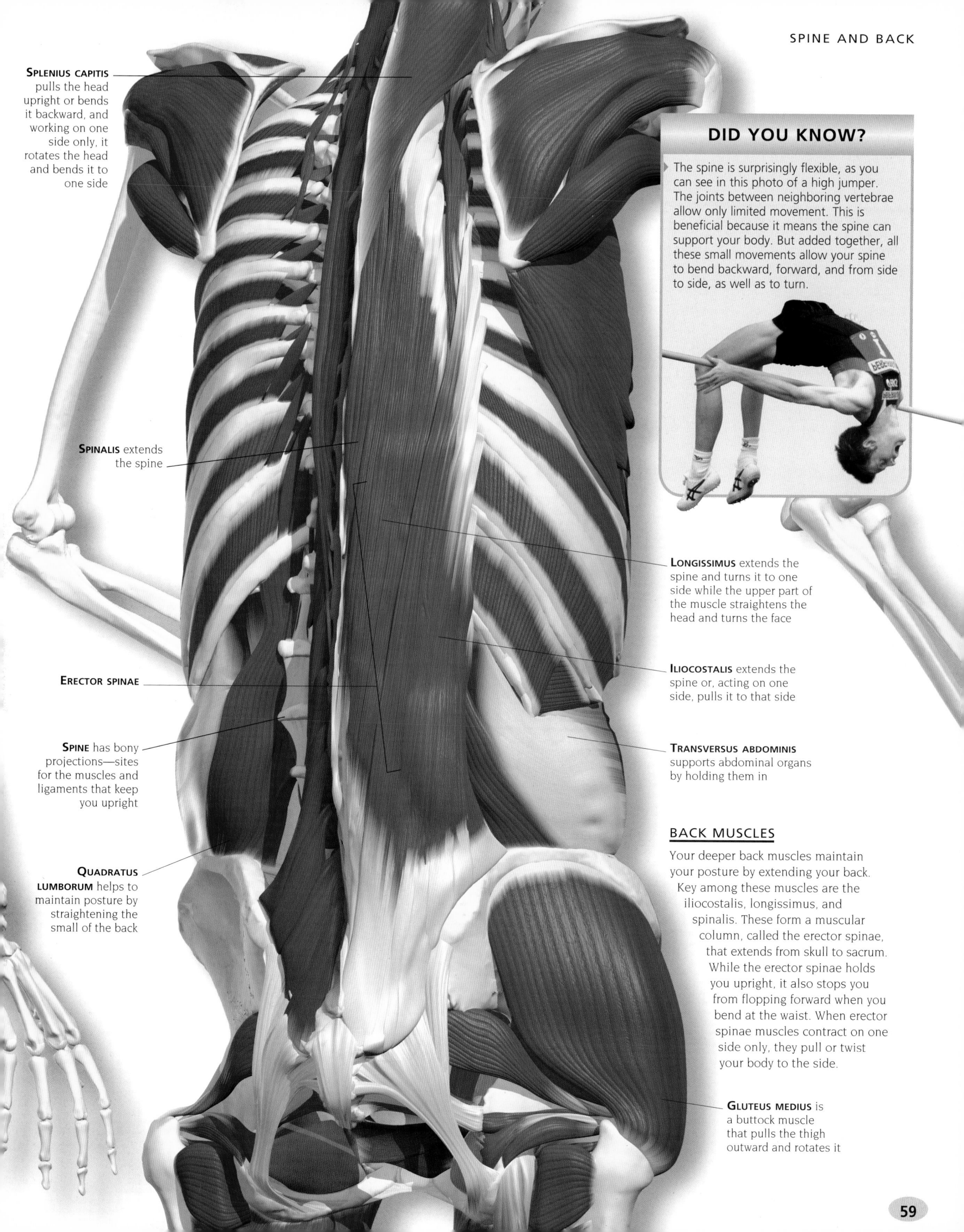

SPLENIUS CAPITIS pulls the head upright or bends it backward, and working on one side only, it rotates the head and bends it to one side

SPINALIS extends the spine

ERECTOR SPINAE

SPINE has bony projections—sites for the muscles and ligaments that keep you upright

QUADRATUS LUMBORUM helps to maintain posture by straightening the small of the back

DID YOU KNOW?

The spine is surprisingly flexible, as you can see in this photo of a high jumper. The joints between neighboring vertebrae allow only limited movement. This is beneficial because it means the spine can support your body. But added together, all these small movements allow your spine to bend backward, forward, and from side to side, as well as to turn.

LONGISSIMUS extends the spine and turns it to one side while the upper part of the muscle straightens the head and turns the face

ILIOCOSTALIS extends the spine or, acting on one side, pulls it to that side

TRANSVERSUS ABDOMINIS supports abdominal organs by holding them in

BACK MUSCLES

Your deeper back muscles maintain your posture by extending your back. Key among these muscles are the iliocostalis, longissimus, and spinalis. These form a muscular column, called the erector spinae, that extends from skull to sacrum. While the erector spinae holds you upright, it also stops you from flopping forward when you bend at the waist. When erector spinae muscles contract on one side only, they pull or twist your body to the side.

GLUTEUS MEDIUS is a buttock muscle that pulls the thigh outward and rotates it

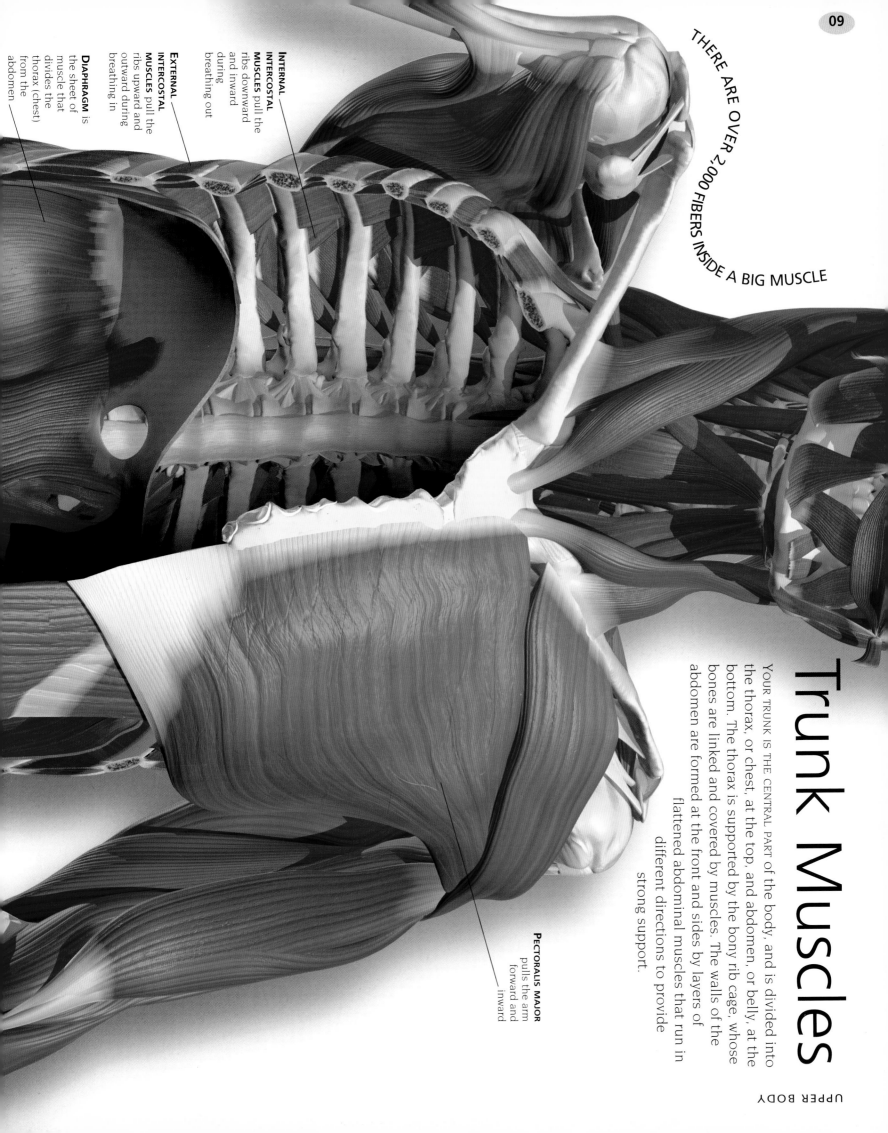

THERE ARE OVER 2,000 FIBERS INSIDE A BIG MUSCLE

Trunk Muscles

YOUR TRUNK IS THE CENTRAL PART of the body, and is divided into the thorax, or chest, at the top, and abdomen, or belly, at the bottom. The thorax is supported by the bony rib cage, whose bones are linked and covered by muscles. The walls of the abdomen are formed at the front and sides by layers of flattened abdominal muscles that run in different directions to provide strong support.

INTERNAL INTERCOSTAL MUSCLES pull the ribs downward and inward during breathing out

EXTERNAL INTERCOSTAL MUSCLES pull the ribs upward and outward during breathing in

DIAPHRAGM is the sheet of muscle that divides the thorax (chest) from the abdomen

PECTORALIS MAJOR pulls the arm forward and inward

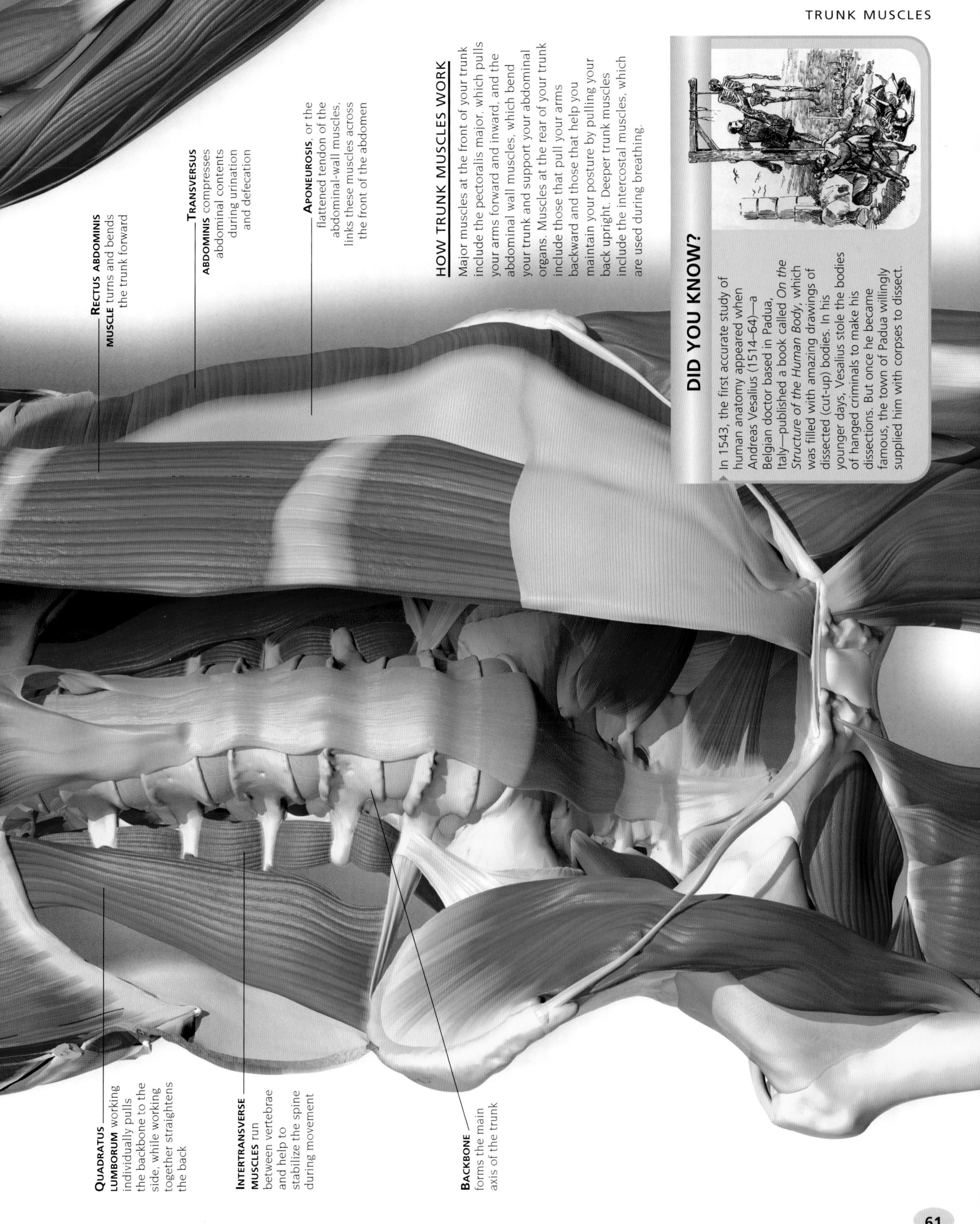

RECTUS ABDOMINIS MUSCLE turns and bends the trunk forward

TRANSVERSUS ABDOMINIS compresses abdominal contents during urination and defecation

APONEUROSIS, or the flattened tendon of the abdominal-wall muscles, links these muscles across the front of the abdomen

HOW TRUNK MUSCLES WORK

Major muscles at the front of your trunk include the pectoralis major, which pulls your arms forward and inward, and the abdominal wall muscles, which bend your trunk and support your abdominal organs. Muscles at the rear of your trunk include those that pull your arms backward and those that help you maintain your posture by pulling your back upright. Deeper trunk muscles include the intercostal muscles, which are used during breathing.

DID YOU KNOW?

In 1543, the first accurate study of human anatomy appeared when Andreas Vesalius (1514–64)—a Belgian doctor based in Padua, Italy—published a book called *On the Structure of the Human Body*, which was filled with amazing drawings of dissected (cut-up) bodies. In his younger days, Vesalius stole the bodies of hanged criminals to make his dissections. But once he became famous, the town of Padua willingly supplied him with corpses to dissect.

QUADRATUS LUMBORUM working individually pulls the backbone to the side, while working together straightens the back

INTERTRANSVERSE MUSCLES run between vertebrae and help to stabilize the spine during movement

BACKBONE forms the main axis of the trunk

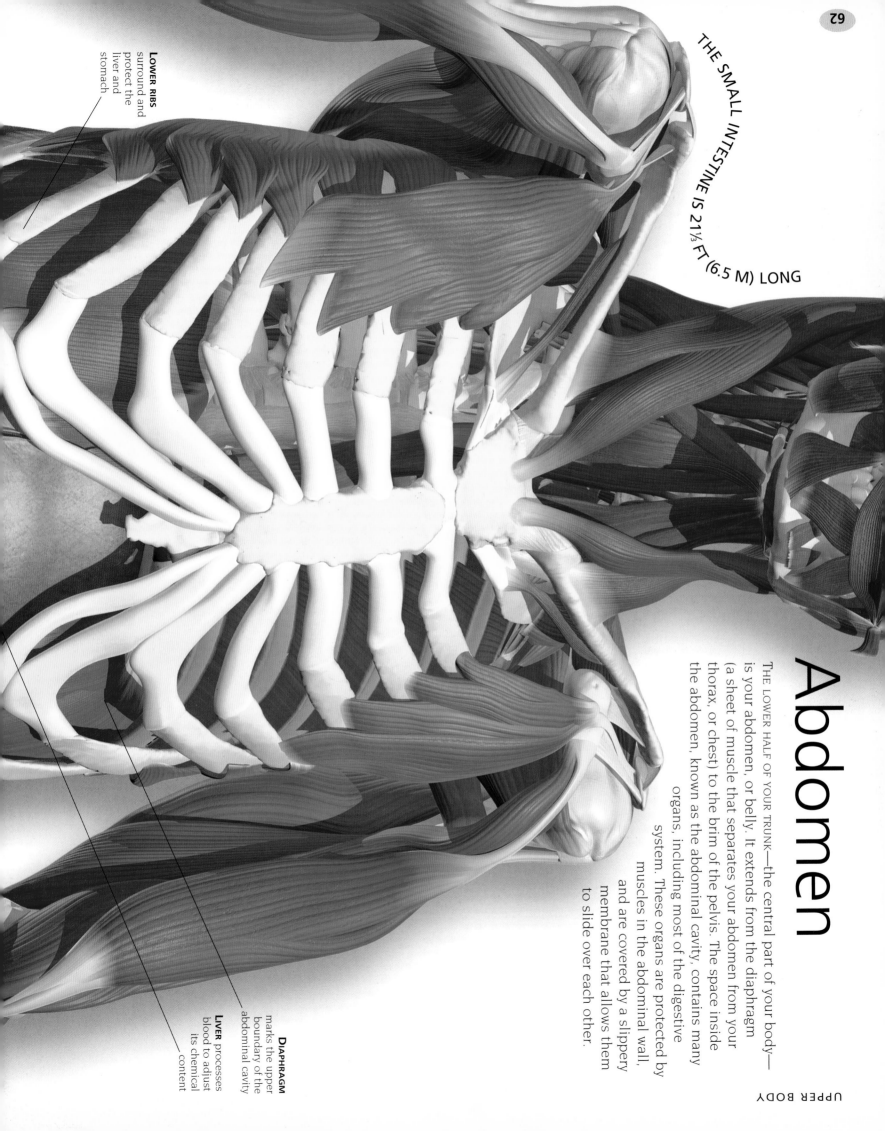

THE SMALL INTESTINE IS 21⅓ FT (6.5 M) LONG

Abdomen

THE LOWER HALF OF YOUR TRUNK—the central part of your body—is your abdomen, or belly. It extends from the diaphragm (a sheet of muscle that separates your abdomen from your thorax, or chest) to the brim of the pelvis. The space inside the abdomen, known as the abdominal cavity, contains many organs, including most of the digestive system. These organs are protected by muscles in the abdominal wall, and are covered by a slippery membrane that allows them to slide over each other.

LOWER RIBS surround and protect the liver and stomach

DIAPHRAGM marks the upper boundary of the abdominal cavity

LIVER processes blood to adjust its chemical content

GALL BLADDER releases bile into the small intestine

SMALL INTESTINE is where most digestion of food takes place

LARGE INTESTINE is the last section of the digestive system

APPENDIX

STOMACH churns up and digests food

ABDOMINAL ORGANS

Your abdominal cavity is packed with organs. These include the stomach, the small and large intestines—which occupy most of the space in the abdominal cavity—and the liver. The abdominal cavity is lined with, and its organs are covered by, a membrane called the peritoneum. This forms folds that hold the digestive organs in place. The peritoneum also carries blood vessels and nerves to and from the organs.

PERITONEUM is a membrane that holds the digestive organs in place

PELVIS supports organs in the lower abdomen

DID YOU KNOW?

▶ During pregnancy, a woman's abdomen bulges outward as the fetus grows inside her uterus. This woman is tracking the development of her baby by measuring how big the bulge is. Before pregnancy, the uterus is the size of a small fist. After 16 weeks of pregnancy, it fills the pelvis. It then pushes upward, displacing digestive organs and the diaphragm and forcing the woman's abdominal wall outward. Not surprisingly, this expansion can cause discomfort, and the extra weight—averaging almost 29 lb (13 kg) after nine months of pregnancy—can often cause backaches.

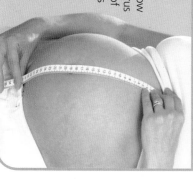

Digestive System

FOOD SUPPLIES YOUR CELLS with energy and the raw materials for growth and repair. But before cells can use food, it has to be processed by being digested, or broken down, into simple nutrients. This is the job of your digestive system. It chews and churns food into small pieces, then exposes it to chemicals called enzymes that convert complex nutrients into simple ones. These are then absorbed (taken in) by your bloodstream and carried to your cells. Any undigested waste is removed.

LIVER processes absorbed nutrients and makes bile

STOMACH churns and digests food into a creamy liquid

DIGESTIVE ORGANS

The main part of your digestive system is a long tube—the alimentary canal—that runs from mouth to anus. It consists of the mouth, esophagus, stomach, small intestine, and large intestine. Other organs attached to the alimentary canal aid digestion. These are the teeth, tongue, and salivary glands, and the liver, pancreas, and gall bladder.

DID YOU KNOW?

▶ The lining of your stomach releases a very acidic digestive liquid called gastric juice. It contains powerful hydrochloric acid—corrosive enough to strip paint. The acidity of gastric juice provides the best environment for the action of pepsin, an enzyme that digests proteins.

ESOPHAGUS, which passes behind the heart, carries chewed food from the throat to the stomach

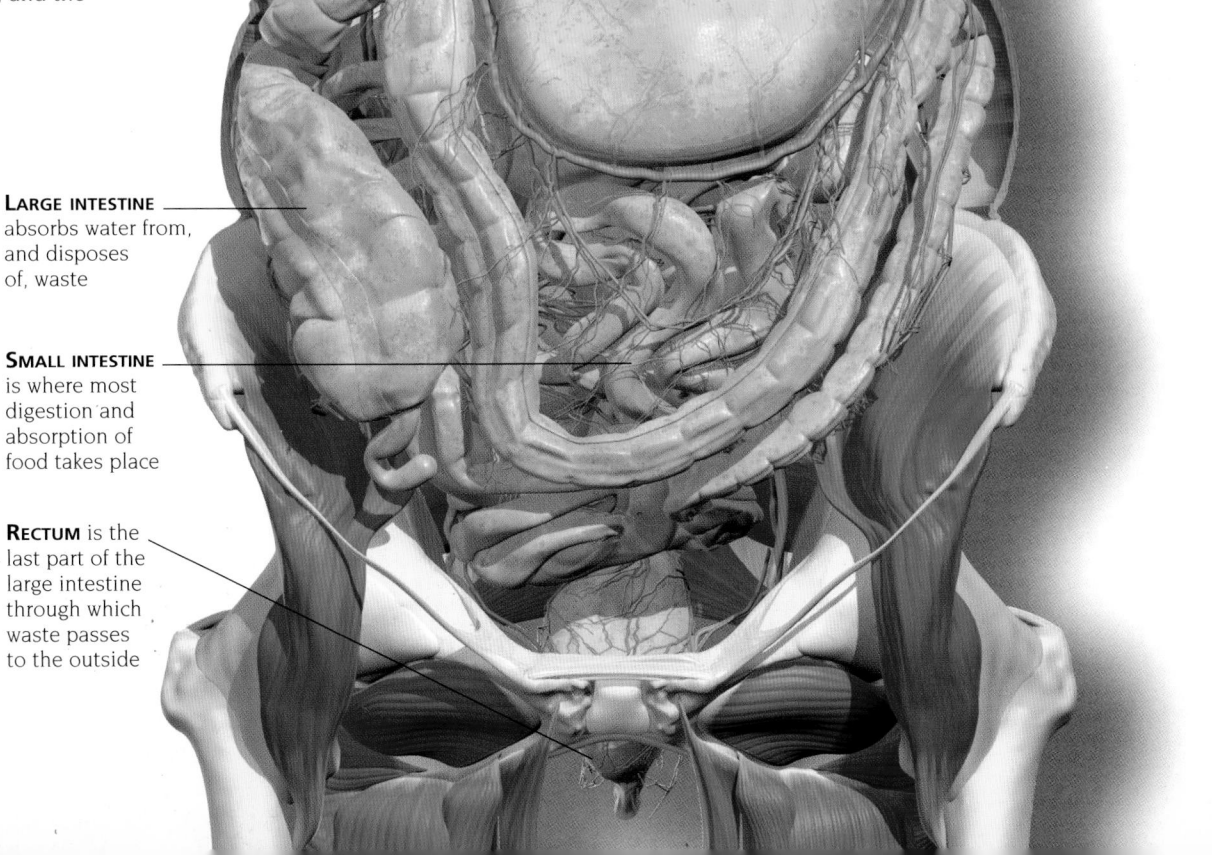

LARGE INTESTINE absorbs water from, and disposes of, waste

SMALL INTESTINE is where most digestion and absorption of food takes place

RECTUM is the last part of the large intestine through which waste passes to the outside

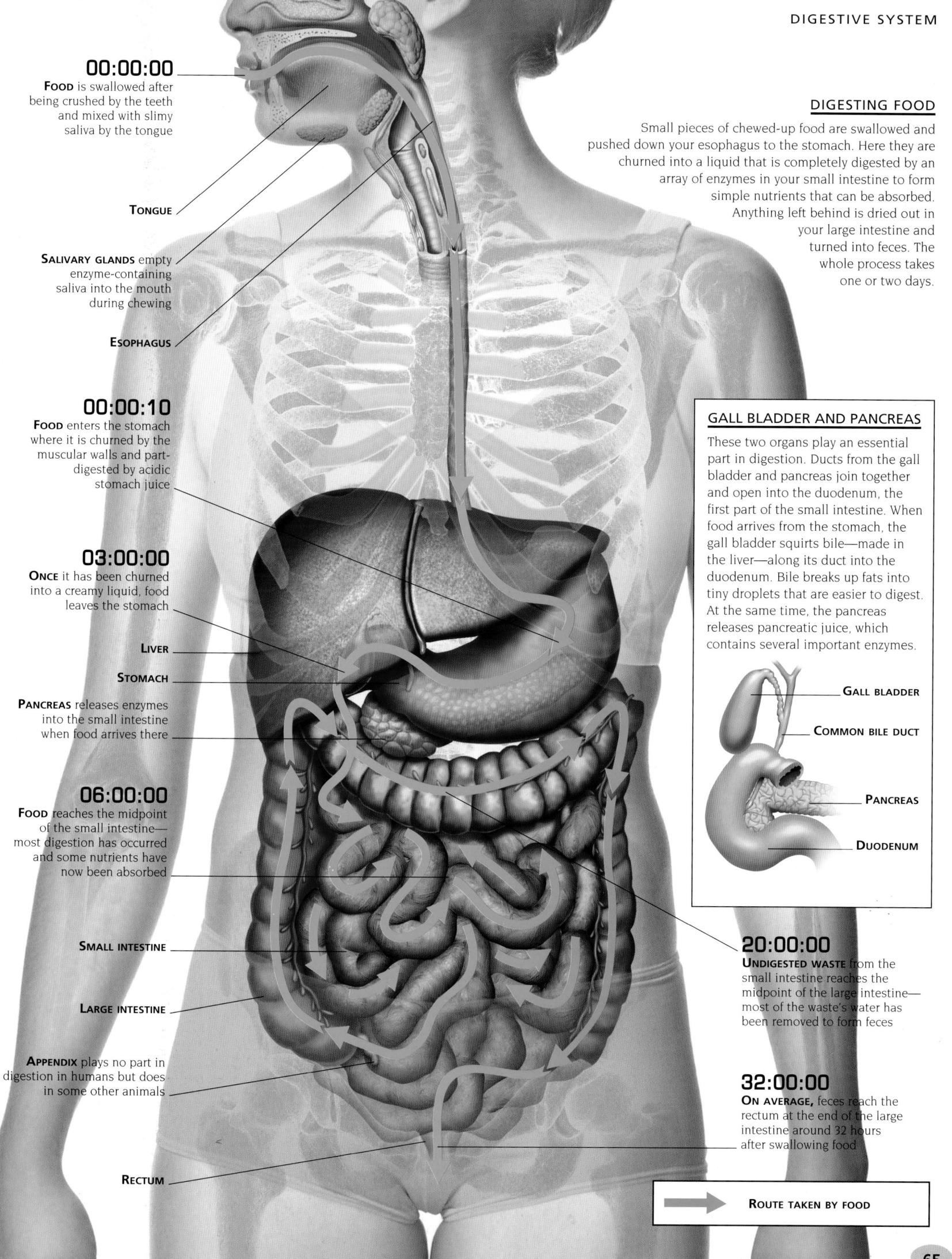

00:00:00

FOOD is swallowed after being crushed by the teeth and mixed with slimy saliva by the tongue

TONGUE

SALIVARY GLANDS empty enzyme-containing saliva into the mouth during chewing

ESOPHAGUS

00:00:10

FOOD enters the stomach where it is churned by the muscular walls and part-digested by acidic stomach juice

03:00:00

ONCE it has been churned into a creamy liquid, food leaves the stomach

LIVER

STOMACH

PANCREAS releases enzymes into the small intestine when food arrives there

06:00:00

FOOD reaches the midpoint of the small intestine— most digestion has occurred and some nutrients have now been absorbed

SMALL INTESTINE

LARGE INTESTINE

APPENDIX plays no part in digestion in humans but does in some other animals

RECTUM

DIGESTING FOOD

Small pieces of chewed-up food are swallowed and pushed down your esophagus to the stomach. Here they are churned into a liquid that is completely digested by an array of enzymes in your small intestine to form simple nutrients that can be absorbed. Anything left behind is dried out in your large intestine and turned into feces. The whole process takes one or two days.

GALL BLADDER AND PANCREAS

These two organs play an essential part in digestion. Ducts from the gall bladder and pancreas join together and open into the duodenum, the first part of the small intestine. When food arrives from the stomach, the gall bladder squirts bile—made in the liver—along its duct into the duodenum. Bile breaks up fats into tiny droplets that are easier to digest. At the same time, the pancreas releases pancreatic juice, which contains several important enzymes.

GALL BLADDER

COMMON BILE DUCT

PANCREAS

DUODENUM

20:00:00

UNDIGESTED WASTE from the small intestine reaches the midpoint of the large intestine— most of the waste's water has been removed to form feces

32:00:00

ON AVERAGE, feces reach the rectum at the end of the large intestine around 32 hours after swallowing food

→ **ROUTE TAKEN BY FOOD**

Stomach

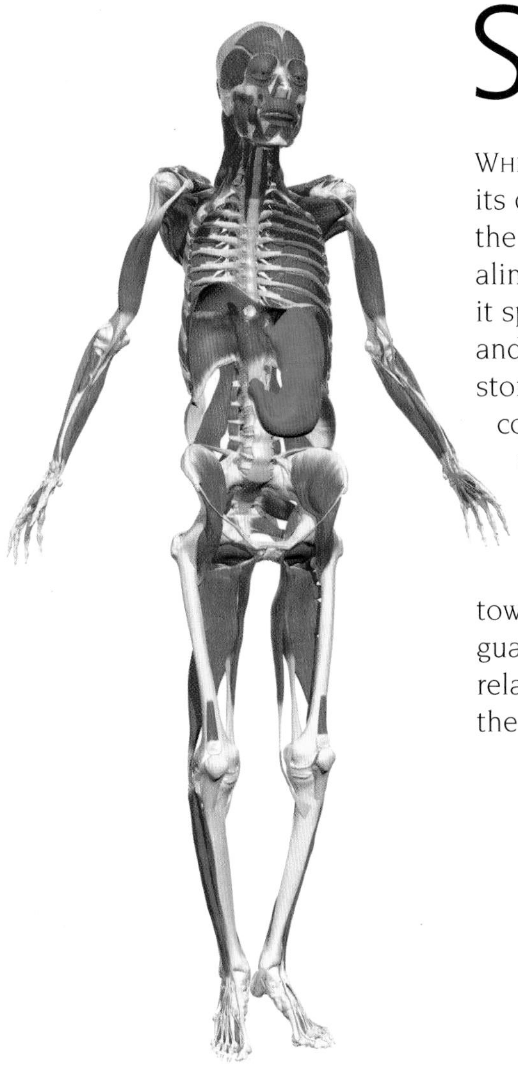

WHEN FOOD TRAVELS down your esophagus, its destination is your J-shaped stomach, the widest and most elastic part of the alimentary canal. During the three hours that it spends in your stomach, food is pummeled and churned by the contraction of muscles in the stomach wall. It is also doused in enzyme-containing gastric juice. This acidic juice does not digest your stomach's lining because this is coated with a protective layer of thick mucus. The action of churning and the gastric juice turn food into a partially digested creamy liquid called chyme. This chyme is pushed toward the funnel-shaped exit from the stomach, which is guarded by a ring of muscle called the pyloric sphincter. This relaxes slightly, allowing squirts of chyme to enter the duodenum, the first part of your small intestine, where digestion begins in earnest.

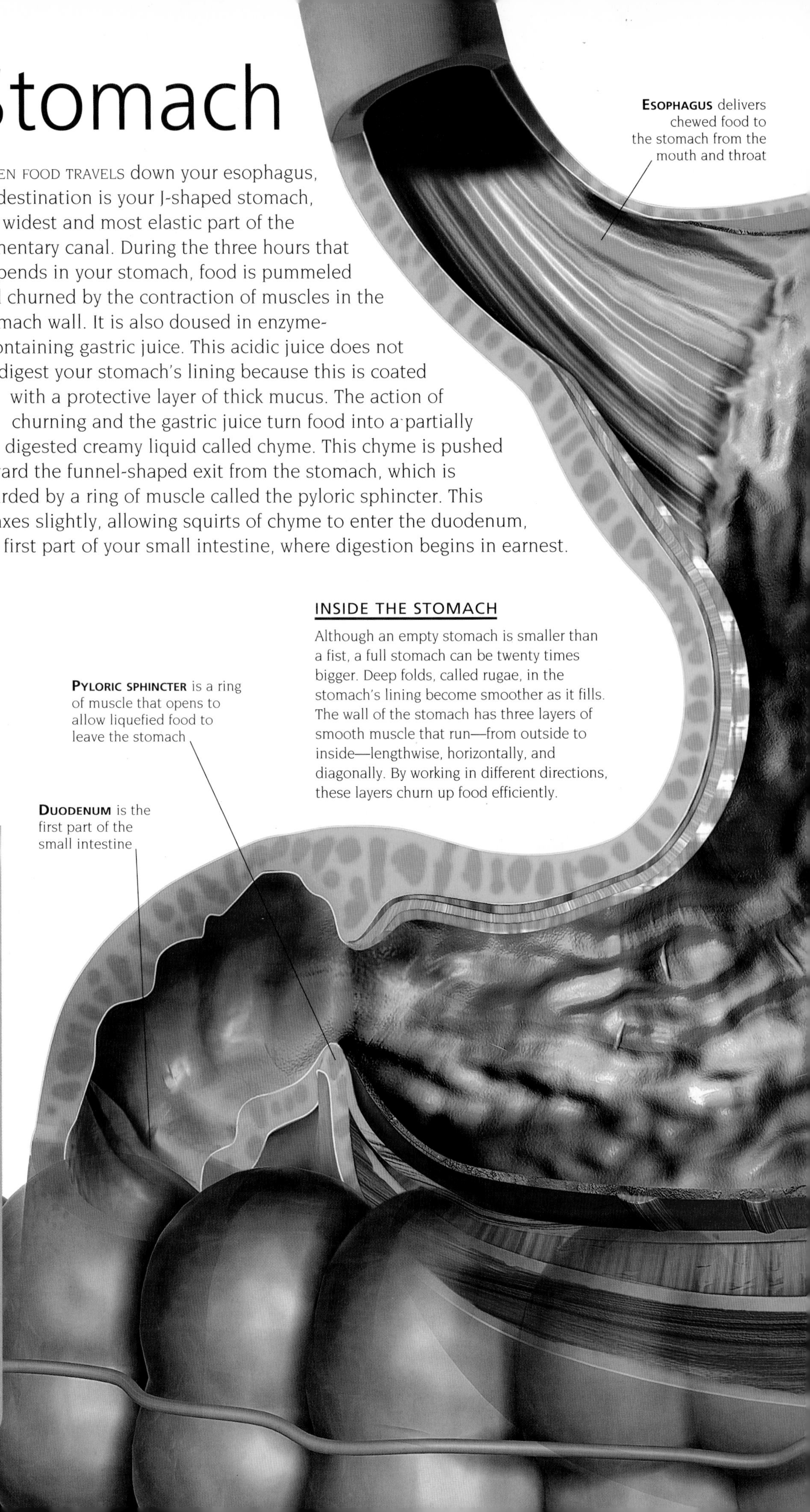

ESOPHAGUS delivers chewed food to the stomach from the mouth and throat

INSIDE THE STOMACH

Although an empty stomach is smaller than a fist, a full stomach can be twenty times bigger. Deep folds, called rugae, in the stomach's lining become smoother as it fills. The wall of the stomach has three layers of smooth muscle that run—from outside to inside—lengthwise, horizontally, and diagonally. By working in different directions, these layers churn up food efficiently.

PYLORIC SPHINCTER is a ring of muscle that opens to allow liquefied food to leave the stomach

DUODENUM is the first part of the small intestine

DID YOU KNOW?

A great advance in understanding the process of digestion resulted from a freak accident. In 1822, fur trapper Alexis St. Martin accidentally shot himself in the side, causing a wound that left a permanent opening to his stomach. St. Martin was treated by US Army surgeon Dr. William Beaumont. Over the next 11 years, Beaumont carried out a series of experiments on St. Martin's stomach, including dangling different types of food in the stomach to see how long they took to digest. Beaumont published his findings to great acclaim in 1833.

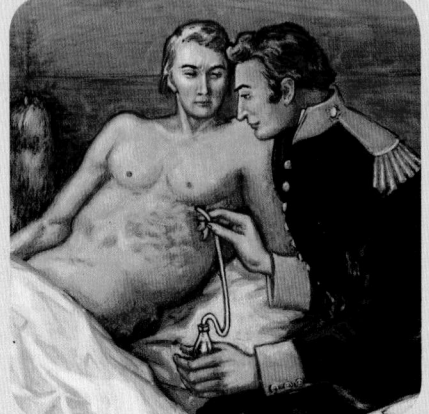

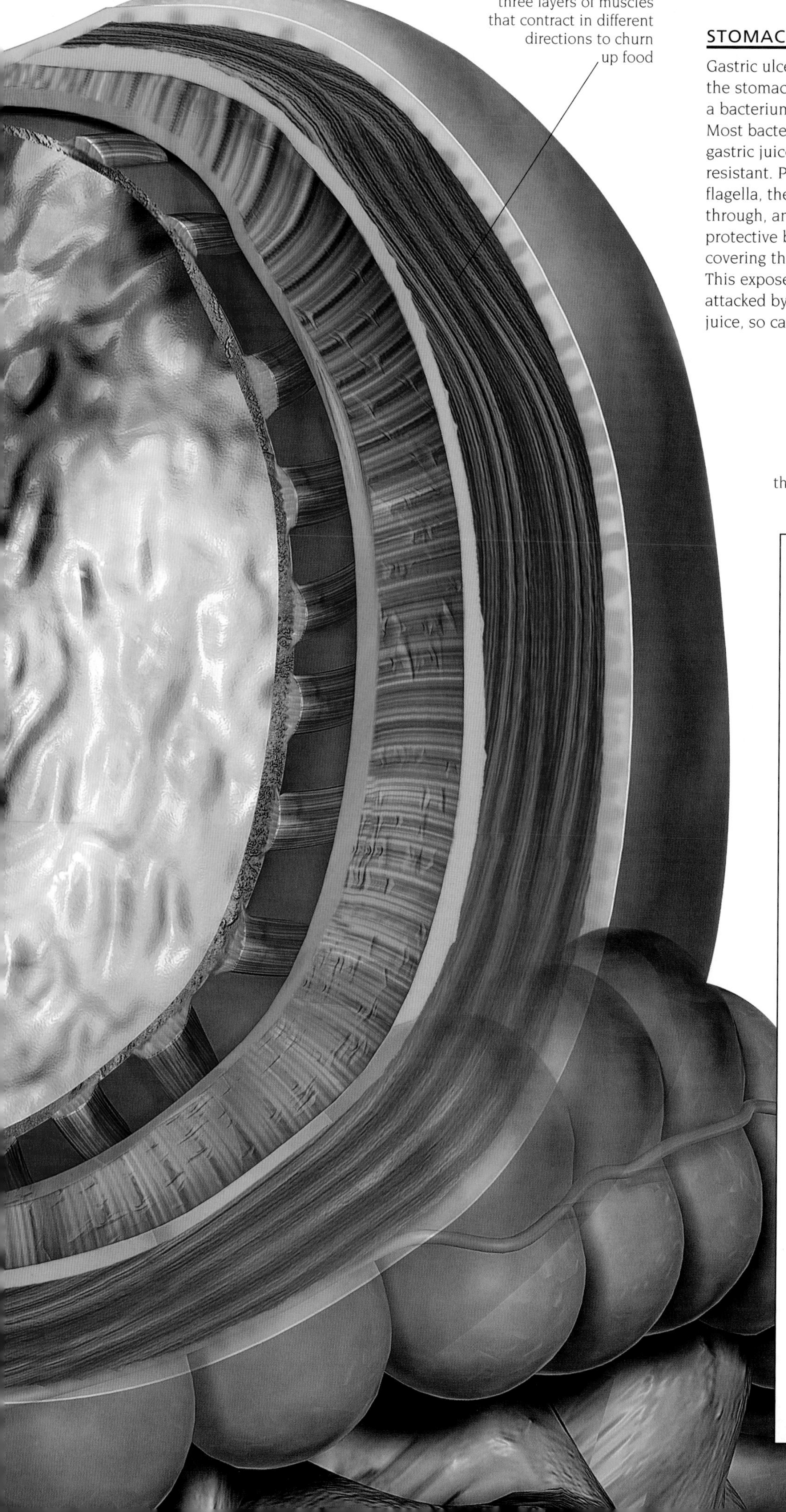

WALL OF STOMACH contains three layers of muscles that contract in different directions to churn up food

STOMACH BUG ▶

Gastric ulcers are painful, open sores in the stomach's lining, generally caused by a bacterium called *Helicobacter pylori*. Most bacteria are destroyed by gastric juice, but H. *pylori* is acid-resistant. Propelled by its beating flagella, the bacterium burrows through, and destroys, the protective barrier of mucus covering the stomach lining. This exposed lining is attacked by acidic gastric juice, so causing the ulcer.

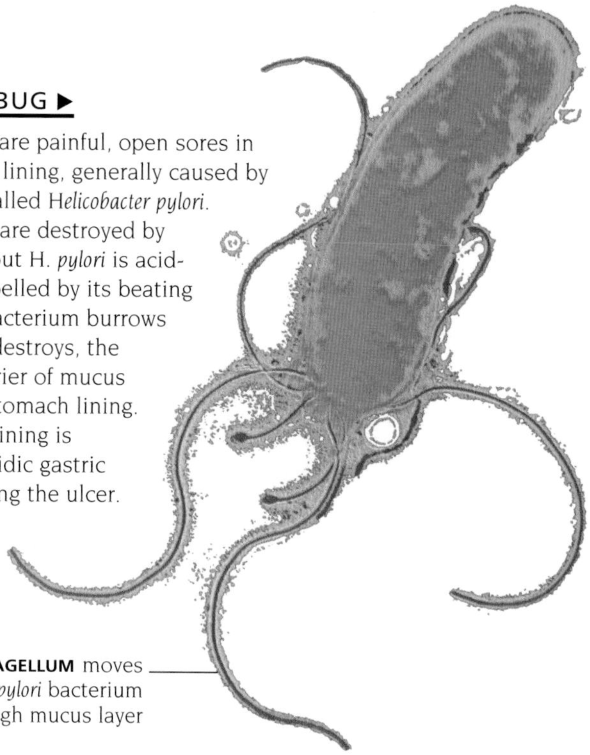

FLAGELLUM moves H. *pylori* bacterium through mucus layer

STOMACH LINING

As this section of the stomach's lining shows, it is dotted with millions of deep holes called gastric pits. Each of these pits leads to an even deeper gastric gland, which contains cells that produce the various components that make up gastric juice. These include mucus, powerful hydrochloric acid, and the enzyme pepsin, which digests proteins.

GASTRIC JUICE is released through the opening of a gastric pit in the stomach's lining

GASTRIC GLAND cells secrete the components of gastric juice

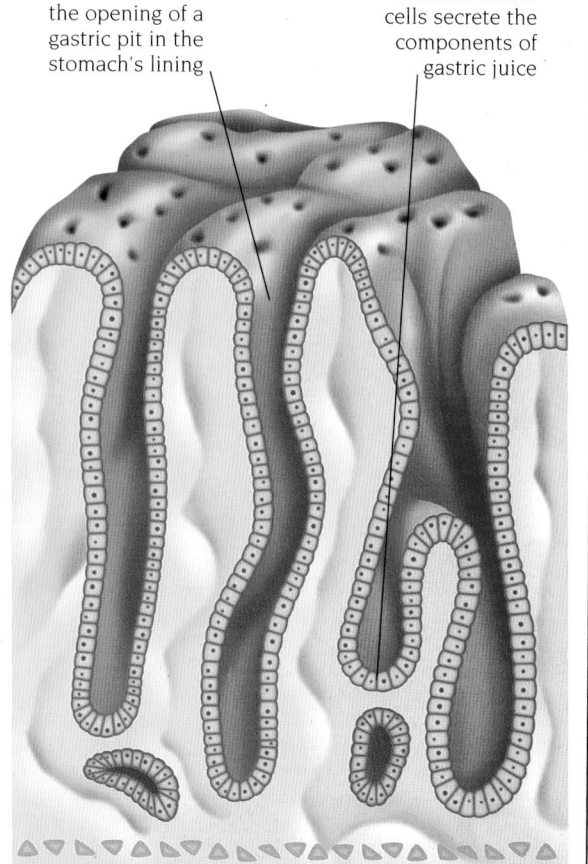

Liver and Gall bladder

YOUR BODY'S CELLS NEED WARM, stable conditions to work at their best and to keep you feeling healthy. Your liver plays a key role in maintaining the right conditions for these cells by controlling the composition of the blood that supplies them. Like tiny chemical factories, liver cells perform more than 500 functions, many to do with processing the products of digestion. These include storing and releasing glucose, storing fats, storing vitamins and minerals, removing poisons from the blood, making bile, and removing bacteria and old blood cells. All this activity releases lots of heat to keep your body warm. Tucked behind your liver, the kiwi-fruit-sized gall bladder is a green bag that stores bile.

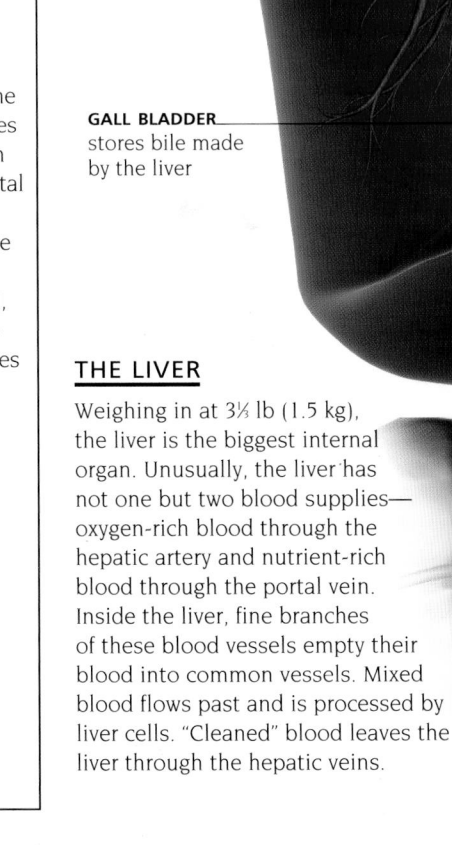

HEPATIC VEIN empties blood processed by the liver into the inferior vena cava

HEPATIC DUCT collects bile from liver cells

RIGHT LOBE of the liver is the larger of the two lobes

GALL BLADDER stores bile made by the liver

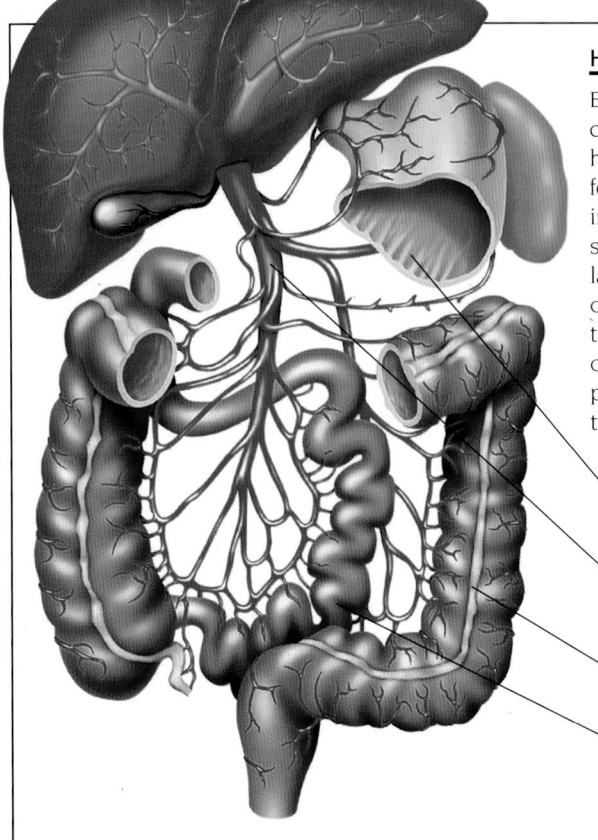

HEPATIC PORTAL SYSTEM

Blood normally travels through capillaries to a vein and back to the heart. In a portal system, capillaries feed into veins, which then branch into capillaries. In the hepatic portal system, capillaries collect blood laden with nutrients from digestive organs, and merge to form veins that empty into the hepatic portal, or portal, vein. Inside the liver the portal vein branches into capillaries that supply liver cells.

STOMACH

PORTAL VEIN carries blood into the liver

LARGE INTESTINE

SMALL INTESTINE is where most digestion takes place

THE LIVER

Weighing in at 3⅓ lb (1.5 kg), the liver is the biggest internal organ. Unusually, the liver has not one but two blood supplies—oxygen-rich blood through the hepatic artery and nutrient-rich blood through the portal vein. Inside the liver, fine branches of these blood vessels empty their blood into common vessels. Mixed blood flows past and is processed by liver cells. "Cleaned" blood leaves the liver through the hepatic veins.

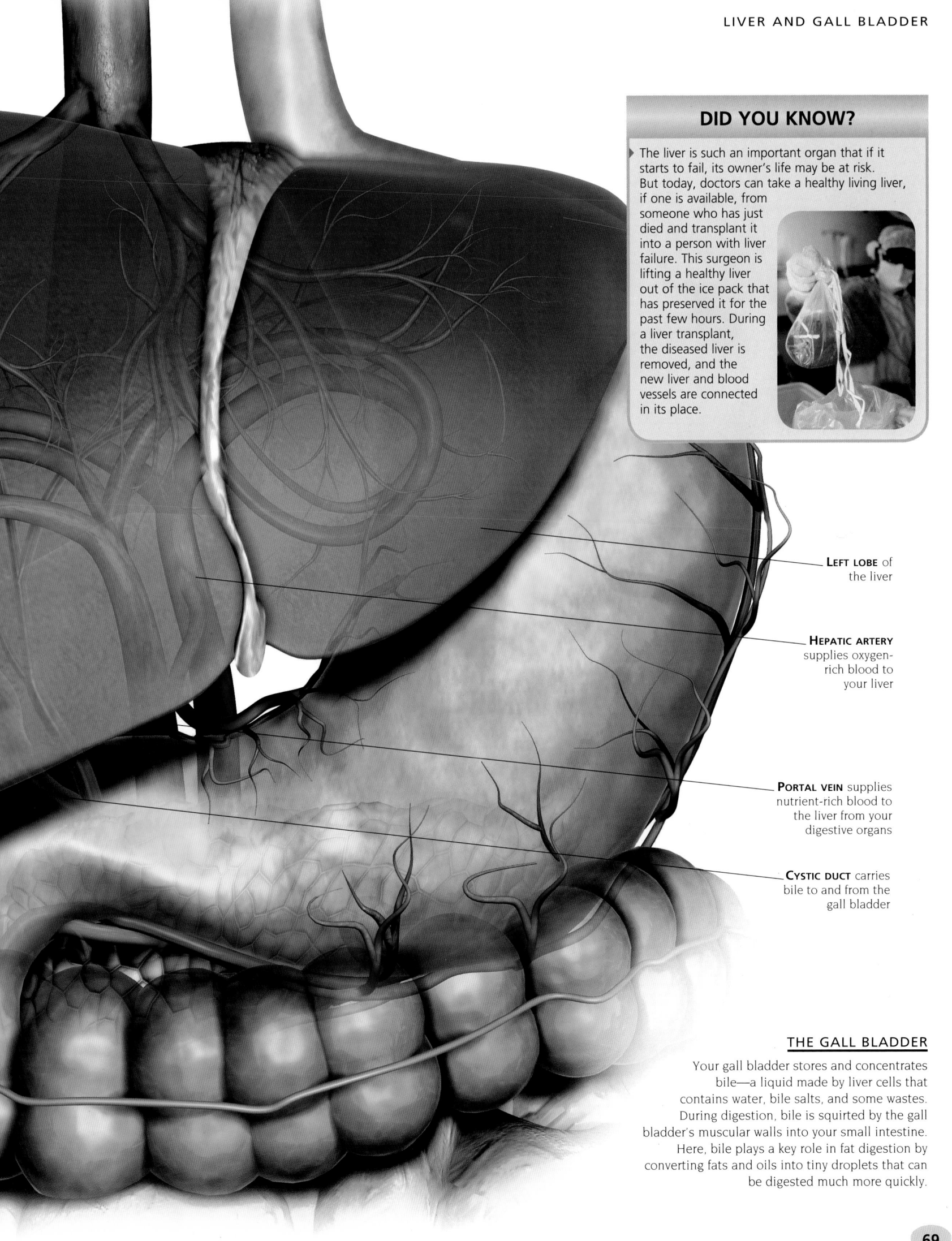

DID YOU KNOW?

▶ The liver is such an important organ that if it starts to fail, its owner's life may be at risk. But today, doctors can take a healthy living liver, if one is available, from someone who has just died and transplant it into a person with liver failure. This surgeon is lifting a healthy liver out of the ice pack that has preserved it for the past few hours. During a liver transplant, the diseased liver is removed, and the new liver and blood vessels are connected in its place.

LEFT LOBE of the liver

HEPATIC ARTERY supplies oxygen-rich blood to your liver

PORTAL VEIN supplies nutrient-rich blood to the liver from your digestive organs

CYSTIC DUCT carries bile to and from the gall bladder

THE GALL BLADDER

Your gall bladder stores and concentrates bile—a liquid made by liver cells that contains water, bile salts, and some wastes. During digestion, bile is squirted by the gall bladder's muscular walls into your small intestine. Here, bile plays a key role in fat digestion by converting fats and oils into tiny droplets that can be digested much more quickly.

Intestines

PACKED INSIDE YOUR ABDOMINAL CAVITY, your small and large intestines are two linked tubes that form the longest part of your alimentary canal. It takes several hours to thoroughly process the food or waste passing through them. Inside your small intestine, food is digested into simple substances that are absorbed into your bloodstream. Any leftover waste passes into the colon, the longest part of your large intestine, where water is absorbed back into the bloodstream along with vitamins produced by millions of bacteria. Waste is converted into semisolid feces that are pushed out of the body.

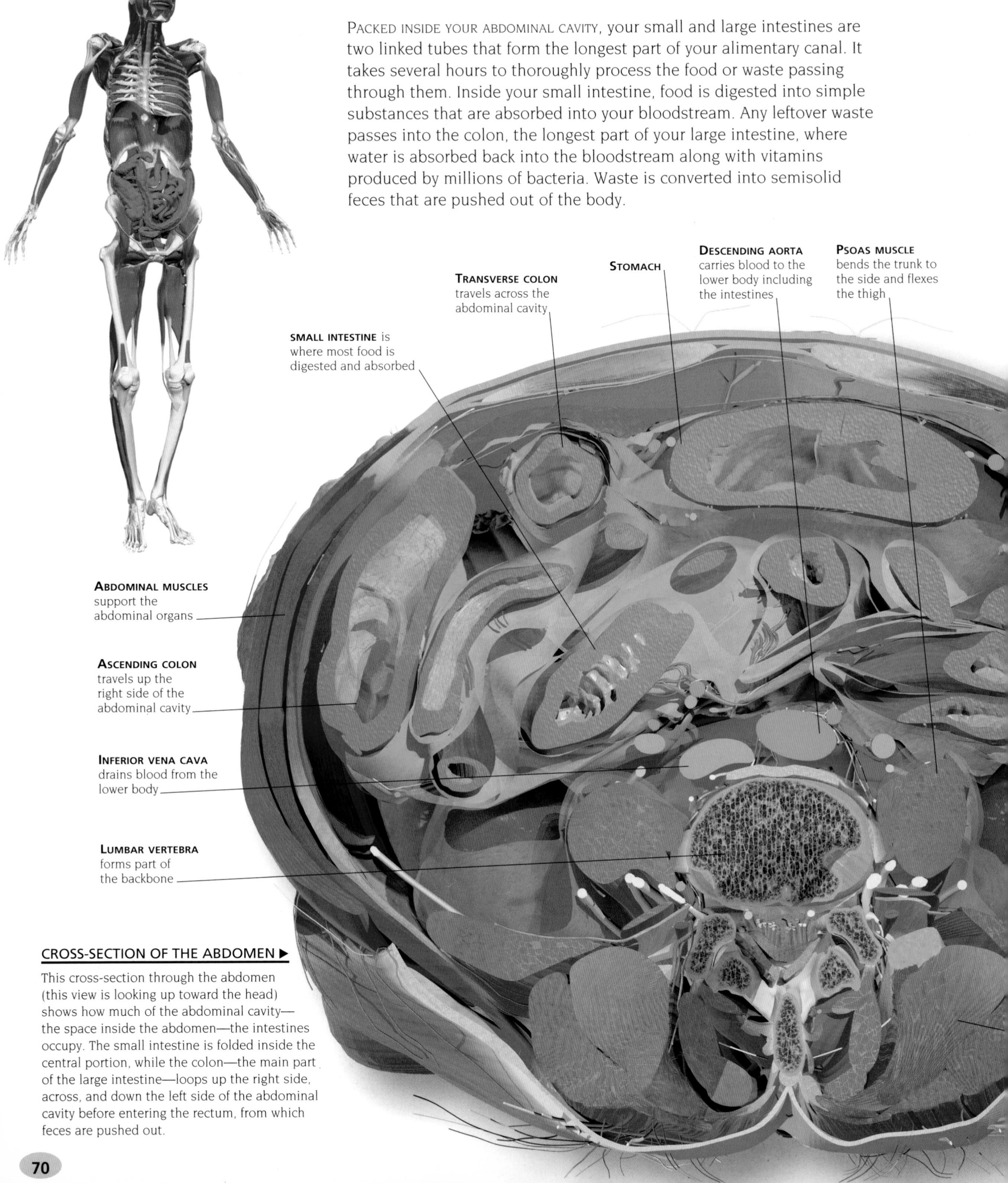

TRANSVERSE COLON travels across the abdominal cavity

STOMACH

DESCENDING AORTA carries blood to the lower body including the intestines

PSOAS MUSCLE bends the trunk to the side and flexes the thigh

SMALL INTESTINE is where most food is digested and absorbed

ABDOMINAL MUSCLES support the abdominal organs

ASCENDING COLON travels up the right side of the abdominal cavity

INFERIOR VENA CAVA drains blood from the lower body

LUMBAR VERTEBRA forms part of the backbone

CROSS-SECTION OF THE ABDOMEN ▶

This cross-section through the abdomen (this view is looking up toward the head) shows how much of the abdominal cavity—the space inside the abdomen—the intestines occupy. The small intestine is folded inside the central portion, while the colon—the main part of the large intestine—loops up the right side, across, and down the left side of the abdominal cavity before entering the rectum, from which feces are pushed out.

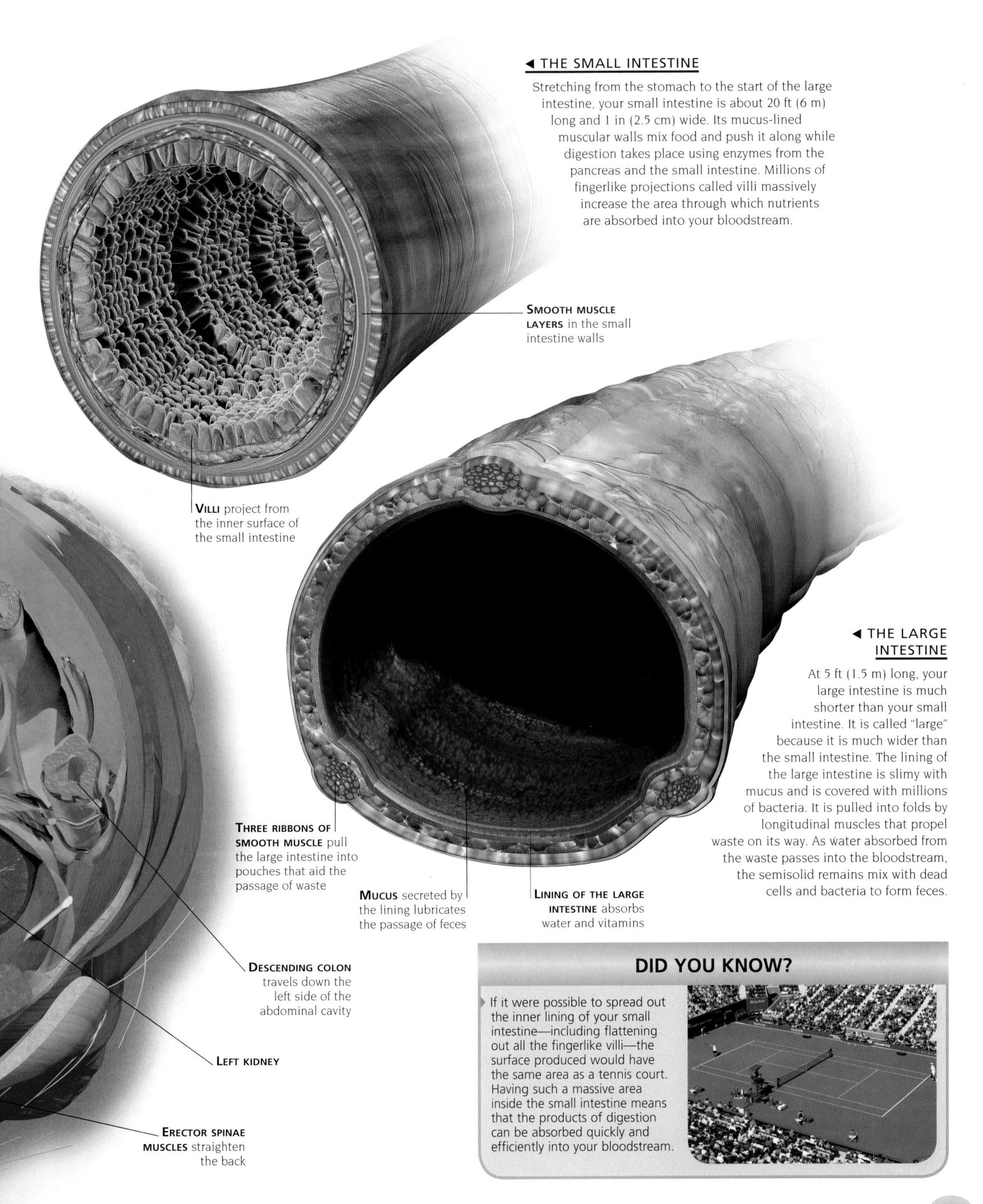

◄ THE SMALL INTESTINE

Stretching from the stomach to the start of the large intestine, your small intestine is about 20 ft (6 m) long and 1 in (2.5 cm) wide. Its mucus-lined muscular walls mix food and push it along while digestion takes place using enzymes from the pancreas and the small intestine. Millions of fingerlike projections called villi massively increase the area through which nutrients are absorbed into your bloodstream.

SMOOTH MUSCLE LAYERS in the small intestine walls

VILLI project from the inner surface of the small intestine

◄ THE LARGE INTESTINE

At 5 ft (1.5 m) long, your large intestine is much shorter than your small intestine. It is called "large" because it is much wider than the small intestine. The lining of the large intestine is slimy with mucus and is covered with millions of bacteria. It is pulled into folds by longitudinal muscles that propel waste on its way. As water absorbed from the waste passes into the bloodstream, the semisolid remains mix with dead cells and bacteria to form feces.

THREE RIBBONS OF SMOOTH MUSCLE pull the large intestine into pouches that aid the passage of waste

MUCUS secreted by the lining lubricates the passage of feces

LINING OF THE LARGE INTESTINE absorbs water and vitamins

DESCENDING COLON travels down the left side of the abdominal cavity

LEFT KIDNEY

ERECTOR SPINAE MUSCLES straighten the back

DID YOU KNOW?

If it were possible to spread out the inner lining of your small intestine—including flattening out all the fingerlike villi—the surface produced would have the same area as a tennis court. Having such a massive area inside the small intestine means that the products of digestion can be absorbed quickly and efficiently into your bloodstream.

Pelvis

IF YOU PUT YOUR HANDS on your hips, you can feel the bones of your pelvis—the lowest part of your trunk. Strong and bowl-shaped, your pelvis surrounds, protects, and supports the organs inside your pelvic cavity. It attaches your legs to your trunk and helps you maintain an upright posture. With its large bony surface, your pelvis provides attachment points for the muscles that go upward to move your trunk, and the muscles that go downward to move your legs.

THE PELVIC SKELETON

Your pelvis has three bony components—two hip bones, or coxal bones, and the part of the backbone (the sacrum and coccyx) to which they are attached. Each of the two hip bones is made up of three separate bones—the ilium, ischium, and pubis—that fuse together in teenage years. These three bones meet at the acetabulum, the cup-shaped socket into which the head of the femur fits. Together, the two hip bones form the pelvic girdle, which anchors your legs to the rest of your body.

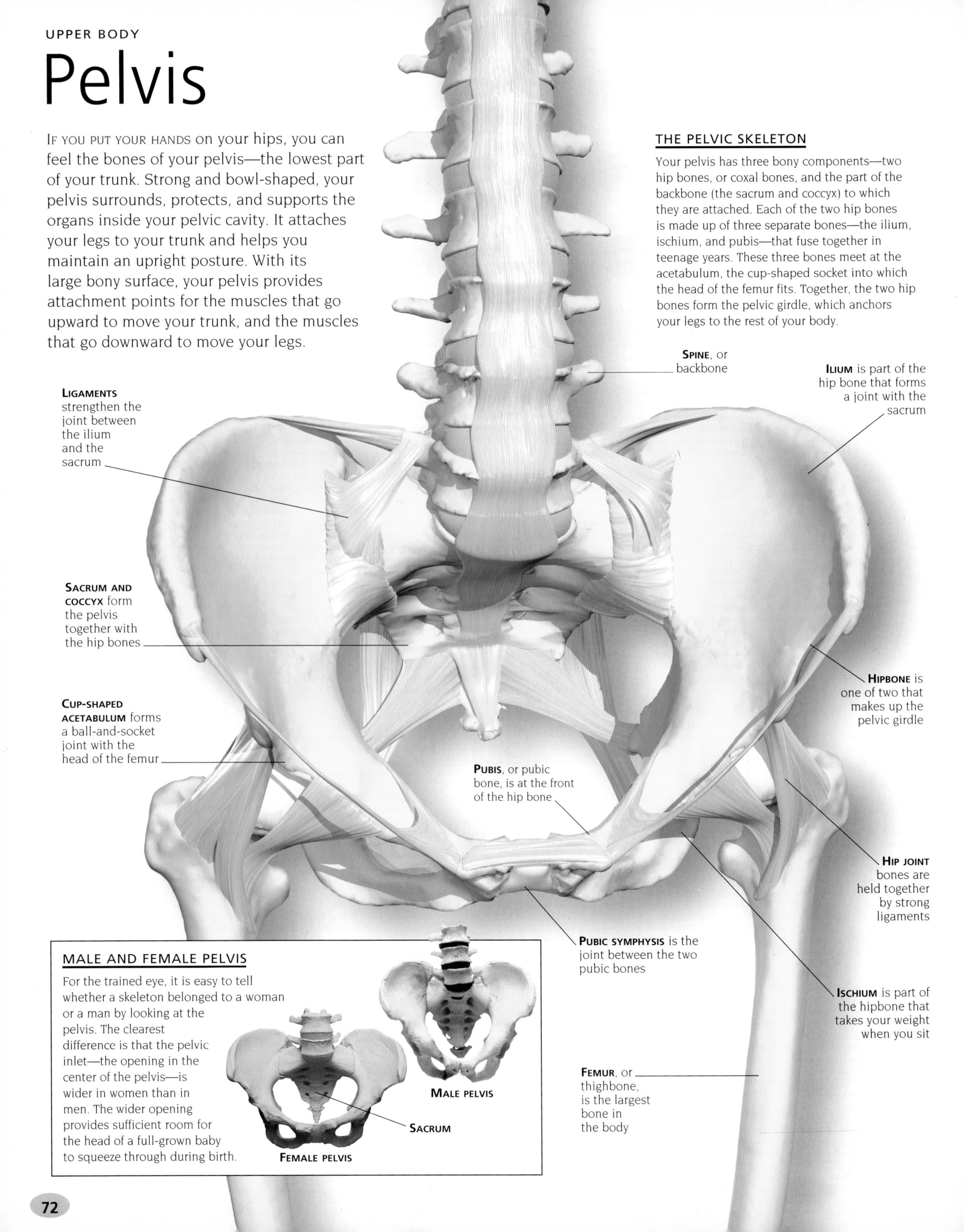

LIGAMENTS strengthen the joint between the ilium and the sacrum

SACRUM AND COCCYX form the pelvis together with the hip bones

CUP-SHAPED ACETABULUM forms a ball-and-socket joint with the head of the femur

SPINE, or backbone

ILIUM is part of the hip bone that forms a joint with the sacrum

HIPBONE is one of two that makes up the pelvic girdle

PUBIS, or pubic bone, is at the front of the hip bone

HIP JOINT bones are held together by strong ligaments

PUBIC SYMPHYSIS is the joint between the two pubic bones

ISCHIUM is part of the hipbone that takes your weight when you sit

FEMUR, or thighbone, is the largest bone in the body

MALE AND FEMALE PELVIS

For the trained eye, it is easy to tell whether a skeleton belonged to a woman or a man by looking at the pelvis. The clearest difference is that the pelvic inlet—the opening in the center of the pelvis—is wider in women than in men. The wider opening provides sufficient room for the head of a full-grown baby to squeeze through during birth.

MALE PELVIS

SACRUM

FEMALE PELVIS

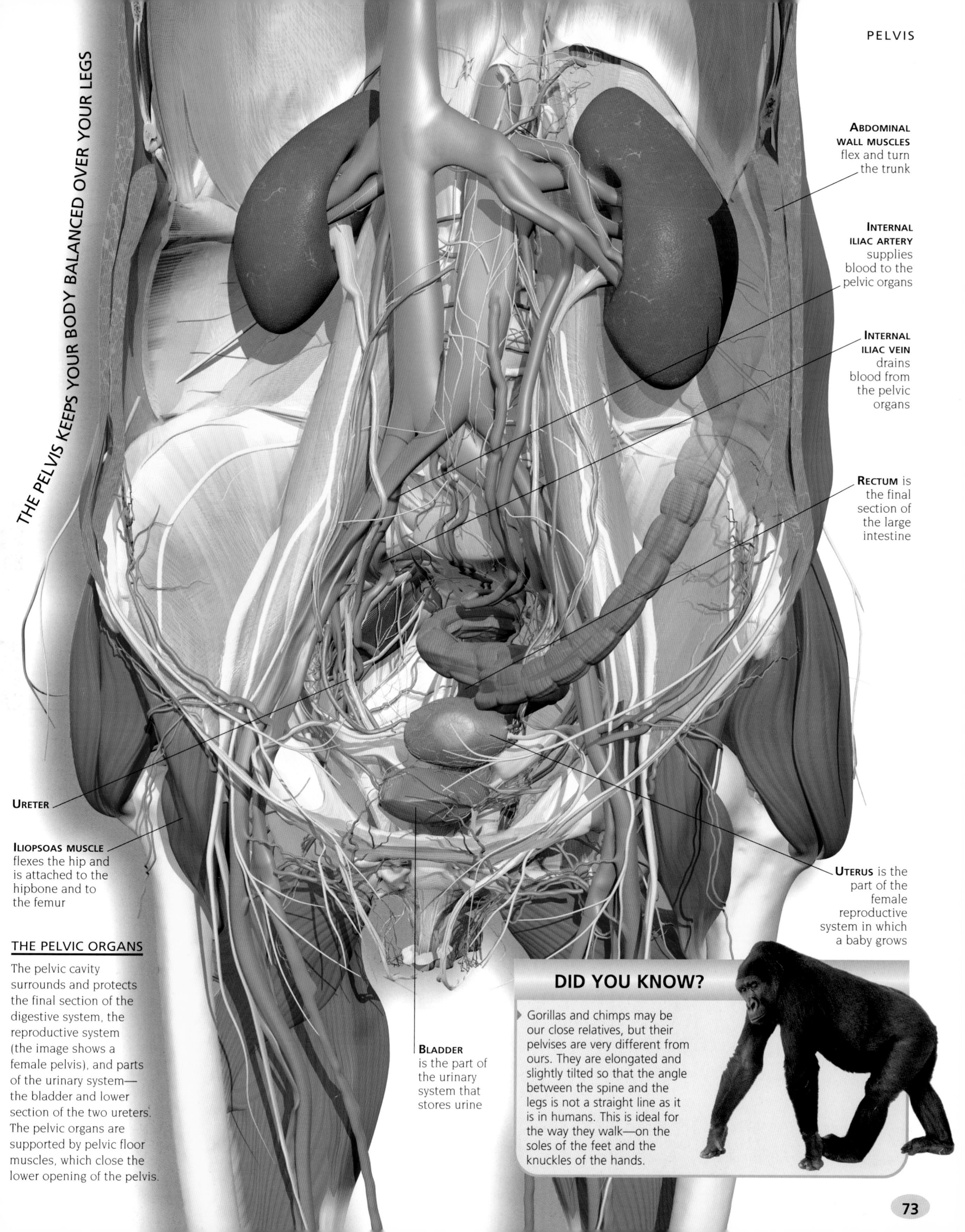

THE PELVIS KEEPS YOUR BODY BALANCED OVER YOUR LEGS

ABDOMINAL WALL MUSCLES flex and turn the trunk

INTERNAL ILIAC ARTERY supplies blood to the pelvic organs

INTERNAL ILIAC VEIN drains blood from the pelvic organs

RECTUM is the final section of the large intestine

UTERUS is the part of the female reproductive system in which a baby grows

URETER

ILIOPSOAS MUSCLE flexes the hip and is attached to the hipbone and to the femur

THE PELVIC ORGANS

The pelvic cavity surrounds and protects the final section of the digestive system, the reproductive system (the image shows a female pelvis), and parts of the urinary system—the bladder and lower section of the two ureters. The pelvic organs are supported by pelvic floor muscles, which close the lower opening of the pelvis.

BLADDER is the part of the urinary system that stores urine

DID YOU KNOW?

▶ Gorillas and chimps may be our close relatives, but their pelvises are very different from ours. They are elongated and slightly tilted so that the angle between the spine and the legs is not a straight line as it is in humans. This is ideal for the way they walk—on the soles of the feet and the knuckles of the hands.

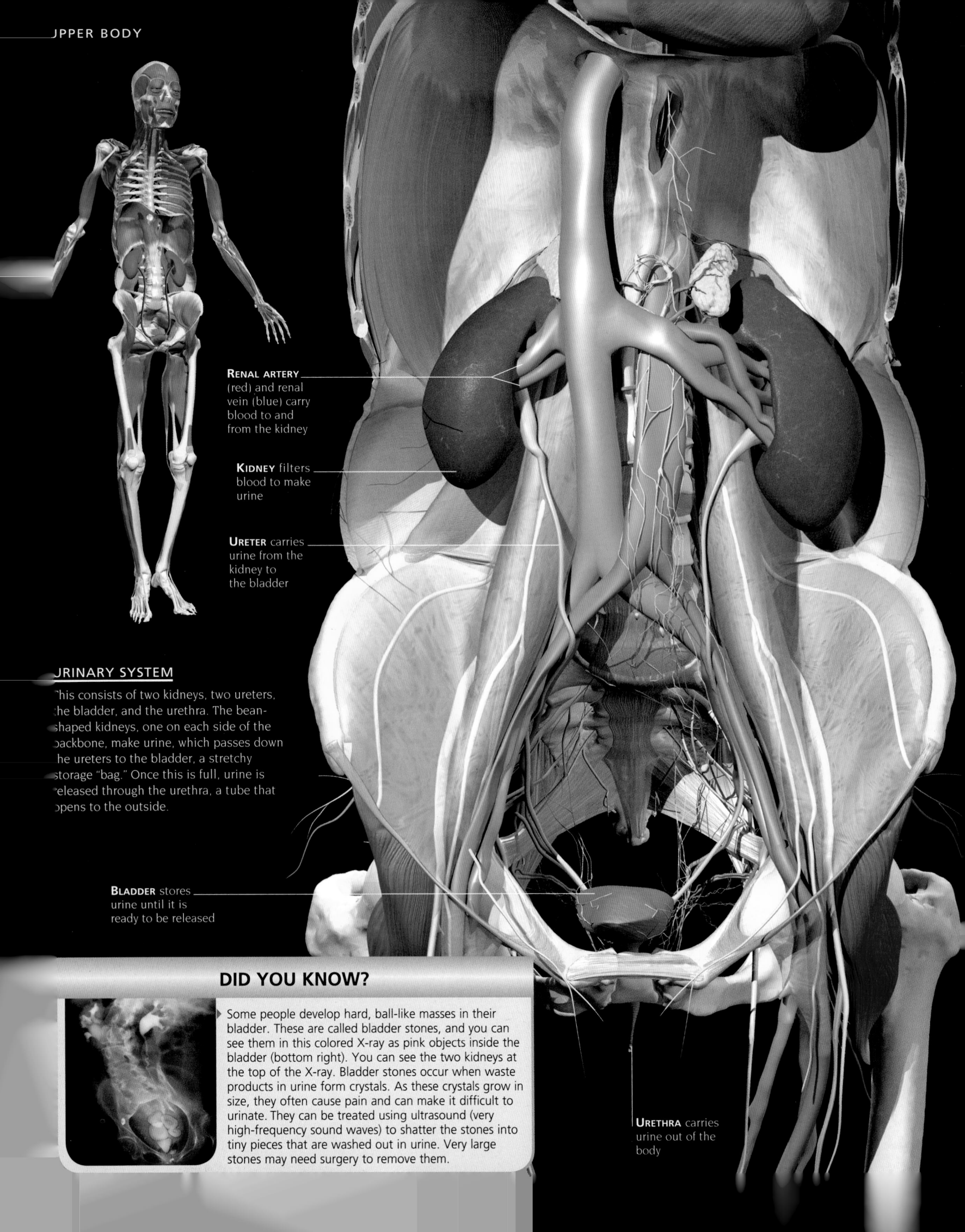

RENAL ARTERY
(red) and renal
vein (blue) carry
blood to and
from the kidney

KIDNEY filters
blood to make
urine

URETER carries
urine from the
kidney to
the bladder

URINARY SYSTEM

This consists of two kidneys, two ureters,
the bladder, and the urethra. The bean-
shaped kidneys, one on each side of the
backbone, make urine, which passes down
the ureters to the bladder, a stretchy
storage "bag." Once this is full, urine is
released through the urethra, a tube that
opens to the outside.

BLADDER stores
urine until it is
ready to be released

DID YOU KNOW?

Some people develop hard, ball-like masses in their
bladder. These are called bladder stones, and you can
see them in this colored X-ray as pink objects inside the
bladder (bottom right). You can see the two kidneys at
the top of the X-ray. Bladder stones occur when waste
products in urine form crystals. As these crystals grow in
size, they often cause pain and can make it difficult to
urinate. They can be treated using ultrasound (very
high-frequency sound waves) to shatter the stones into
tiny pieces that are washed out in urine. Very large
stones may need surgery to remove them.

URETHRA carries
urine out of the
body

Kidneys and Bladder

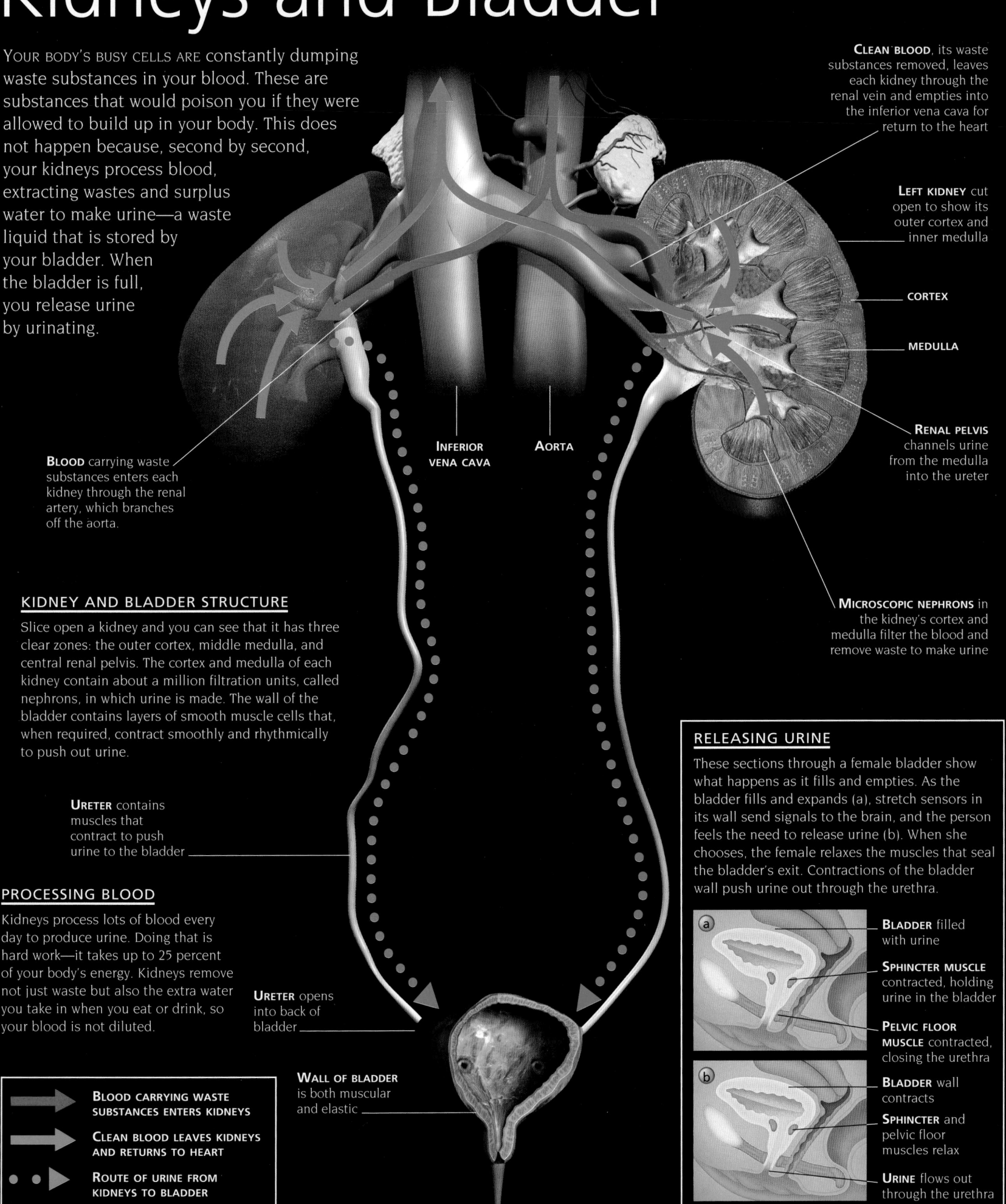

YOUR BODY'S BUSY CELLS ARE constantly dumping waste substances in your blood. These are substances that would poison you if they were allowed to build up in your body. This does not happen because, second by second, your kidneys process blood, extracting wastes and surplus water to make urine—a waste liquid that is stored by your bladder. When the bladder is full, you release urine by urinating.

CLEAN BLOOD, its waste substances removed, leaves each kidney through the renal vein and empties into the inferior vena cava for return to the heart

LEFT KIDNEY cut open to show its outer cortex and inner medulla

CORTEX

MEDULLA

RENAL PELVIS channels urine from the medulla into the ureter

BLOOD carrying waste substances enters each kidney through the renal artery, which branches off the aorta.

INFERIOR VENA CAVA

AORTA

MICROSCOPIC NEPHRONS in the kidney's cortex and medulla filter the blood and remove waste to make urine

KIDNEY AND BLADDER STRUCTURE

Slice open a kidney and you can see that it has three clear zones: the outer cortex, middle medulla, and central renal pelvis. The cortex and medulla of each kidney contain about a million filtration units, called nephrons, in which urine is made. The wall of the bladder contains layers of smooth muscle cells that, when required, contract smoothly and rhythmically to push out urine.

URETER contains muscles that contract to push urine to the bladder

PROCESSING BLOOD

Kidneys process lots of blood every day to produce urine. Doing that is hard work—it takes up to 25 percent of your body's energy. Kidneys remove not just waste but also the extra water you take in when you eat or drink, so your blood is not diluted.

URETER opens into back of bladder

WALL OF BLADDER is both muscular and elastic

RELEASING URINE

These sections through a female bladder show what happens as it fills and empties. As the bladder fills and expands (a), stretch sensors in its wall send signals to the brain, and the person feels the need to release urine (b). When she chooses, the female relaxes the muscles that seal the bladder's exit. Contractions of the bladder wall push urine out through the urethra.

(a)

BLADDER filled with urine

SPHINCTER MUSCLE contracted, holding urine in the bladder

PELVIC FLOOR MUSCLE contracted, closing the urethra

(b)

BLADDER wall contracts

SPHINCTER and pelvic floor muscles relax

URINE flows out through the urethra

BLOOD CARRYING WASTE SUBSTANCES ENTERS KIDNEYS

CLEAN BLOOD LEAVES KIDNEYS AND RETURNS TO HEART

ROUTE OF URINE FROM KIDNEYS TO BLADDER

Female Reproduction

FROM HER EARLY TEENS, WHEN PUBERTY HAPPENS, to her early to mid-fifties, a woman's reproductive system prepares itself each month for the possibility of nurturing a new life. During a regular sequence of events, known as the menstrual cycle, a female sex cell—called an egg, or ovum—is released from an ovary. If fertilized by a sperm—the male sex cell—the resulting fertilized egg settles in the lining of the uterus, or womb. Protected within the uterus, the fertilized egg develops and grows into a baby. After nine months, the muscular walls of the uterus begin a series of powerful contractions that push the baby out of the woman's body during childbirth.

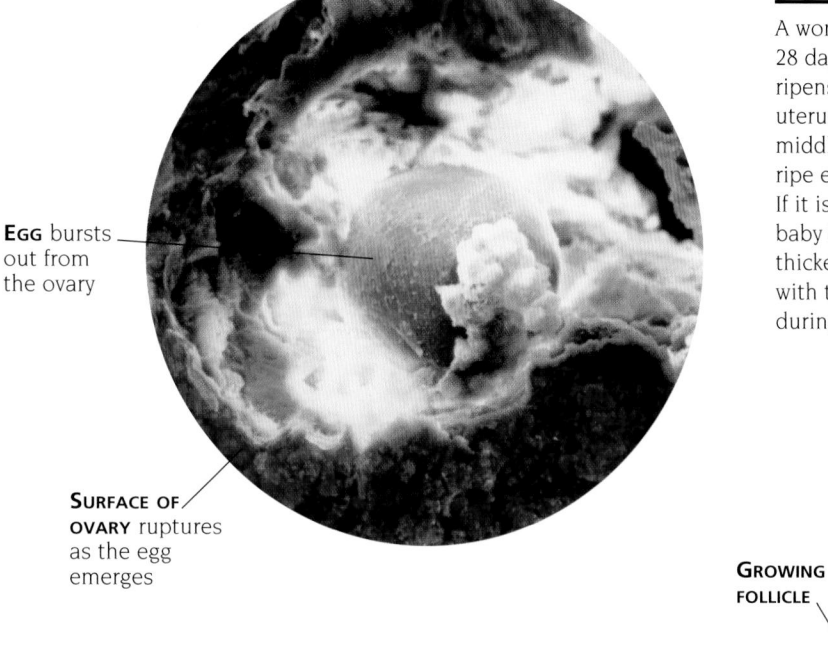

EGG bursts out from the ovary

SURFACE OF OVARY ruptures as the egg emerges

MENSTRUAL CYCLE AND OVULATION

A woman's monthly menstrual cycle lasts about 28 days. Under the control of hormones, an egg ripens within an ovary, and the lining of the uterus thickens to receive a fertilized egg. In the middle of the cycle, ovulation occurs when the ripe egg bursts out from the surface of the ovary. If it is fertilized by a sperm, it develops into a baby in the uterus. If it is not fertilized, the thickened lining of the uterus breaks down and, with the egg, passes out through the vagina during menstruation. The cycle then starts again.

DID YOU KNOW?

▶ Infertility may be caused when a man produces only a few, slow-moving sperm. In this case, intracytoplasmic sperm injection (ICSI) may help. A single sperm is injected directly into an egg (below) that has been removed from his partner's ovary. The fertilized egg is then placed in the woman's uterus to develop.

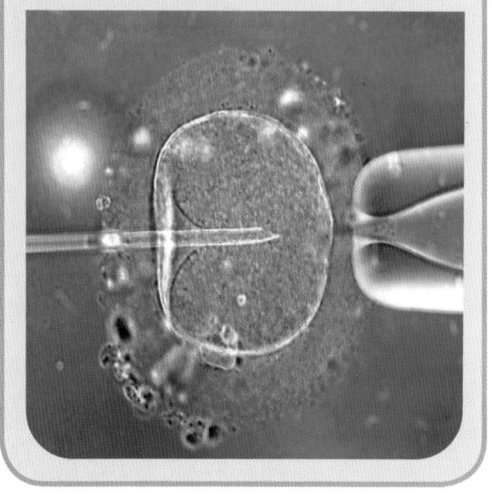

EGG RIPENING

At birth, the ovaries already contain hundreds of thousands of immature eggs, each in a baglike follicle. Every month, several follicles start to mature, grow, and fill with fluid as the egg inside them ripens. One follicle outgrows the others, forms a swelling under the ovary's surface, then bursts during ovulation to release the egg.

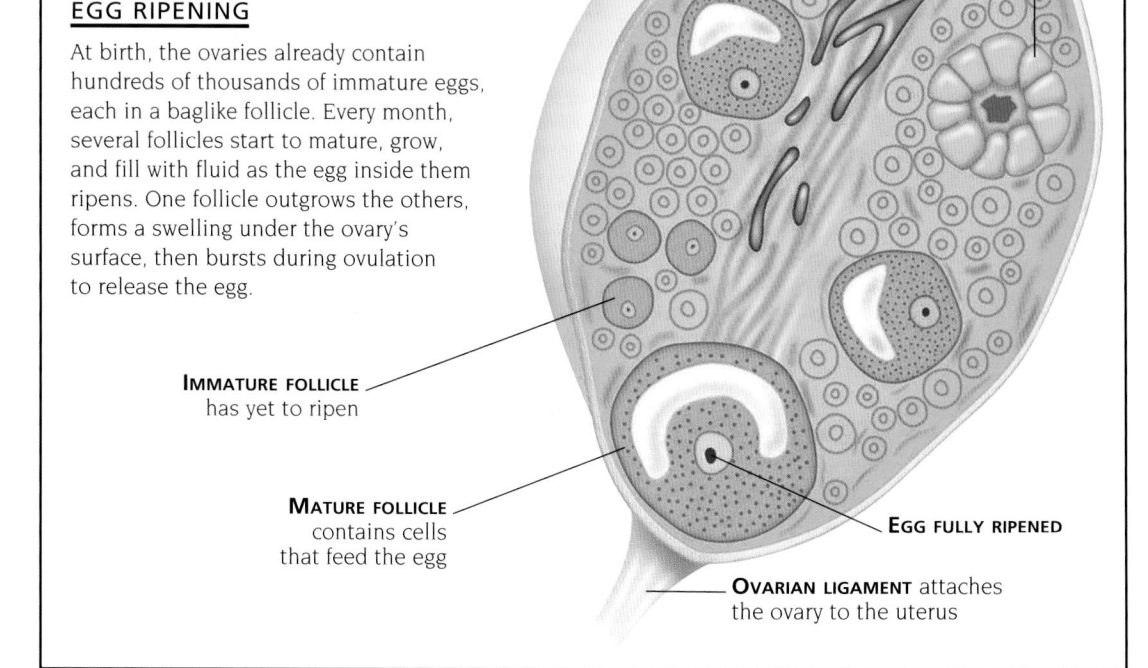

MEDULLA contains ovarian blood vessels and nerves

GROWING FOLLICLE

EMPTY FOLLICLE breaks down at the end of the menstrual cycle

SURFACE OF OVARY becomes more pitted during a woman's life

IMMATURE FOLLICLE has yet to ripen

MATURE FOLLICLE contains cells that feed the egg

EGG FULLY RIPENED

OVARIAN LIGAMENT attaches the ovary to the uterus

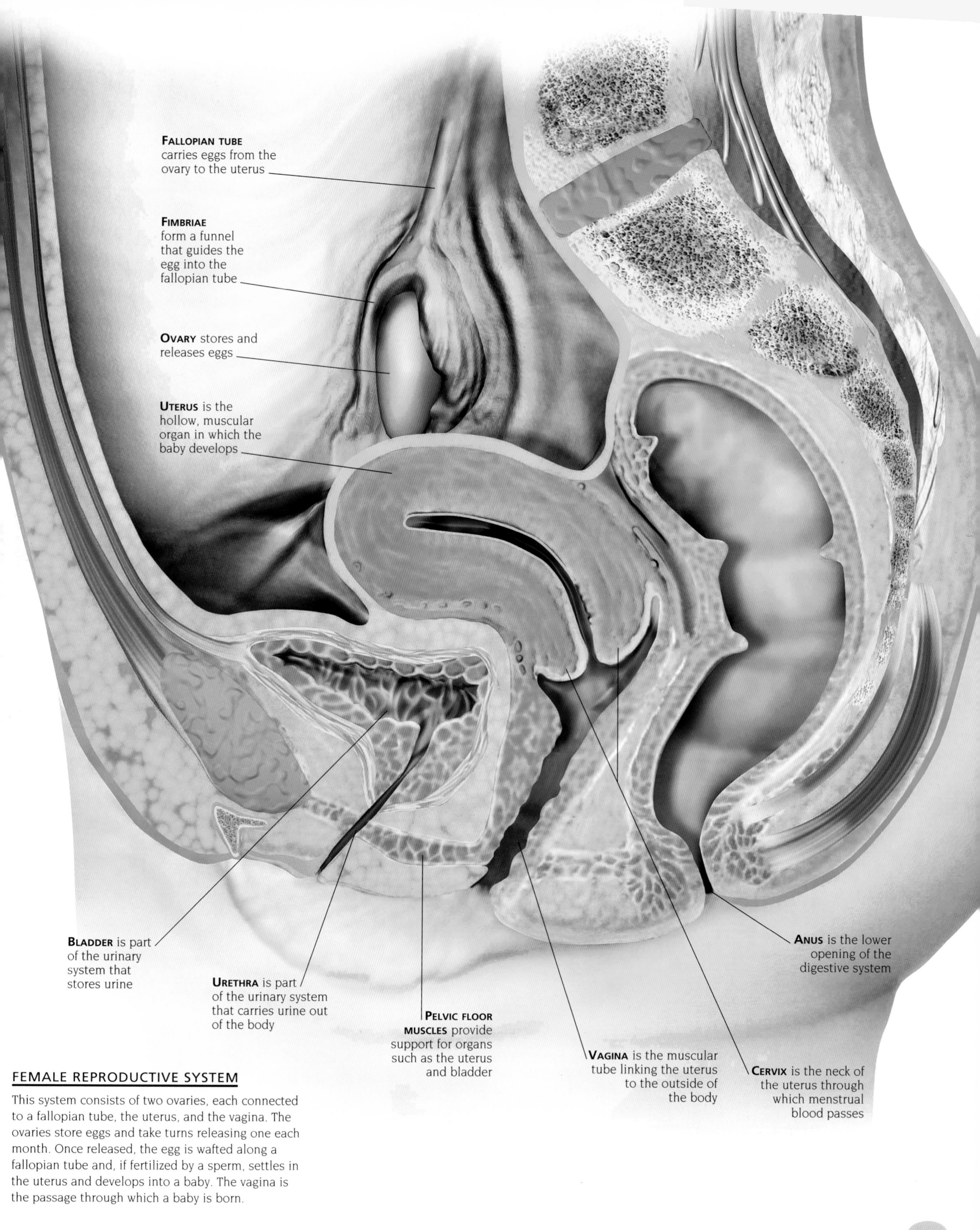

Fallopian tube carries eggs from the ovary to the uterus

Fimbriae form a funnel that guides the egg into the fallopian tube

Ovary stores and releases eggs

Uterus is the hollow, muscular organ in which the baby develops

Bladder is part of the urinary system that stores urine

Urethra is part of the urinary system that carries urine out of the body

Pelvic floor muscles provide support for organs such as the uterus and bladder

Vagina is the muscular tube linking the uterus to the outside of the body

Cervix is the neck of the uterus through which menstrual blood passes

Anus is the lower opening of the digestive system

FEMALE REPRODUCTIVE SYSTEM

This system consists of two ovaries, each connected to a fallopian tube, the uterus, and the vagina. The ovaries store eggs and take turns releasing one each month. Once released, the egg is wafted along a fallopian tube and, if fertilized by a sperm, settles in the uterus and develops into a baby. The vagina is the passage through which a baby is born.

Male Reproduction

FROM PUBERTY ONWARD, THE MALE REPRODUCTIVE SYSTEM makes sex cells called sperm. Their role is to find and fuse with a female egg to create a fertilized egg that will develop into a baby. Each sperm is perfectly adapted for this role by having a streamlined shape and by being able to move. Millions of sperm are released into a woman's body during an intimate act called sexual intercourse. Only a few hundred survive the journey to find an egg.

ZONA PELLUCIDA is the jellylike layer surrounding the egg

FLAGELLUM, or tail, beats to propel the sperm forward

OVARIAN FOLLICLE CELLS form the outer coat

HEAD OF SPERM carrying the nucleus

SPERM trying to burrow through the outer covering of the egg

NUCLEUS of the egg

MIDPIECE OF SPERM contains energy-releasing mitochondria

FERTILIZATION

Hundreds of sperm swim toward and crowd around a recently released egg in a woman's fallopian tube. Each sperm tries to penetrate the egg's outer barrier and get into the egg itself. Eventually one succeeds. Its nucleus fuses with the nucleus of the egg. Fertilization has happened and a new life begins.

DID YOU KNOW?

▶ When sperm were first discovered in 1677, many scientists believed that each one contained a tiny, perfectly formed human called a homunculus (below) that could grow into a baby inside the uterus. Only in the 19th century was it shown that babies develop after fertilization.

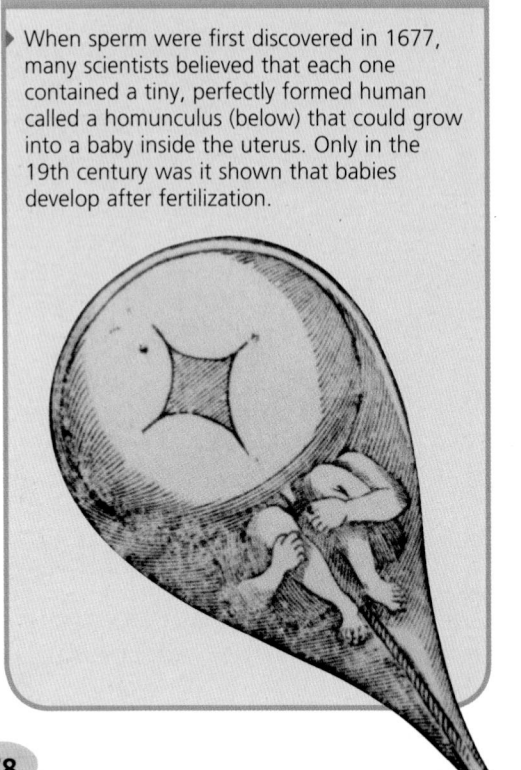

MAKING SPERM

The two testes hang outside the body to ensure each testis temperature is just right for making sperm—that is, about 5°F (3°C) below normal body temperature of 98.6°F (37°C). More than 250 million sperm are produced daily inside coiled tubes called seminiferous tubules, which, if stretched out, would reach more than 1,640 ft (500 m). Immature sperm are moved to the comma-shaped epididymis, where they mature and start to swim. Mature sperm are stored both in the epididymis and in the first section of the vas deferens.

VAS DEFERENS transport the sperm toward the penis

EPIDIDYMIS is the long, coiled tube where sperm mature

SEMINIFEROUS TUBULES are the site of sperm production

SCROTUM MUSCLES move testes up or down to keep them at the correct temperature

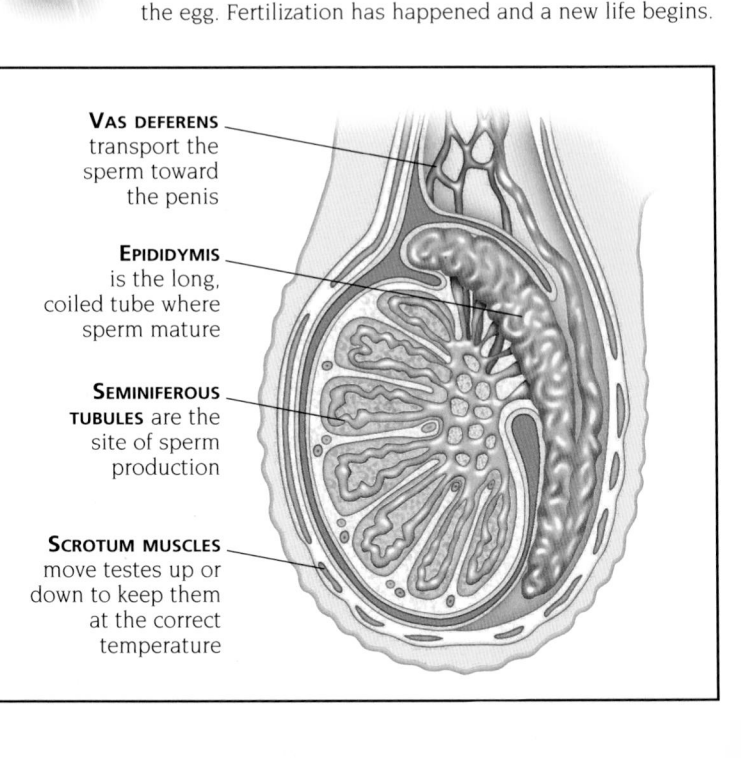

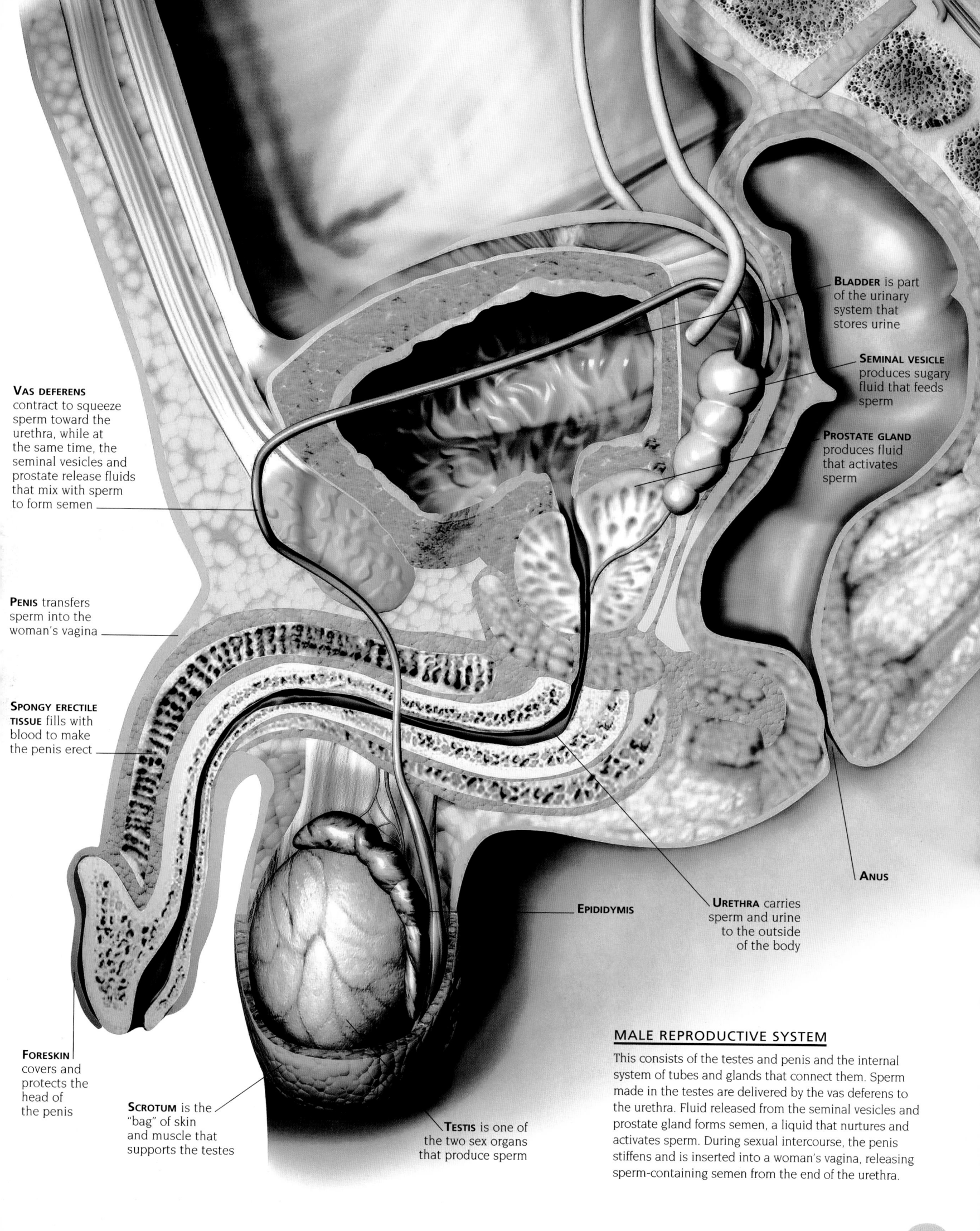

VAS DEFERENS contract to squeeze sperm toward the urethra, while at the same time, the seminal vesicles and prostate release fluids that mix with sperm to form semen

PENIS transfers sperm into the woman's vagina

SPONGY ERECTILE TISSUE fills with blood to make the penis erect

FORESKIN covers and protects the head of the penis

SCROTUM is the "bag" of skin and muscle that supports the testes

TESTIS is one of the two sex organs that produce sperm

EPIDIDYMIS

BLADDER is part of the urinary system that stores urine

SEMINAL VESICLE produces sugary fluid that feeds sperm

PROSTATE GLAND produces fluid that activates sperm

ANUS

URETHRA carries sperm and urine to the outside of the body

MALE REPRODUCTIVE SYSTEM

This consists of the testes and penis and the internal system of tubes and glands that connect them. Sperm made in the testes are delivered by the vas deferens to the urethra. Fluid released from the seminal vesicles and prostate gland forms semen, a liquid that nurtures and activates sperm. During sexual intercourse, the penis stiffens and is inserted into a woman's vagina, releasing sperm-containing semen from the end of the urethra.

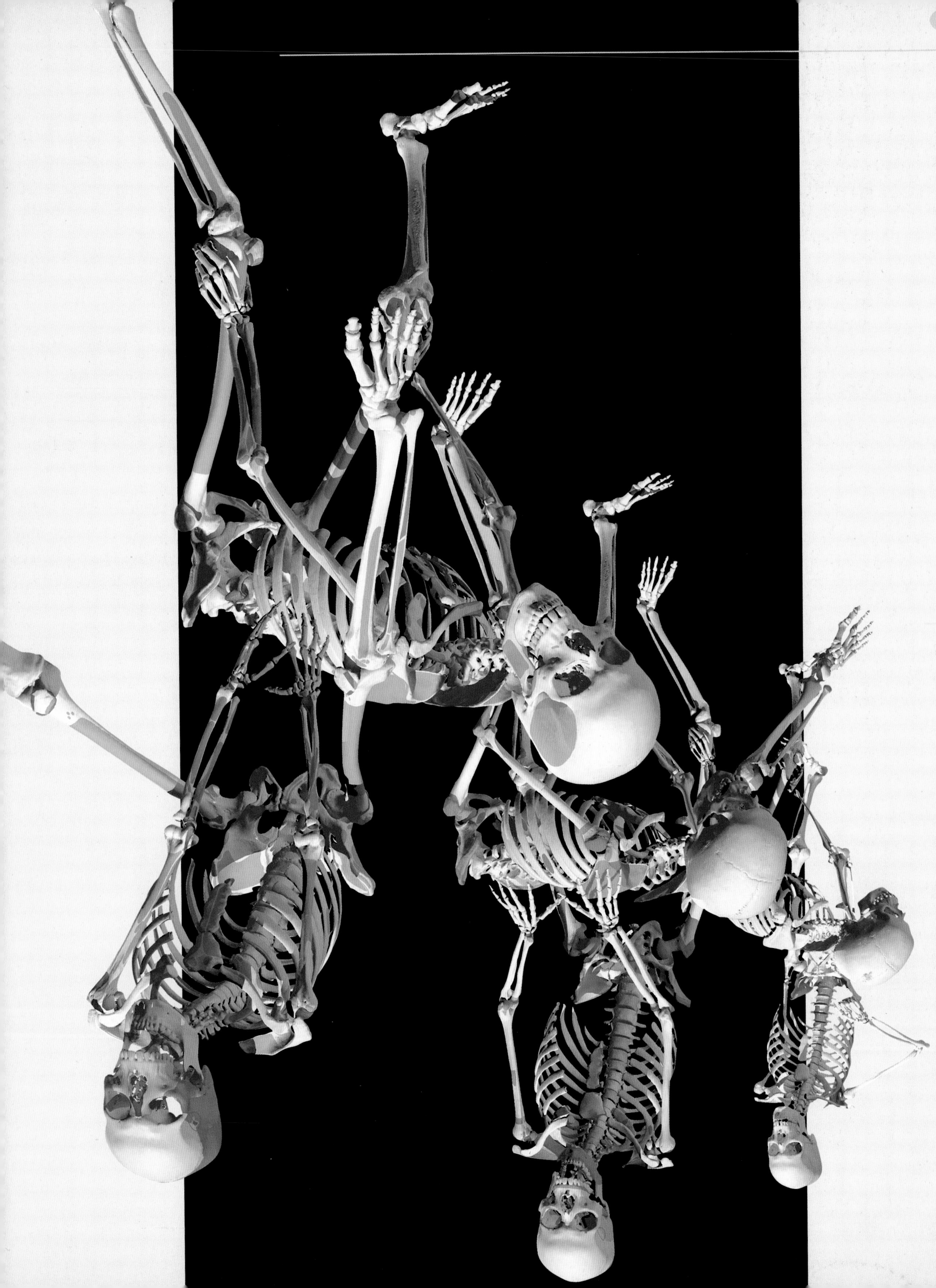

SECTION FOUR: LOWER BODY

Travel from hip to toe to see the intricacies of the muscles, bones, blood vessels, and nerves. Find out how these lower body parts work together to make you stand up, walk, or run.

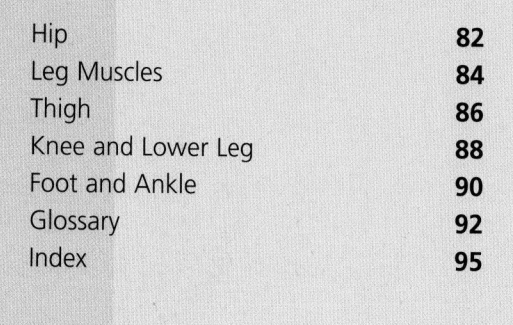

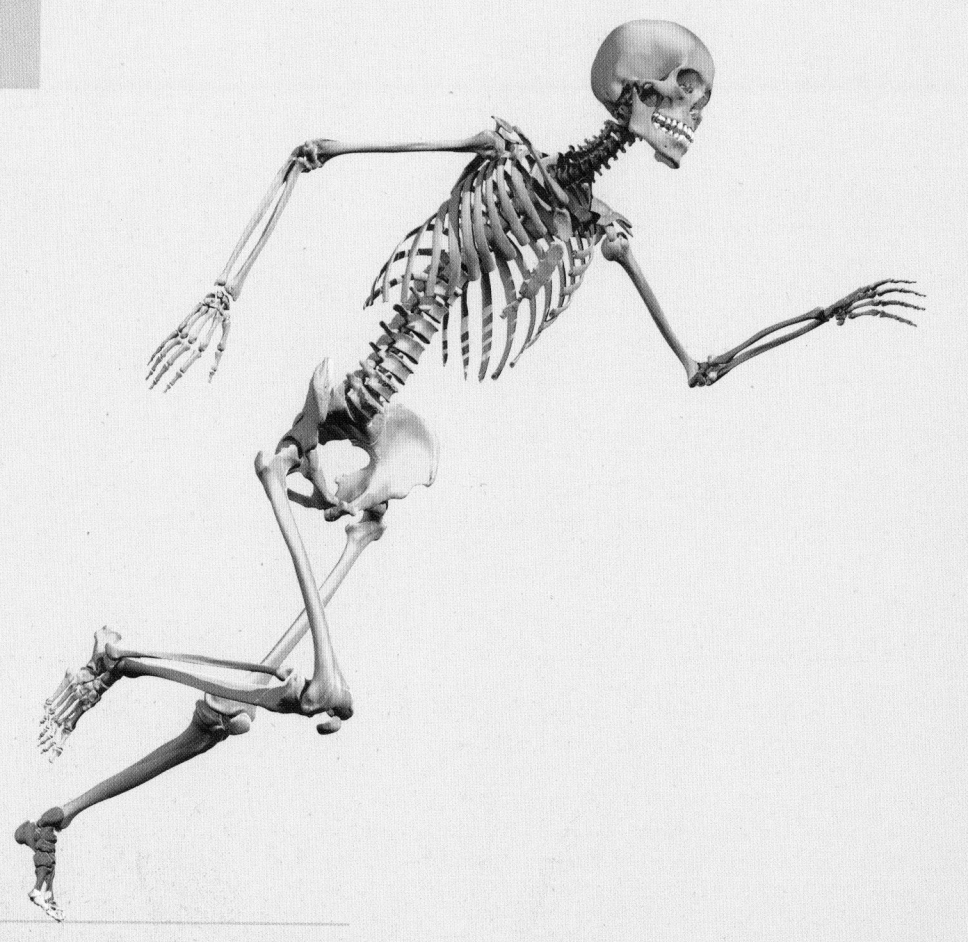

Hip

EVERY DAY WHEN YOU WALK, run, jump, or even just stand, your legs have to support the downward push of your body weight without collapsing under the strain. Such support is achieved by your hips—your pelvic girdle, hip joints, and associated muscles. The strong, basin-shaped pelvic girdle attaches your legs to your backbone through the two hip joints. Reinforced by strong ligaments, this heavy-duty arrangement supports your body weight. At the same time, the flexibility of your hip joints allows powerful muscles to move your legs in various directions.

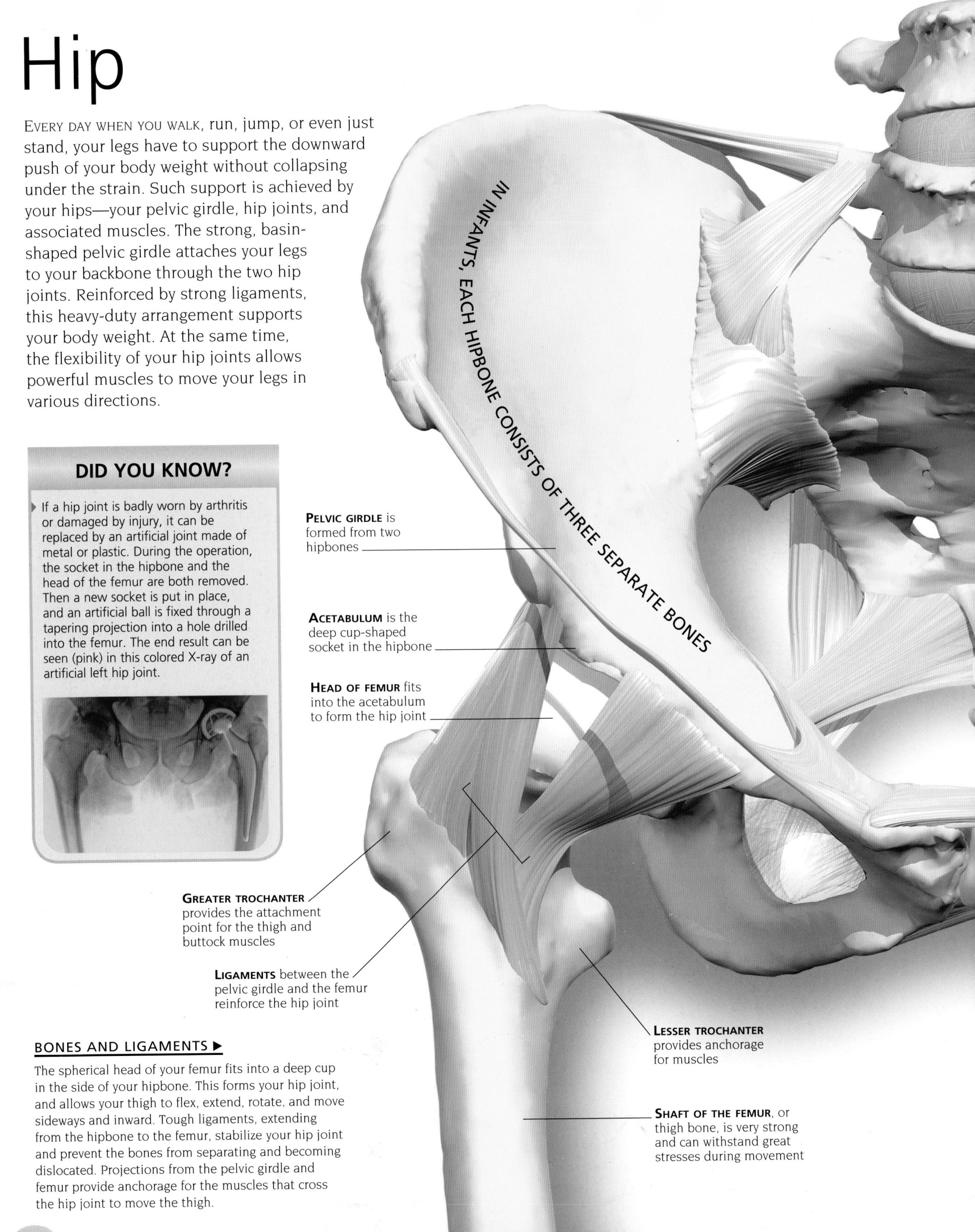

IN INFANTS, EACH HIPBONE CONSISTS OF THREE SEPARATE BONES

DID YOU KNOW?

▶ If a hip joint is badly worn by arthritis or damaged by injury, it can be replaced by an artificial joint made of metal or plastic. During the operation, the socket in the hipbone and the head of the femur are both removed. Then a new socket is put in place, and an artificial ball is fixed through a tapering projection into a hole drilled into the femur. The end result can be seen (pink) in this colored X-ray of an artificial left hip joint.

PELVIC GIRDLE is formed from two hipbones

ACETABULUM is the deep cup-shaped socket in the hipbone

HEAD OF FEMUR fits into the acetabulum to form the hip joint

GREATER TROCHANTER provides the attachment point for the thigh and buttock muscles

LIGAMENTS between the pelvic girdle and the femur reinforce the hip joint

LESSER TROCHANTER provides anchorage for muscles

SHAFT OF THE FEMUR, or thigh bone, is very strong and can withstand great stresses during movement

BONES AND LIGAMENTS ▶

The spherical head of your femur fits into a deep cup in the side of your hipbone. This forms your hip joint, and allows your thigh to flex, extend, rotate, and move sideways and inward. Tough ligaments, extending from the hipbone to the femur, stabilize your hip joint and prevent the bones from separating and becoming dislocated. Projections from the pelvic girdle and femur provide anchorage for the muscles that cross the hip joint to move the thigh.

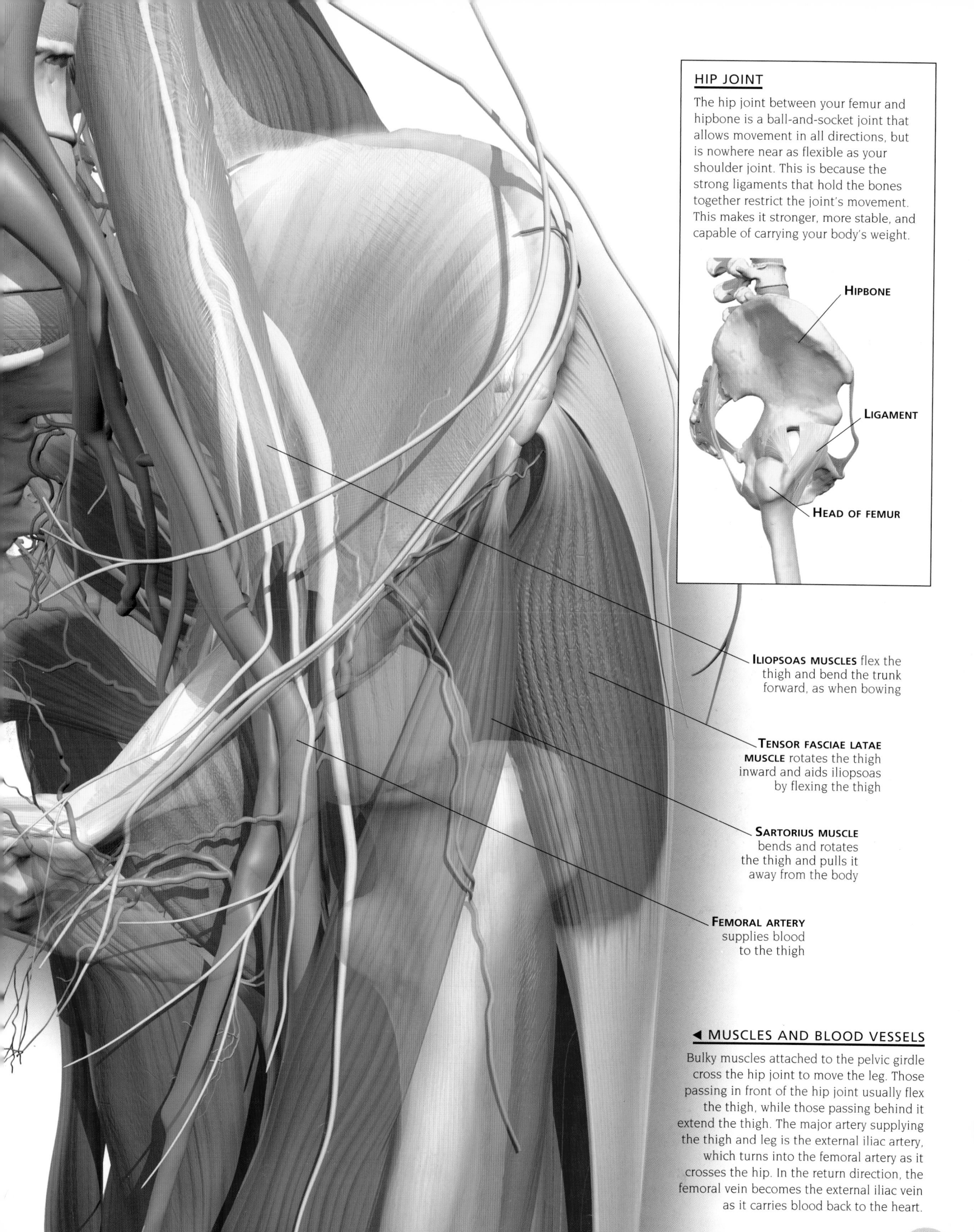

HIP JOINT

The hip joint between your femur and hipbone is a ball-and-socket joint that allows movement in all directions, but is nowhere near as flexible as your shoulder joint. This is because the strong ligaments that hold the bones together restrict the joint's movement. This makes it stronger, more stable, and capable of carrying your body's weight.

HIPBONE

LIGAMENT

HEAD OF FEMUR

ILIOPSOAS MUSCLES flex the thigh and bend the trunk forward, as when bowing

TENSOR FASCIAE LATAE MUSCLE rotates the thigh inward and aids iliopsoas by flexing the thigh

SARTORIUS MUSCLE bends and rotates the thigh and pulls it away from the body

FEMORAL ARTERY supplies blood to the thigh

◄ MUSCLES AND BLOOD VESSELS

Bulky muscles attached to the pelvic girdle cross the hip joint to move the leg. Those passing in front of the hip joint usually flex the thigh, while those passing behind it extend the thigh. The major artery supplying the thigh and leg is the external iliac artery, which turns into the femoral artery as it crosses the hip. In the return direction, the femoral vein becomes the external iliac vein as it carries blood back to the heart.

Leg Muscles

YOUR LEGS HAVE TO BE STRONG ENOUGH to support your body when you are standing still and to move it when you run or jump. That is why your legs are the most muscular parts of your body, and why they have the most powerful muscles. Muscles in the thigh (the upper part of the leg) act at the hip joint or the knee joint, or both, to bend or straighten the hip and the knee. Muscles in the lower leg move your foot up or down.

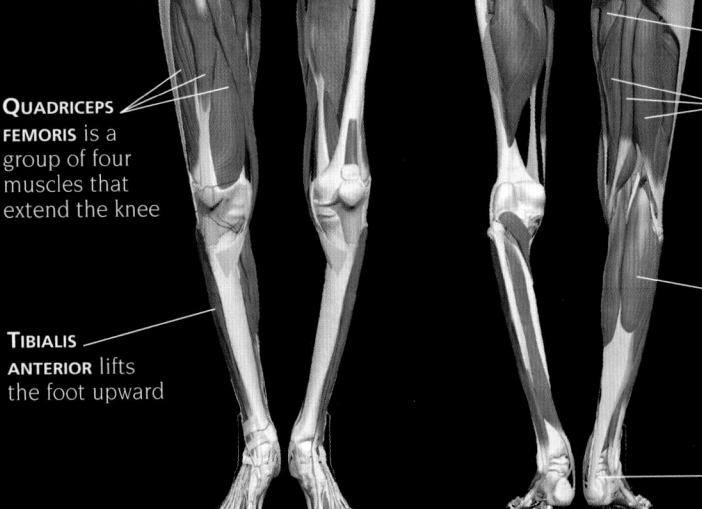

QUADRICEPS FEMORIS is a group of four muscles that extend the knee

TIBIALIS ANTERIOR lifts the foot upward

ADDUCTOR MAGNUS

HAMSTRINGS are three muscles in the back of the thigh that bend the knee

GASTROCNEMIUS

ACHILLES TENDON connects the gastrocnemius and soleus to the ankle bone

FRONT   BACK

▲ FRONT AND BACK VIEW

Muscles at the front of your thigh flex (bend) your hip to bring your thigh forward and extend (straighten) your knee—this is the forward-swinging part of walking. Muscles at the back of your thigh extend your hip by pulling the thigh backward and flex the knee—this is the backward-swinging part of walking.

KICKING A BALL ▲

As the kicker prepares to kick, hamstring muscles flex (bend) the knee and pull the thigh backward. Then the opposing quadriceps femoris contracts, flexing the thigh at the hip, extending (straightening) the knee, and giving the ball a powerful kick.

QUADRICEPS FEMORIS IS ONE OF YOUR BODY'S STRONGEST MUSCLES

TIBIA, or shinbone, carries most of the body's weight in the lower leg

FIBULA is the smaller of the lower leg bones

GASTROCNEMIUS bends the foot downward

SOLEUS bends the foot downward

PERONEUS LONGUS bends the foot upward and turns it outward

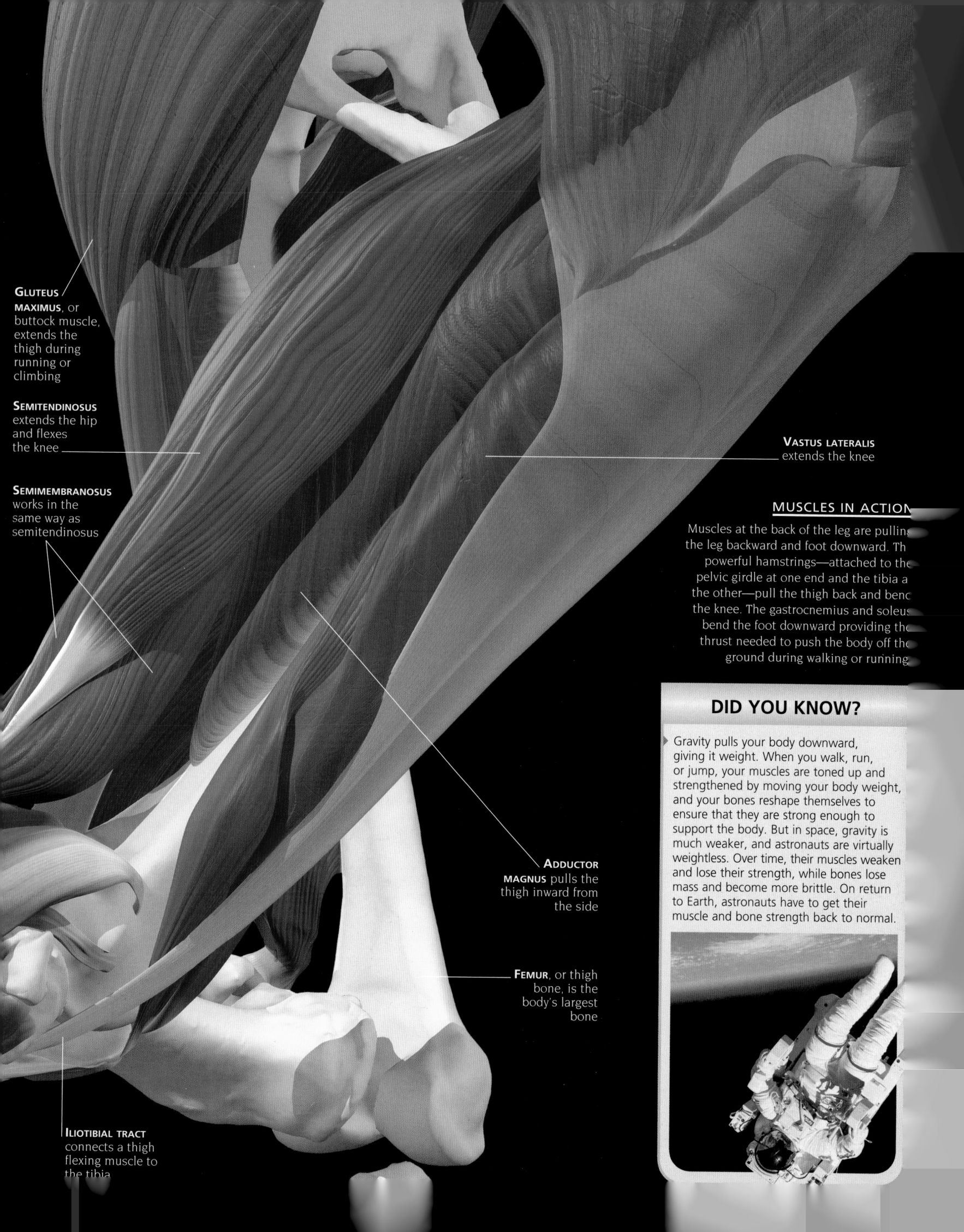

GLUTEUS MAXIMUS, or buttock muscle, extends the thigh during running or climbing

SEMITENDINOSUS extends the hip and flexes the knee

SEMIMEMBRANOSUS works in the same way as semitendinosus

VASTUS LATERALIS extends the knee

MUSCLES IN ACTION

Muscles at the back of the leg are pulling the leg backward and foot downward. The powerful hamstrings—attached to the pelvic girdle at one end and the tibia at the other—pull the thigh back and bend the knee. The gastrocnemius and soleus bend the foot downward providing the thrust needed to push the body off the ground during walking or running.

DID YOU KNOW?

Gravity pulls your body downward, giving it weight. When you walk, run, or jump, your muscles are toned up and strengthened by moving your body weight, and your bones reshape themselves to ensure that they are strong enough to support the body. But in space, gravity is much weaker, and astronauts are virtually weightless. Over time, their muscles weaken and lose their strength, while bones lose mass and become more brittle. On return to Earth, astronauts have to get their muscle and bone strength back to normal.

ADDUCTOR MAGNUS pulls the thigh inward from the side

FEMUR, or thigh bone, is the body's largest bone

ILIOTIBIAL TRACT connects a thigh flexing muscle to the tibia

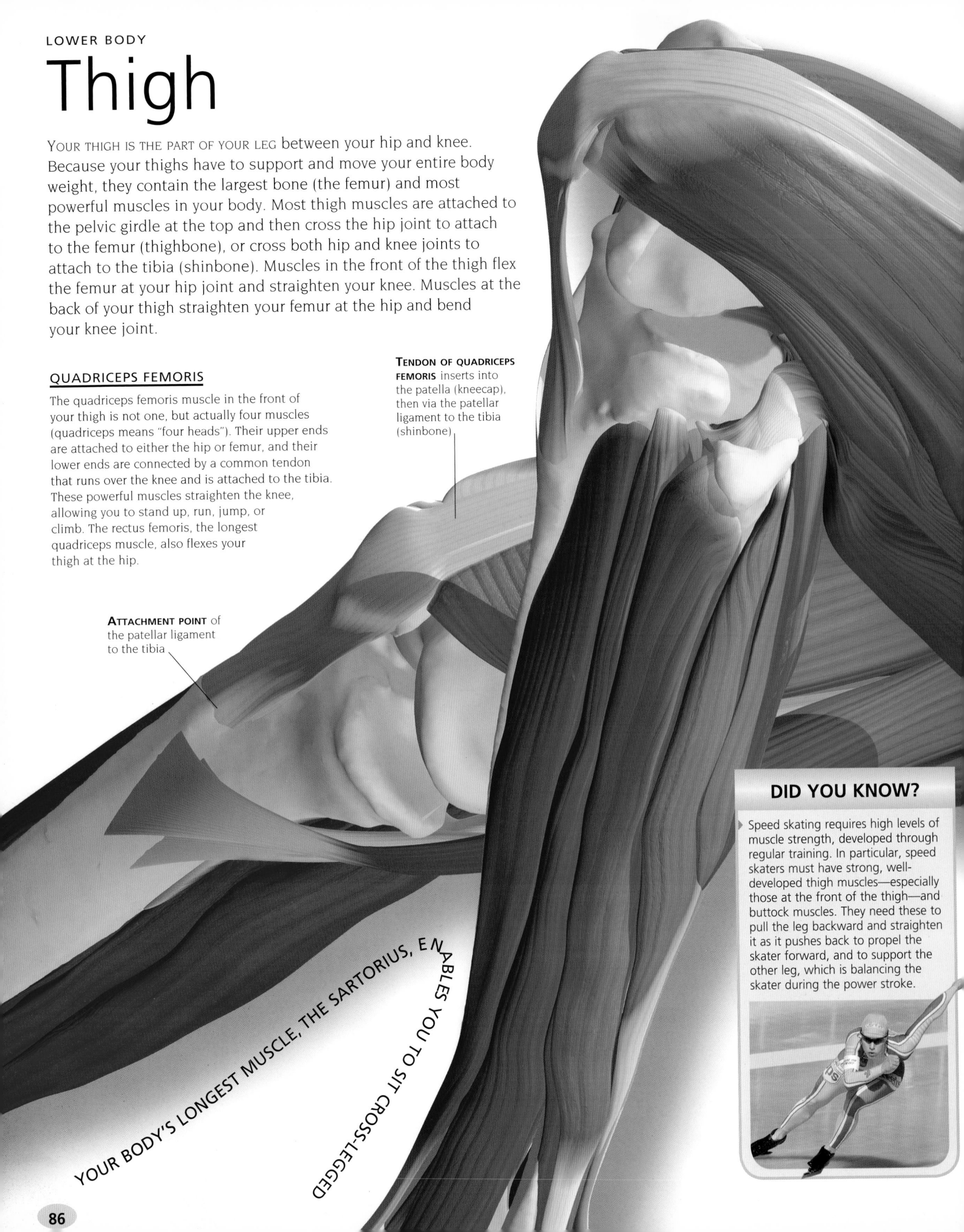

Thigh

Your thigh is the part of your leg between your hip and knee. Because your thighs have to support and move your entire body weight, they contain the largest bone (the femur) and most powerful muscles in your body. Most thigh muscles are attached to the pelvic girdle at the top and then cross the hip joint to attach to the femur (thighbone), or cross both hip and knee joints to attach to the tibia (shinbone). Muscles in the front of the thigh flex the femur at your hip joint and straighten your knee. Muscles at the back of your thigh straighten your femur at the hip and bend your knee joint.

QUADRICEPS FEMORIS

The quadriceps femoris muscle in the front of your thigh is not one, but actually four muscles (quadriceps means "four heads"). Their upper ends are attached to either the hip or femur, and their lower ends are connected by a common tendon that runs over the knee and is attached to the tibia. These powerful muscles straighten the knee, allowing you to stand up, run, jump, or climb. The rectus femoris, the longest quadriceps muscle, also flexes your thigh at the hip.

TENDON OF QUADRICEPS FEMORIS inserts into the patella (kneecap), then via the patellar ligament to the tibia (shinbone)

ATTACHMENT POINT of the patellar ligament to the tibia

YOUR BODY'S LONGEST MUSCLE, THE SARTORIUS, ENABLES YOU TO SIT CROSS-LEGGED

DID YOU KNOW?

▶ Speed skating requires high levels of muscle strength, developed through regular training. In particular, speed skaters must have strong, well-developed thigh muscles—especially those at the front of the thigh—and buttock muscles. They need these to pull the leg backward and straighten it as it pushes back to propel the skater forward, and to support the other leg, which is balancing the skater during the power stroke.

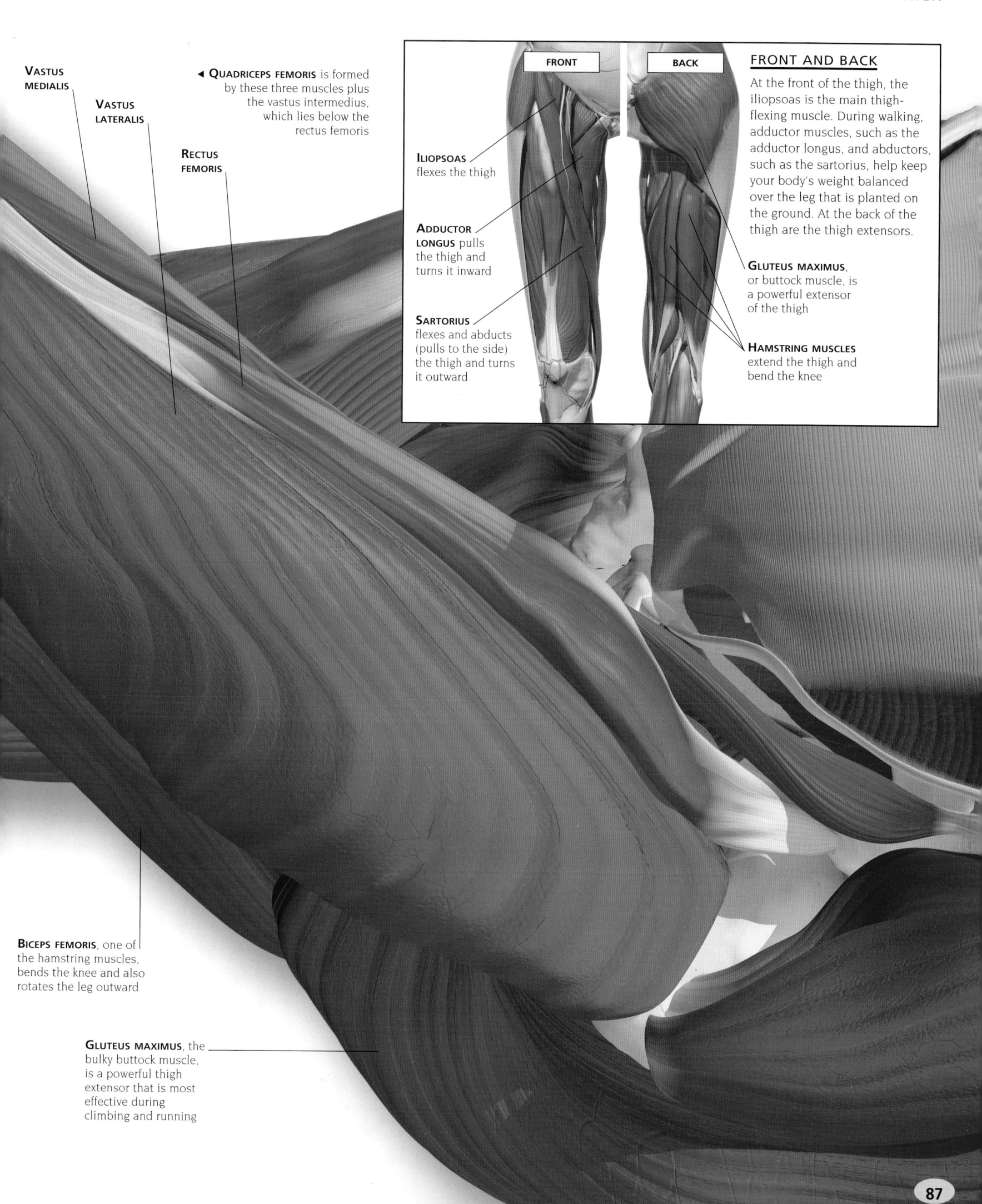

VASTUS MEDIALIS

VASTUS LATERALIS

RECTUS FEMORIS

◄ **QUADRICEPS FEMORIS** is formed by these three muscles plus the vastus intermedius, which lies below the rectus femoris

FRONT

BACK

FRONT AND BACK

At the front of the thigh, the iliopsoas is the main thigh-flexing muscle. During walking, adductor muscles, such as the adductor longus, and abductors, such as the sartorius, help keep your body's weight balanced over the leg that is planted on the ground. At the back of the thigh are the thigh extensors.

ILIOPSOAS flexes the thigh

ADDUCTOR LONGUS pulls the thigh and turns it inward

SARTORIUS flexes and abducts (pulls to the side) the thigh and turns it outward

GLUTEUS MAXIMUS, or buttock muscle, is a powerful extensor of the thigh

HAMSTRING MUSCLES extend the thigh and bend the knee

BICEPS FEMORIS, one of the hamstring muscles, bends the knee and also rotates the leg outward

GLUTEUS MAXIMUS, the bulky buttock muscle, is a powerful thigh extensor that is most effective during climbing and running

87

Knee and Lower Leg

HUMANS WALK UPRIGHT, so legs have the body's strongest bones and joints to support the weight and to withstand the stresses caused by walking and running. The knee joint between your thighbone and shinbone is strong and stable, yet still allows you to move. Your lower leg extends down from the knee to the ankle. Muscles in the front and back of your lower leg bend the feet and toes to help you walk.

THE KNEE ▶

The hinge joint in your knee allows your leg to extend or straighten, but not much else. It is held in place by tough ligaments that are found not just outside the joint but also inside. In addition, C-shaped cartilages, called menisci, between the ends of the femur and tibia, absorb shocks transmitted through the knee during walking.

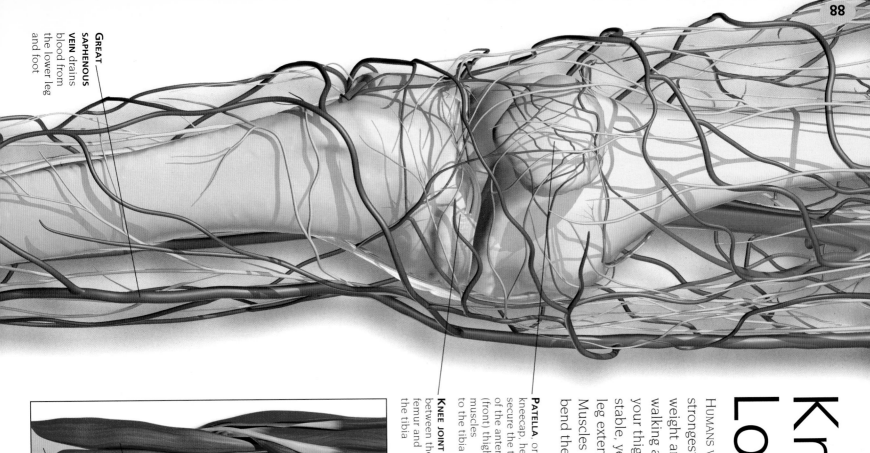

GREAT SAPHENOUS VEIN drains blood from the lower leg and foot

KNEE JOINT between the femur and the tibia

PATELLA, or kneecap, helps secure the tendon of the anterior (front) thigh muscles to the tibia

CALF MUSCLES

Two muscles, the gastrocnemius and soleus, shape the calf at the back of your lower leg and pull on your heel bone to bend your foot downward, providing the push you need to walk or run or stand on tiptoe.

SOLEUS works with the gastrocnemius and helps to maintain posture during movement

GASTROCNEMIUS bends the foot downward when the knee is extended

TENDON OF GASTROCNEMIUS joins the tendon of the soleus farther down the calf to form the Achilles tendon

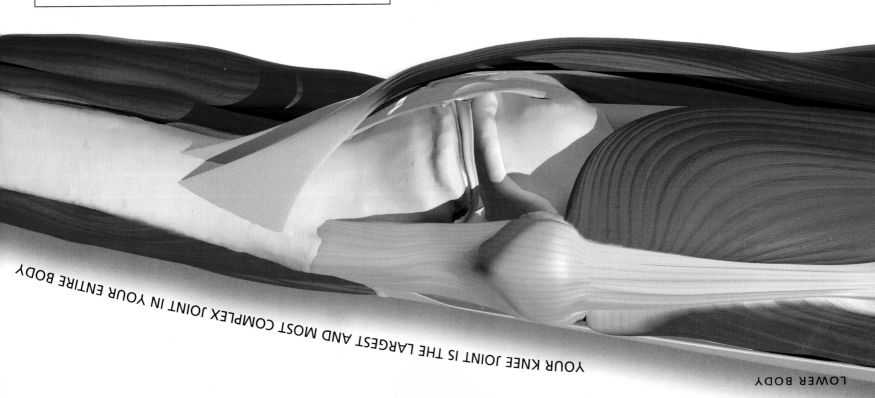

YOUR KNEE JOINT IS THE LARGEST AND MOST COMPLEX JOINT IN YOUR ENTIRE BODY

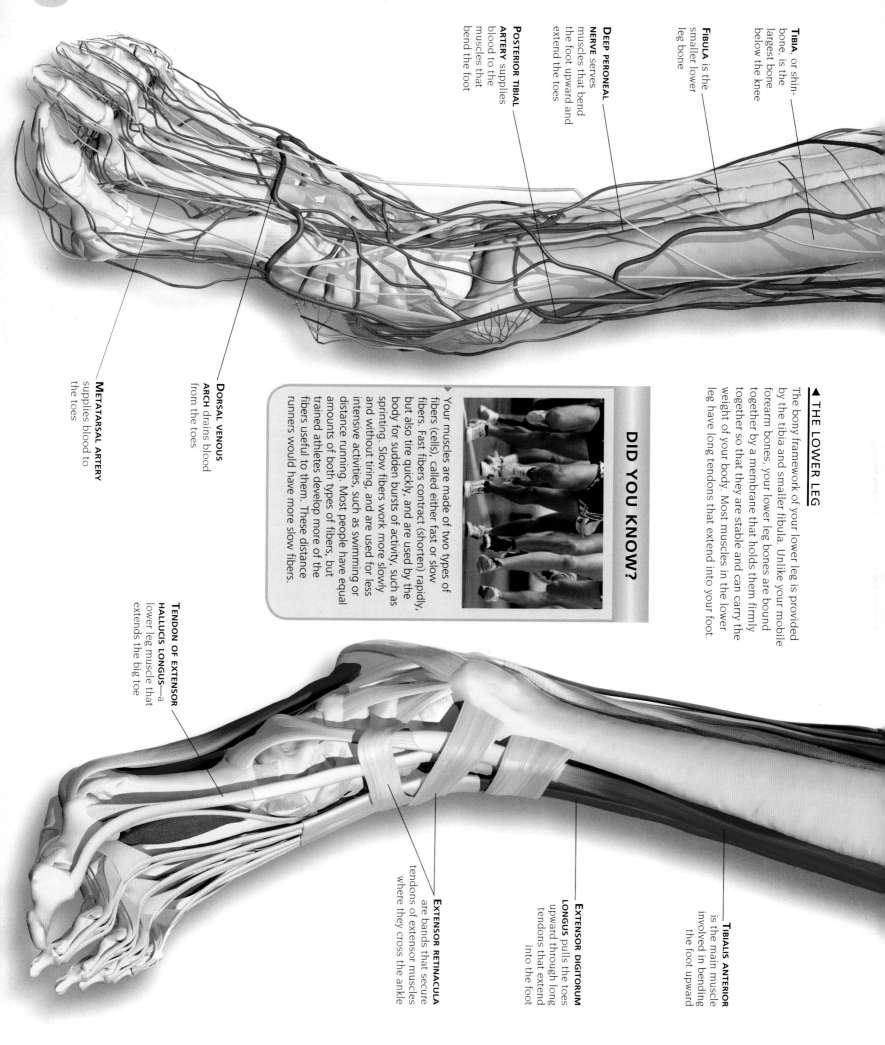

TIBIA, or shin-bone, is the largest bone below the knee

FIBULA is the smaller lower leg bone

DEEP PERONEAL NERVE serves muscles that bend the foot upward and extend the toes

POSTERIOR TIBIAL ARTERY supplies blood to the muscles that bend the foot

METATARSAL ARTERY supplies blood to the toes

DORSAL VENOUS ARCH drains blood from the toes

▲ THE LOWER LEG

The bony framework of your lower leg is provided by the tibia and smaller fibula. Unlike your mobile forearm bones, your lower leg bones are bound together by a membrane that holds them firmly together so that they are stable and can carry the weight of your body. Most muscles in the lower leg have long tendons that extend into your foot.

DID YOU KNOW?

Your muscles are made of two types of fibers (cells), called either fast or slow fibers. Fast fibers contract (shorten) rapidly, but also tire quickly, and are used by the body for sudden bursts of activity, such as sprinting. Slow fibers work more slowly and without tiring, and are used for less intensive activities, such as swimming or distance running. Most people have equal amounts of both types of fibers, but trained athletes develop more of the fibers useful to them. These distance runners would have more slow fibers.

TENDON OF EXTENSOR HALLUCIS LONGUS—a lower leg muscle that extends the big toe

EXTENSOR RETINACULA are bands that secure tendons of extensor muscles where they cross the ankle

EXTENSOR DIGITORUM LONGUS pulls the toes upward through long tendons that extend into the foot

TIBIALIS ANTERIOR is the main muscle involved in bending the foot upward

Foot and Ankle

YOUR HARD-WORKING FEET CARRY YOUR BODY WEIGHT, often for hours on end, and keep your body balanced whether you are moving or standing still. Feet are also flexible springboards that, when moved by muscles, allow you to walk, run, or jump. The ankle is formed where the shin bone of the lower leg forms a joint with the talus, the uppermost foot bone. This hinge joint allows your foot to bend upward or downward when pulled by lower leg muscles, which, helped by muscles in the foot itself, also move your toes.

FOOT AND ANKLE (FROM ABOVE) ▶

This top view of the right foot shows foot bones (see opposite for more details), tendons, and muscles. The long tendons arise from muscles in the front of the lower leg, cross the ankle, and are fixed to the foot bones. These muscles pull the foot upward and, aided by muscles in the foot itself, straighten the toes. This stops the toes from dragging along the ground when we take a step forward.

EXTENSOR DIGITORUM BREVIS bends the toes upward

TENDONS OF EXTENSOR DIGITORUM LONGUS, a lower leg muscle, help to pull the toes upward

ARCUATE ARTERY curves over the foot, producing branches that supply blood to the toes

METATARSAL BONES are pulled into springy arches by tendons and ligaments, so helping to spread the body's weight

INTEROSSEOUS MUSCLES pull the toes apart

SHINBONE, or tibia, has a bulging end that forms the ankle joint with the talus

GREAT SAPHENOUS VEIN helps to drain blood from the foot

RETINACULUM is a band that holds the long tendons in place

SUPERFICIAL FIBULAR NERVE gives sensation to the skin and muscles of the toes

◀ ACHILLES TENDON

Easy to feel at the back of your ankle, the Achilles tendon is a tough strap that connects your calf muscles to the heel bone. Calf muscles pull the heel bone to bend your foot downward when you walk, or stand, on tiptoe.

ACHILLES TENDON is the strongest tendon in the body

DID YOU KNOW?

In this scene from ancient Greek mythology, the nymph Thetis holds her son Achilles by the heel as she dips him in the magical waters of the river Styx. This should make Achilles immortal, but Thetis fails to dip the heel she is holding. Years later, Achilles fights bravely in the Trojan war but is killed by a poison arrow that pierces his heel. Today, people refer to a person's weak, or vulnerable, point as their "Achilles' heel."

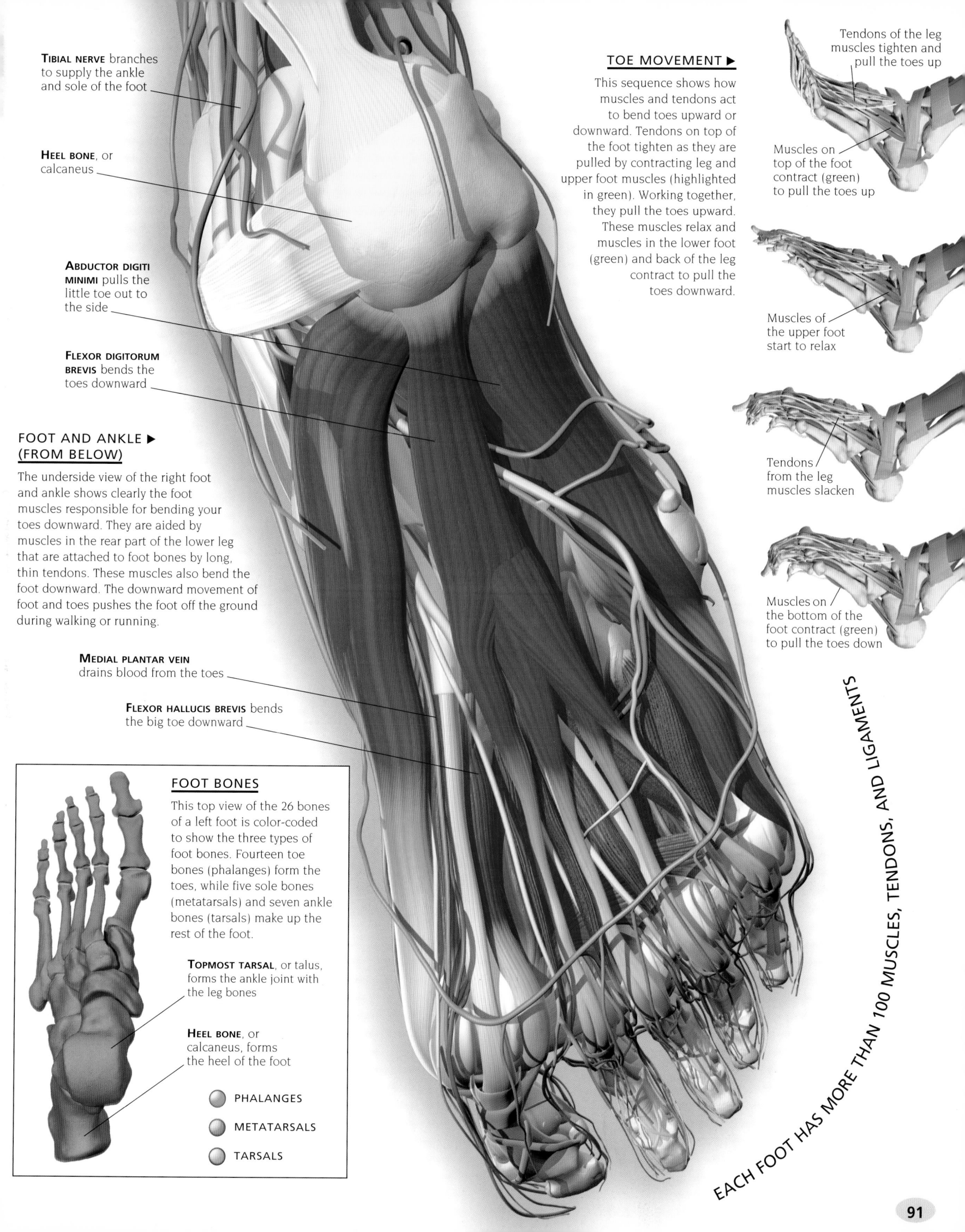

TIBIAL NERVE branches to supply the ankle and sole of the foot

HEEL BONE, or calcaneus

ABDUCTOR DIGITI MINIMI pulls the little toe out to the side

FLEXOR DIGITORUM BREVIS bends the toes downward

FOOT AND ANKLE ▶ (FROM BELOW)

The underside view of the right foot and ankle shows clearly the foot muscles responsible for bending your toes downward. They are aided by muscles in the rear part of the lower leg that are attached to foot bones by long, thin tendons. These muscles also bend the foot downward. The downward movement of foot and toes pushes the foot off the ground during walking or running.

MEDIAL PLANTAR VEIN drains blood from the toes

FLEXOR HALLUCIS BREVIS bends the big toe downward

FOOT BONES

This top view of the 26 bones of a left foot is color-coded to show the three types of foot bones. Fourteen toe bones (phalanges) form the toes, while five sole bones (metatarsals) and seven ankle bones (tarsals) make up the rest of the foot.

TOPMOST TARSAL, or talus, forms the ankle joint with the leg bones

HEEL BONE, or calcaneus, forms the heel of the foot

- ● PHALANGES
- ● METATARSALS
- ○ TARSALS

TOE MOVEMENT ▶

This sequence shows how muscles and tendons act to bend toes upward or downward. Tendons on top of the foot tighten as they are pulled by contracting leg and upper foot muscles (highlighted in green). Working together, they pull the toes upward. These muscles relax and muscles in the lower foot (green) and back of the leg contract to pull the toes downward.

Tendons of the leg muscles tighten and pull the toes up

Muscles on top of the foot contract (green) to pull the toes up

Muscles of the upper foot start to relax

Tendons from the leg muscles slacken

Muscles on the bottom of the foot contract (green) to pull the toes down

EACH FOOT HAS MORE THAN 100 MUSCLES, TENDONS, AND LIGAMENTS

Glossary

ABDOMEN
The lower part of the trunk (central part of the body), between the thorax (chest) and pelvis, which contains most of the digestive organs, including the stomach.

ABDUCTOR
Muscle that pulls a body part away from the midline of the body.

ADDUCTOR
Muscle that pulls a body part toward the midline of the body.

ALVEOLI (SINGULAR ALVEOLUS)
Tiny air sacs found inside the lungs through which oxygen enters, and carbon dioxide leaves, the bloodstream during breathing.

ANATOMY
The study of the structure of the human body.

AORTA
Body's largest artery, which arises from the left side of the heart and supplies oxygen-rich blood to all other arteries except for the pulmonary artery.

ARTERY
Thick-walled blood vessel that carries blood away from the heart.

ATRIUM (PLURAL ATRIA)
One of two chambers (left and right) in the upper part of the heart.

AXON
Also called a nerve fiber; the long fiberlike extension of a neuron (nerve cell) that carries nerve impulses at high speed away from the cell body.

BACTERIA (SINGULAR BACTERIUM)
Abundant group of single-celled microscopic organisms. Some bacteria live in human bodies. Some bacteria, often called germs, can cause disease.

BASOPHIL
A type of white blood cell that is full of toxic chemical granules which can digest microorganisms.

BLOOD
Red liquid, consisting of billions of cells floating in a watery fluid, which supplies and maintains the body's cells and helps defend the body against infection.

BLOOD VESSEL
Living tube that transports blood.

BRAINSTEM
The lower part of the brain, which controls vital functions such as breathing and heartbeat.

BRONCHI
The two main branches of the trachea, a tube leading to the lungs.

CAPILLARY
Microscopic blood vessel that links the smallest arteries to the smallest veins, and supplies individual cells in the tissues.

CARBON DIOXIDE
Gas that is a waste product of cell respiration and is breathed out from the lungs.

CARDIAC MUSCLE
Type of muscle, found only in the heart, which contracts without tiring.

CARDIOVASCULAR SYSTEM
Also called the circulatory system, this body system consists of the heart, blood, and a vast network of blood vessels.

CARTILAGE
Tough, flexible skeletal tissue that covers the ends of bones in joints and helps to support the body.

CELL
One of the trillions of tiny living units that form a human body.

CELL BODY
Part of a neuron (nerve cell) that contains its nucleus.

CELL RESPIRATION
Process going on inside all body cells, which uses oxygen to release energy from glucose and releases carbon dioxide as a waste product.

CENTRAL NERVOUS SYSTEM (CNS)
The part of the nervous system that consists of the brain and spinal cord.

CEREBRUM
Largest and most complex part of the brain, responsible for thinking, feeling, and controlling movement.

CILIA
Microscopic hairlike structures that project from the surface of certain body cells.

CLAVICLE
One of two slender bones that make up part of the shoulder girdle. Also called the collarbone.

CONTRACTION
The shortening of a muscle to move part of the body.

CRANIAL NERVE
One of the 12 pairs of nerves that emerge from the brain stem.

CRANIUM
Upper, dome-shaped part of the skull, which is made of eight interlocking bones and surrounds, supports, and protects the brain.

CT (COMPUTER TOMOGRAPHY) SCAN
Imaging technique that uses X-rays and a computer to produce "slices" through living tissues.

DENDRITE
Short branch of a neuron that carries nerve impulses toward the neuron's cell body.

DENTINE
Hard, bonelike material that shapes a tooth and forms its root.

DIAPHRAGM
Dome-shaped sheet of muscle that separates the thorax from the abdomen and plays a key role in breathing.

ENAMEL
The hardest material in the body, consisting mainly of calcium, enamel covers the exposed part of a tooth with a thin, hard layer.

ENDOCRINE GLAND
A gland, such as the adrenal gland, that makes hormones and releases them into the bloodstream.

ENERGY
The ability to do work or vigorous activity, such as moving the body.

ENZYME
Substance that greatly accelerates the speed of chemical reactions, including the breakdown of food during digestion.

EOSINOPHIL
A type of white blood cell that contains many enzyme granules. These react against foreign organisms such as bacteria.

ESOPHAGUS
The muscular tube through which food passes from the pharynx down to the stomach.

EXTENSOR
Muscle that extends or straightens a bone joint by moving its bones farther apart, such as the triceps brachii, which straightens the arm at the elbow.

FECES
Solid waste consisting of undigested food, dead cells, and bacteria that is pushed out of the body from the end of the large intestine.

FEMUR
The largest bone in the body, located in the leg between the pelvis and the knee.

FERTILIZATION
Joining together of a male sex cell (sperm) and female sex cell (egg) to make a new human being.

FLEXOR
A muscle that flexes or bends a joint by bringing its bones closer together—for example, the biceps brachii, which bends the arm at the elbow.

FORAMEN
Hole or opening in a bone through which blood vessels and nerves can pass.

FORENSIC SCIENCE
The application of science to law and the investigation of criminal activity. Forensic scientists examine evidence from crime scenes, such as fingerprints and saliva.

FORENSIC SCULPTING
The attempt by a sculptor to create a likeness of a specific individual using his or her skull.

FRONTAL LOBE
The foremost of the four lobes that make up each hemisphere of the cerebrum. The frontal lobes help with higher mental faculties, such as planning and decision-making.

GASTRIC
Describes something related to the stomach, such as gastric juice.

GLAND
Tissue or organ that produces a substance, such as a hormone or sweat, which is released into or onto the body.

GRAVITY
A pulling force that attracts objects to each other, such as the attraction between planet Earth and everything on its surface.

HEPATIC
Describes something related to the liver, such as the hepatic vein.

HORMONE
Substances that are released into the blood by endocrine glands, and act as chemical messengers by altering the activities of target cells.

HUMERUS
The long arm bone that extends from the shoulder to the elbow.

HYPOTHALAMUS
Part of the brain that links the nervous and endocrine systems by controlling the pituitary gland.

IMMUNE SYSTEM
Defense system consisting of white cells in the blood and lymphatic system, which protect the body from infection by pathogens.

JOINT
Part of the skeleton where two bones meet.

LARYNX
The part of the respiratory tract containing the vocal cords, covered in folds of mucous membrane.

LIGAMENT
Tough bands of tissue that hold bones together where they meet at joints.

LUNG
One of two spongy respiratory organs in the chest cavity, which removes carbon dioxide from the blood and provides it with oxygen.

LYMPH
Liquid that is picked up in the tissue, flows through the lymphatic system, and is returned to the bloodstream.

LYMPHATIC SYSTEM
Body system that returns excess fluid from the tissues to the bloodstream and helps to fight infections.

LYMPHOCYTE
Type of white blood cell that plays a key role in the immune system.

MACROPHAGE
Type of white blood cell that engulfs pathogens and plays a part in the immune system.

METABOLIC RATE
The rate at which body cells use energy.

METABOLISM
The sum total of all the chemical reactions going on inside the body's cells.

MINERAL
One of about 20 substances, including iron and calcium, which a person must eat to stay healthy.

MONOCYTE
A large white blood cell that defends the body by engulfing and digesting foreign particles.

MRI (MAGNETIC RESONANCE IMAGING) SCAN
Imaging technique that uses magnetism, radio waves, and a computer to produce images of the interior of the body.

MUCUS
A thick, slimy fluid produced by the respiratory and digestive systems to protect and lubricate.

MUSCLE
An organ that contracts (gets shorter) in order to move part of the body.

MUSCLE FIBER
One of the cells that make up a muscle.

NASAL CAVITY
The hollow space behind the nose through which air flows during breathing.

NERVE
Cablelike bundle of the axons (nerve fibers) of neurons that relays nerve impulses between the central nervous system (brain and spinal cord) and the body.

NERVE FIBER
Alternative name for an axon.

NERVE IMPULSE
Tiny electrical signal that moves quickly along a neuron (nerve cell).

NEURON
One of the billions of inter-connected nerve cells that make up the nervous system.

NEUTROPHIL
The most common type of white blood cell, which targets and defends the body from harmful bacteria.

NUCLEUS
Control center of a cell that contains instructions needed to build and maintain that cell.

NUTRIENT
Substance a person needs to eat in order to keep their body functioning normally.

OCCIPITAL LOBE
One of the four lobes that make up each hemisphere of the cerebrum. The occipital lobe is responsible for sight.

OLFACTORY
Describes something related to the sense of smell, such as the olfactory nerve.

ORGAN
A major part of the body, such as the heart or kidney, which has a key role or roles and is made up of two or more different types of tissues.

OXYGEN
Gas found in the air that is taken into the lungs during breathing in, and is used by body cells to release energy during cell respiration.

PARIETAL LOBE
One of the four lobes that make up each hemisphere of the cerebrum. The parietal lobe is involved in the interpretation of touch, pain, and temperature.

PATHOGEN
A disease-causing microscopic organism such as a bacterium or virus.

PELVIC FLOOR MUSCLES
Muscles that close the lower opening of the pelvis and help support organs in the abdomen.

PELVIS
Basin-shaped bony structure, consisting of the pelvic girdle, sacrum, and coccyx, which attaches the legs to the body.

PHAGOCYTE
General name for white blood cells, such as a macrophage, which track down, surround, and eat pathogens.

PHALANGES (SINGULAR PHALANX)
The bones of the fingers, thumbs, and toes.

PHARYNX
A tube that extends from the nasal cavity down the neck to the esophagus. Also called the throat.

PHOTORECEPTOR
A type of nerve cell found in the eye, which sends nerve impulses to the brain when it detects light.

Glossary

PLEXUS

A network of nerves that joins together, then separates.

PORTAL SYSTEM

Veins, such as the hepatic portal system, that carry blood from one organ to another rather than toward the heart.

PROTEIN

Nutrient used by the body for growth and repair.

PULMONARY

Describes something related to the lungs, such as the pulmonary artery and pulmonary vein.

PULMONARY ARTERY

The artery that carries oxygen-poor blood to the lungs to pick up oxygen. Other arteries carry oxygen-rich blood.

PULMONARY VEIN

The vein that carries oxygen-rich blood from the lungs to the heart. Other veins carry oxygen-poor blood.

RECEPTOR

Nerve cell, or the ending of a neuron, which responds to a stimulus or change in surroundings, such as sound or light.

RENAL

Describes something related to the kidney, such as the renal artery.

RIB CAGE

The bony enclosing wall which protects the soft organs inside the chest, such as the heart, liver, and kidneys.

SALIVA

The watery mixture of secretions from the salivary glands, which lubricate and clean the mouth.

SCAPULA

One of the two large, flat bones forming the back of the shoulder. Also called the shoulder blade.

SENSE ORGAN

An organ, such as the eye or ear, which contains receptors that detect changes inside or outside the body and sends nerve signals to the brain that enable us to see, hear, balance, taste, and smell.

SEX CELL

A cell, either a sperm in males or an egg in females, which is involved in reproduction.

SKELETAL MUSCLE

Type of muscle that is attached to the bones of the skeleton and moves the body.

SMOOTH MUSCLE

Type of muscle found in the walls of hollow organs, such as the bladder and small intestine, which contracts slowly and rhythmically.

SPHINCTER

A ring of muscle surrounding an opening in the body, such as the outlet between the stomach and the duodenum. It can open or close to control the flow of food.

SPINAL NERVE

One of the 31 pairs of nerves that arises from the spinal cord.

SUTURE

Immovable joint between the bones that make up the skull and pelvis.

SYMPHYSIS

A joint in which the bones are connected by cartilage.

SYNAPSE

A junction between two neurons (nerve cells) in which they are close to each other but do not touch.

SYNOVIAL JOINT

A freely movable joint, such as the knee joint, in which a space between bones is filled with lubricating synovial fluid.

SYSTEM

A group of linked organs that work together to perform a particular task or tasks, such as the lung and various air passages that make up the respiratory system.

TASTE BUD

A receptor located in the surface of the tongue that detects tastes in food and drink.

TEMPORAL LOBE

One of the four lobes that make up each cerebral hemisphere of the brain. The temporal lobe is involved in hearing, speech, and memory.

TENDON

Tough cord or sheet that attaches a muscle to a bone and transmits the force exerted by the muscle.

THALAMUS

A mass of gray matter (nerve tissue) that lies deep within the brain. The thalamus receives and coordinates sensory information.

THORACIC CAVITY

The area inside the thorax containing the heart, lungs, and other major blood vessels.

THORAX

Also called the chest, the upper part of the trunk (central part of the body), between the neck and abdomen, which contains the heart and lungs.

TISSUE

Group of cells of the same or similar type that work together to perform a particular task, such as neurons carrying nerve impulses.

TONGUE

The movable, muscular organ attached to the floor of the mouth. It is the main organ for taste and is also used for speech.

TONSIL

One of six small organs, located around the entrance to the throat, which help destroy pathogens entering the body in food and air.

TRACHEA

A thin-walled tube going from the larynx to the bronchi. It carries air to the lungs and is sometimes called the windpipe.

TRANSPLANT

Replacement of a diseased tissue or organ using a healthy tissue or organ donated by another person, usually someone who has just died.

TRUNK

Also called the torso, this is the central part of the body to which the head, arms, and legs are attached.

ULTRAVIOLET (UV) RAYS

Radiation that occurs naturally in sunlight, but can be harmful if the skin is exposed to too much of it.

VENTRICLE

One of two chambers (left and right) in the lower part of the heart.

VEIN

Thin-walled blood vessel that returns blood to the heart from body tissues. Veins contain valves to prevent backflow of blood.

VILLI (SINGULAR VILLUS)

Tiny, fingerlike projections on the lining of the small intestine, which greatly increase the surface available for absorbing digested food into the bloodstream.

VITAMINS

One of more than 13 substances, including vitamins A and C, that are required in small amounts in food to keep the body healthy.

X-RAY

Imaging technique that reveals body structures, especially bones, by projecting a type of radiation through the body onto a photographic film.

Index

Credits

The publisher would like to thank the following for their kind permission to reproduce their photographs:
Abbreviations key: t-top, b-bottom, r-right, l-left, c-center, a-above, f-far

13 Getty Images: The Image Bank/Ellen Schuster (br). 19 Corbis: David Butow (br). 21 Science Photo Library: Francis Leroy, Biocosmos (tl). 22 Science Photo Library: Steve Gschmeissner (bl). 23 Science Photo Library: Mauro Fermariello (br). 28 Corbis: Bettmann (br). 31 Science Photo Library: Michael Donne, University of Manchester (br). 36 Science Photo Library: James King-Holmes (br). 38 Science Photo Library: (br). 46 Corbis: K.J. Historical (br). 48 Corbis: Stephen Frink (bl). 50 Corbis: Reuters/Stefano Rellandini (bl). 53 Corbis: D. Robert and Lorri Franz (cr). 54 Zefa Visual Media: Sagel and Kranefeld (br). 57 Corbis: George D. Lepp (bl). 59 Corbis: Sean Aidan; Eye Ubiquitous (tr). 61 Corbis: Bettmann (tr). 63 Science Photo Library: Paul Whitehill (tr). 66 Corbis: Bettmann (bl). 67 Science Photo Library: P. Hawtin, University of Southampton (tr). 69 Science Photo Library: J.L. Martra, Publiphoto Diffusion (tr). 71 Corbis: Duomo (br). 74 Science Photo Library: (bl). 76 Science Photo Library: National Library of Medicine (bl). 78 Science Photo Library: Professors P. M. Motta and J. Van Blerkom (tr); Zephyr (bl). 82 Science Photo Library: BSIP (cl). 85 NASA: (br). 86 Corbis: Reuters (br). 89 Corbis: Duomo (cf). 90 The Picture Desk: The Art Archive/Galleria Nazionale Parma/Dagli Orti (A) (br).

All other images © Dorling Kindersley.
For further information, see www.dkimages.com

The publisher would also like to thank CG Anatomy Images: Simon Barrick, Joe Barrow, Richard Wilson, Nik Clifford, Fiona Morgan, Giles Lord, and Michael Jones. For Dorling Kindersley: Jacqui Swan, Spencer Holbrook, Joe Conneally, Andrea Mills, Julie Ferris, Susmita Dey, Supriya Mahajan, and Bimlesh Tiwary.